The Purbrook Heath Story

(Jottings on a Cricket Ground)

By Andy Cragg

Copyright © 2010 Andrew Cragg. First published in the UK in 2010 by Andrew Cragg.

Book designed and produced by Ralph Murray. Website: ralphmurray.co.uk
Cartoons by Peter Beilby.

Printed by MPG Books Limited

The email address for Andrew Cragg is andrew.cragg@care4free.net

A CIP catalogue record for this book is available from The British Library.

ISBN: 978-0-9565226-0-3

The right of Andrew Cragg to be identified as the author of this work has been asserted.

In memory of
Win and Alec

ACKNOWLEDGEMENTS

I am indebted to many people who helped me with my research for this book. Sadly a number of them passed away before I completed publication, and consequently the names recorded below acknowledge friends and helpers past and present:

Brian Andrews, Phil Andrews, "Archaeology and Historic Buildings" at Hampshire County Council, John Austin, Stan Baynham, Peter Beilby, Trevor Biffen, June Blythe, Roger Boulton, John Bradley, British Museum, Brian Browne, Sharon Bryan, Buriton Heritage Bank, John Burrell, Greg Carson, Brian Churcher, Roger Clarke, Dave Cleeve, Joss Cleeve, Pete Connor, Kingsley Daniels, Brian Davis, Ernie Davis, Doug Doe, Jean Doe, Laurie Farmer, Sheila Farmer, Alan Figgins, Roger Flake, Richard Gale, Hampshire Record Office, Mark Hamson, Trevor Harfield, Havant Borough Council, Havant Museum, Norman Hayward, Andy Holder, Jim Holder, Sylvia Holder, James Iles, Toni James, Bob Jenkins, Steve Jones, Russell Kyte, Annie Lamont, Ted Lamont, my sister Jean Leaver, Ian Limb, Mervyn Liversidge, John Mackney, Richard Manning, Dave Martin, Pete Martin, John Masson, Dave May, Dianne Mazzetelli, Graham McCoy, Alan Mengham, Colin Mills, Paul Musselwhite, Wayne Musselwhite, The News Portsmouth, Bruce Oliver, John Page, Steve Pethybridge, Portsmouth Central Library, Portsmouth Museums and Records Office, Diane Bourne and Andy Neve at Portsmouth Water, Brian Robbins, Peter Rogers, Reverend Karen Schmidt, Bob Smith, Trissie Smith, Southsea Gallery, Keith Todd, Mike Turner, Adey Voss, Paul Walder, Mr & Mrs Stuart Waring, Colin Wearn, Roy West, Andrew Whitmarsh and the D-Day Museum, Brian Woolley, Jean Worthington, Roy Worthington, Jack Wright.

My thanks also go to Ralph Murray who designed and produced the book.

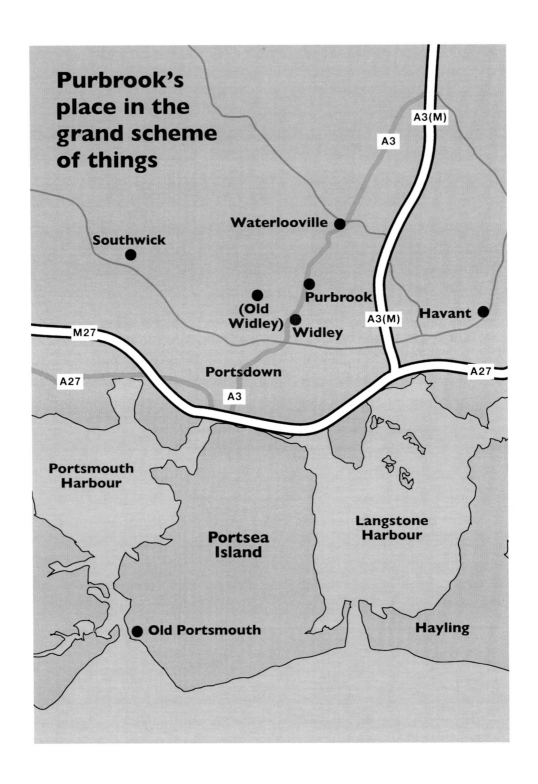

Purbrook's place in the grand scheme of things

Southwick

Waterlooville

A3(M)

A3

(Old Widley)

Purbrook

A3(M)

Havant

Widley

M27

Portsdown

A27

A3

A27

Portsmouth Harbour

Langstone Harbour

Portsea Island

Old Portsmouth

Hayling

CONTENTS

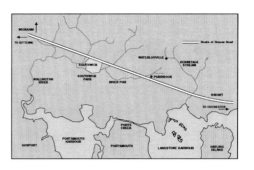

Purbrook Heath – Pretty Common

How old is your Club? The question was posed by the Webmaster of the Southern Premier Cricket League, at the start of the millennium. Nobody knew. This wasn't surprising, because everyone in Purbrook CC's bar that evening was on the right side of 40, except me and a couple of other Zimmers. The query didn't provoke much interest, so we emailed His Worship the Webmaster, saying: "circa 1900," and we got on with our ciders and ciggies.

Stirring my Horlicks later that night, I felt irked that we didn't know our age, and I decided to see whether "circa 1900" was anywhere near correct. I thought of drawing up a timeline for the clubroom wall, but so far all we had were team photographs from 1971 onwards. There had to be more to it. A skeleton or two in the Club cellar would be nice!

So I made a bee-line for Colin Wearn, who had a lively interest in Purbrook's past. The veil began to lift straightaway because Colin had already cracked the toughest part of the problem; he had trawled through papers and magazines and had documented more than 100 years of local history.

This included records of cricket matches played at Purbrook Heath from 1815 on, a revelation to me. Almost a century before the date we had guessed for the illustrious Webmaster. Almost back to the Men of Hambledon and their cradle of cricket. Colin's recording marathon concluded at year 1930 and I resolved to bring the records up to date.

I enjoyed several subsequent discussions with Colin Wearn before, sadly, he died in 2004. But he, along with another village stalwart Ted Lamont, fired my enthusiasm and suggested Purbrook's bigger picture. Cricket at the Heath was just one piece in a much older, more diverse, jigsaw.

My idea of a timeline had to be dumped. I learned that unassuming Purbrook Heath, (a name synonymous with Purbrook Common), is a wedge of common land or common waste that has endured many dates with destiny through the centuries. Cricket is merely an add-on. The tiny stream that dawdles inconspicuously along the Common's southern edge has seen far more than a dribbly ditch is entitled to see. There's a tale in its meanderings; it's been quiet too long.

I began to delve into many a dusty document in Hampshire archives, libraries and museums. An early surprise was the geological significance of Purbrook Heath and its downland neighbour Portsdown Hill. This significance kicked off about two hundred million years ago although, as is the way with geology, things happened very slowly.

So much so that, if we ignore the iguanadons and straight-tusked elephants that once roamed our hills and valleys – and I *have* ignored them because they are someone else's story – there wasn't much competition for headlines until the Romans trampled over southern Britain in AD43.

The all-conquering Romans built a major highway across Purbrook Heath. Not just any old road, but a major route from east to west, essential in their subjugation of south and south west Britain.

A thousand and more years later, following on from another Conquest – this time by the Normans, an arable slice of Purbrook Heath found itself presented as a gift to the burgeoning estate of a priory of Augustinian canons at Southwick. A good move, because it meant that peace broke out for three hundred years at the Heath.

But in the mid 1500s our larger-than-life monarch, Henry VIII, had a ruck with the Pope over power and authority and, as a result, dissolved the monasteries. Southwick Priory became Henry's to dispose of, and he decided to grant it (more likely sell it!) to one of his pals. So part of the Heath had a new owner.

Purbrook Heath is at the southern tip of the ancient Forest of Bere. The 1600s and 1700s saw the emergence of stage wagons, stage coaches and mail coaches making the journey between London and the naval town of Portsmouth. In those days, the trackways through the Forest between Horndean and Purbrook were feared and hated by travellers. It was easy to get lost, the tracks became mud slides in winter, and they harboured too many dodgy, dastardly highwaymen who lurked in these woods, ready to nick your lunchbox and a great deal more besides.

But once travellers reached Purbrook, heading south, they were through the Forest and safe. A community developed at Purbrook to cater for these coachmen, passengers and horses. After many a dry mile, there was water in the brook at the bottom of the hill to refresh the horses. And before long there were inns at the top of the village to refresh the travellers. By the 1850s, however, the railways had pinched the customers and the mail. The Stage Coaches and Mail Coaches disappeared, and Purbrook went to sleep again.

Fifty years on, the Heath's next brush with history witnessed a transport revolution – the Portsdown and Horndean Light Railway. This electric tramway ran a regular service from Portsmouth (Cosham) up and over Portsdown Hill between 1903 and 1935. The stop at Purbrook was popular with Pompey people seeking a whiff of country air on summer weekends. The tram track through Purbrook ran straight down the middle of the road. In 1907 the Company consolidated its Purbrook connection by building its own power station in the village, alongside The Leopard Inn.

The eventual demise of this town and country tramway was inevitable once the petrol engine spluttered into widespread use, but history wasn't finished with Purbrook Heath just yet. A decade later, in spring 1944, the headquarters of the biggest sea-borne invasion the world has ever seen was established a mile away at Southwick House.

Supreme Allied Commander Eisenhower was based there and our man, General Montgomery, hitched up at nearby Broomfield House. The byways, hedgerows and fields all around Purbrook Heath were swarming with Allied troops, their vehicles and their armouries. British, Canadians, Americans....everywhere. The edges of Bere Forest around the Heath provided the camouflage they needed. The whole area was an Exclusion Zone from April 1st, 1944 until some time after the D-Day invasion on June 6th.

When troops filtered home after the War – many of them were not demobbed until 1947 – major efforts were made by national and local government to provide recreation and sports facilities. And so the old cricket ground at the top of Purbrook Heath, adjacent to the Roman road, was chosen for a makeover.

It had gone to rack and ruin in wartime, never to recover properly, and Havant & Waterloo Urban District Council – to their eternal credit – resolved to excavate and level the land which they had purchased for a song from Southwick Estate in 1936. So on May 10th 1953, cricket returned to Purbrook Heath amid much whooping & hollering.

Because the history of Purbrook Common's cricket clubs was in danger of being lost forever, I have endeavoured to bring the clubs' stories to life. But they cover barely two hundred years of the Heath's existence, so a major slice of my tale is given over to Purbrook Heath's encounters with history, as outlined above. The remaining chapters offer a flavour of the cricket clubs: Purbrook CC, Widley CC (who played around the corner at Church Field), Christ Church CC, and Portsdown CC. Purbrook Football Club, our muddy winter cousins, get in on the act too.

Peace In The Valley

If you go down to the woods today (what's left of them), you're sure of a big surprise. Be good to yourself and make that short summer trip along the old Roman road to Purbrook Heath. Wander down to the stream and take five on Doug and Jim's old seat. Because, in the lee of Portsdown, sheltered from the milky breeze just after tea, and with a mellow sun in the western sky, there's no better place on this Earth than a spot by the boundary. Unless you've just been triggered first ball, of course!

I hope you enjoy The Purbrook Heath Story. I enjoyed writing it.

The object of our desire: Purbrook Heath in summertime.

Picture courtesy of Keith Todd

Yesterday's Capers

The summer of 1965 was warm and sunny on the Isle of Wight. I was there with a handy team of cricketers called the Shrewsbury Stragglers. We were touring for a week, playing against Northwood, Ryde, Shanklin, and Newport. Wednesday morning saw four of us in a cafe above Ventnor promenade, stoking up ready for the game at Shanklin that afternoon.

Wicketkeeper Brian Hiscox was our driver and resident comic; his three passengers were young bucks. Our waitress was young, sweet and pretty. She fussed around us encouragingly and we asked her name.

"I'm Catherine du Lac," she said, colouring up. "But everyone says du Lake."

"Oh," replied Hiscox, "we've got a "Canoe Lake" in Southsea. Any relation?"

It was near this Canoe Lake that I was born, nineteen years earlier. Near it, not in it! This was at the fag end of 1945 when much of Portsmouth was a Second World War bombsite. Several months later we settled at 26 The Brow, Widley, a neat residential street with grass verges on the northern slopes of Portsdown Hill. I embarked on a purringly happy childhood with Win and Alec and big sister Jean. Segoina Page-Turner lived two doors away, and Dave Martin lived up the road at number 62.

Dave turned out to be a better cricketer than Segoina, though she enjoyed the more exotic name. What happened to Segoina I have no idea, but I know what happened to Dave. He played cricket at Purbrook Heath for the majority of his adult summers until, at the age of 57, his bowling arm would no longer reach the perpendicular, so he packed it in. Wife Jane mopped his fevered brow and promised him there would be life after cricket. Dave hoped that she was right....she usually was!

Purbrook Heath In Context

Purbrook Heath was referred to as Purbrook Common when I was a lad. I became vaguely aware of it when, on summer Sundays, my mum and I walked the mile from The Brow along the A3 London Road to Sunday School at Purbrook Methodist Church.

In those days of the early 1950s the walk was a pleasant one; the A3 endured a modest sprinkling of traffic and the highway was edged with grassy banks for some of the way. Our walk took us past Widley's tidy parade of shops, The Hampshire Rose, the local co-op at Bushy Mead, Hants & Dorset Caravans, the Allotments and the Old Vicarage, to the outskirts of Purbrook village.

Here the London Road bridged a small stream that, unbeknown to almost everyone, was grandly entitled to call itself the River Pur. Running westwards in the same direction as the stream was Purbrook Heath Road. This area was off limits to a six-year-old and I had no notion that Purbrook Heath would pervade my future life with the cricketing equivalents of ecstasies and enemas.

At the beginning of the 1950s this heathland was a mixture of long grasses, wispy trees and gorse, although a line of tall oaks traced the stream's edge. My earliest recollection of Purbrook Heath is during 1952, when the land was being levelled and developed as a sports field. Havant & Waterloo Urban District Council broke the bank and spent £4,000 to transform the area, including the old cricket ground at the top. The outcome was a cricket table and two football pitches. No sloping off to Purbrook Heath anymore – from 1953 it was flat.

Fun And Games

By the early 1960s the Heath had become a magnet for sports-mad Purbrook and Widley lads. We played football when school broke up in the winter months and cricket through the summer holidays. Football was easier to organise and you could guarantee a game with the likes of Merv Liversidge, Mick Connor, Denny Riley, Dave Bennett and Terry Crump.

In those idyllic times the Heath had a resident groundsman. Bob Scantlebury and his sidekicks Ted Cooper and Kingsley Daniels were kindly men, but they ruled the roost, and they wouldn't think twice about turfing us off should their carefully groomed goalmouths be at risk from our mudlarks. The summer months saw informal games of cricket played by a smaller group of us. Now and then games would shudder to a halt if the kid who owned the solitary bat or ball threw a wobbly and stomped home with his hardware.

7

Cricketing fortunes took me away from Purbrook Heath during school terms. I commuted to Petersfield on Southdown bus number 40 or 42. Churcher's College played a great deal of cricket (cheers), but they also played rugby (boos). The reputable school viewed the round-ball game of football as being suitable only for oiks and banished it altogether. Though we regularly melted away to a remote corner of the playing fields so that we could discreetly kick a tennis ball around during lunch breaks, we risked an hour's detention. Daft but true.

Churcher's was overloaded with long-in-the-tooth teachers who provided a full timetable of oddball and quirk. Goodhearted English master Gus arrived for every lesson topped out in mortar board and flowing gown. A further decoration was his leather slipper, which he wielded to painful effect should any lad misbehave. In gladiatorial tradition he allowed the class to vote on suitable punishment: thumbs-up to be spared, thumbs-down for the slipper. Depending on the bloodlust of classmates, a snivelling offender

"Don't whack him sir, he's only come in to collect the dinner money!"

could end up let off or leathered. Democracy rules, OK?

An exception to this museum of sagging schoolmasters was Bob Pullin, who was simply the best sports master in the world. He also opened the batting for Petersfield, a top club in those days.

Christ Church Cricket Club played at Purbrook Heath and I guested for them a couple of times when I was fifteen. They were adults and I was just a lad, the divide being far more obvious in those days. Playing at Hawkley village one Bank Holiday, I dropped a couple of catches before clinging onto a third. When skipper Paul Christopher gave me a bowl I did OK, but I felt nervous. Scores were miserly in local cricket in those far-off 1960s; at Hawkley one of our batsmen scored 50 and the back slapping went on all evening. It was considered a major feat.

Village Characters

Larger-than-life local characters were alive and well in the fair village of Purbrook. The Brown brothers had been stalwarts of the Purbrook XI between the two World Wars. In their day the Club played on the top part of the Common, where tennis courts are today. By the time the Heath was developed and levelled in 1953, their playing days were almost done, although Reg and Fred (there were four other brothers too) remained loyal supporters into their 70s.

In 1962 I came up against elderly Fred Brown at a Purbrook practice session. Boys were encouraged to attend nets on the Common during summer evenings. In those days the nets were located behind the cricket square, by the stream. Fred Brown was watching proceedings, decked out formally in jacket, waistcoat, shirt and tie. On his feet he wore polished black leather boots, and he looked pretty ancient. I was a lanky teenager who bowled at a lively pace, though a little wayward at times. Fred looked knowingly at me and my pal, stripped down to his waistcoat, strapped one yellowish canvas pad onto his left leg and bellowed to us:

"Come on you young beggars, see if you can get me out."

For the next ten minutes we hurled the kitchen sink at him, but Fred stood firm, his stumps intact. A tough nut was Fred Brown; one of the old school.

Purbrook Football Club

Football kept me in regular touch with Purbrook Heath from 1962 onwards. I sneaked out of school rugby and joined Purbrook Football Club with my pal Dave Martin. Laurie Farmer was the guiding light behind the club, which fielded three teams every Saturday. There was no clubhouse, no social contact after games – it was solely a football club, but it thrived in the 1960s and 1970s.

The Common could become a mudheap in winter, but the first team pitch on the western side of the ground had plenty of width and was great for wingers. The pitch on the other side of the cricket square was smaller, muddier, heavier, bumpier.... great for whingers!

On The Move

Schooldays ended in 1964; time for me to maverick around Hampshire and beyond, playing for half a dozen teams. Sometimes the cricket was good, sometimes it was hit and miss! In 1969 I strayed to the Heath and played several Sunday games for Purbrook. Then, out of a clear blue sky, I was Dugg'd and Jimm'd. Portsdown CC's two evangelists, Douglas Doe and James Holder, came calling. Although I knew Jim, I had never met Doug. He could have sold tea to Earl Grey, and Jim matched his pal's enthusiasm for all things Purbrook Heath and all things Portsdown.

There was a hint of Morecambe & Wise about the duo and, laced with a backdrop of banter, they told me their recruitment plans for this bloke and that. They spun their web and in 20 minutes I was trapped inside. From that epiphany I was soon a Portsdown player, despite being domiciled in London from 1971 on. At first it was Portsdown on Saturdays and Purbrook on Sundays, but soon it became Portsdown full-time. Doug and Jim were true to their word; they had signed up some promising young players. Practically a whole team!

From that moment Bob Scantlebury's soft, green, Purbrook Heath wickets became increasingly familiar. Mind you, in those days of youthful effort and exuberance I never dreamed that, nigh on 40 years later, I'd be trundling in to bowl "right arm over" on a Saturday and shuffling up to draw my pension "left hand under" on a Monday....well, almost.

The times they are a-changing. In days of yore (days of a great deal of yore!) a familiar face in the opposing team might greet me with:

"Hi mate, how's it going? Taking plenty of wickets?"

Decades later, the greeting on the pavilion steps was of a different hue:

"Still going, you old tosser? Ain't it time you jacked it in?"

Reverence, like nostalgia, isn't what it was.

Chapter 1

In The Beginning

The Earth, our hospitality inn three rocks from the Sun, has been spinning around its fiery guardian for almost 4.6 billion years. Four thousand, five hundred and fifty million years is the best estimate – a long haul! The Universe is a good deal older. Data from NASA's WMAP satellite indicates that the Big Bang happened 13.7 billion years ago and that the first stars began to form 400 million years after that.

The Earth was a hostile place during its early life, with stunningly hot volcanoes erupting all over the place, oceans swimming in warm acid, and the entire surface enveloped by toxic fumes. There were no plants and consequently there was no oxygen. But there was water. The mass of volcanic activity saw to that, and copious amounts of water vapour resulted. As far back as 3.5 billion years the earliest, primitive forms of life emerged from these unpromising beginnings: *bacteria* – I've met a few! Their home was the hot, muddy rock pools of the volcanic islands.

Better Late Than Never

From this hot and slimy start way back in the far reaches of time, we have to travel through a dozen periods of geological time, until we reach the epoch when human species began to evolve. We are latecomers to party time on Earth and a great deal else had to happen before mankind put down its first marker. As far as Britain is concerned, tentative roots were put down in East Anglia up to 700,000 years ago by an early version of human kind. These settlers came on foot, crossing a wide bridge of land topped by a chalky ridge that connected what is now Britain and France.

For a majority of the last one million years, this land of ours has not been an island, severe changes in climate causing ice ages to come and go and sea levels to fluctuate. These first East Anglian settlers suffered the same fate as half a dozen later migrations and incursions – they were swept away by extreme environmental changes, both hot and viciously cold. Britain was so unpalatable that, for long stretches of pre-history, it was completely devoid of people.

Homo Sapiens (our lot) began their exodus from Africa almost 100,000 years ago, but it was relatively recently, just 11,500 years back and following the retreat of the last ice age, that they arrived to light their fires on the downland above Purbrook. By then earlier species of mankind had come and gone – the first inhabitants of this region had been Homo Erectus (upright man) who hunted big game through our forests as long as 250,000 years ago.

This Place Rocks

If we leave the Homo Sapiens settlers of Portsdown in their new surroundings and concentrate on the make-up of our planet, we discover that the surface of the Earth has been brought to its present condition by the slow formation of sedimentary rocks – the gradual laying down of volcanic lava, of sands and other particles, of fossils and so on. These rocks, hard and soft, have been slowly compacted and appear as layers, with the oldest at the bottom and the newest on the top, except in the many places where they have been tilted or skewed by pressure from the movement of the tectonic plates that make up the Earth's crust.

The Purbrook Heath story or, more precisely, the Portsdown story began in earnest 200 million years ago. At that time, the world's continents were joined together in one mass that geologists call Pangea. Surrounding the land mass was a huge ocean known as Panthalassa. Some 200 million years ago, this super continent of Pangea began to break up as the crust split into separate blocks. Very gradually the fragments moved apart, slowly drifting to the positions they occupy today. Put bluntly, tectonic activity led to plate movements.

Chalk On Cue

Jumping into the time capsule and setting co-ordinates for the Cretaceous period – between 146 million and 65.5 million years ago – we find Portsdown and Purbrook deep beneath the sea. At various times this area has been semi-arid plain, warm shallow sea, coastal swamp and cold tundra, and geologists believe the sea returned for yet another drenching around 100 million years ago after (perhaps) a 30 million year absence. Chalk symbolises the Cretaceous period and this soft, white rock provides the confirmation that our area was below the waves for millions of years. That's because chalk is the skeletal remains of countless tiny sea creatures and microscopic plants covered by calcite plates. When they died and sank to the seabed they were slowly compacted into chalk. Flint occurs in small lumps in the chalk seams too. It's very hard, much denser than chalk and was formed from the skeletons of sponges that were fossilised in the chalk.

Flint used in Eastney Fort's defences

Other fossils found in Portsdown's chalk include ammonites and belemnites (ancient relatives of squid and octopus), sea urchins, sea snails, shellfish, bony fish, giant lizards and even sharks. But mostly it is the tiny shell fragments of trillions of marine organisms and algae that make up the soft, white limestone we call chalk. It's the thickest and most widespread geological formation in southern England.

The layer of chalk at Portsdown is the oldest rock in the area at between 70 million and 100 million years old. It is also the thickest

– boreholes sunk in Portsdown have measured the chalk to be 400 metres deep. Our chalk-forming seas lasted an incredibly long time, from approximately 100 million to 65 million years ago. After this the seas retreated for a time.

The Purbrook and Portsdown area lies within the Hampshire Basin, a great depression stretching from Lyme Regis to Selsey Bill, and bounded north and south by Butser Hill and Arreton Down on the Isle of Wight. Chalk covers this entire region but between the ridges of Butser and Arreton it dips steeply beneath the Solent, and over time has been covered by clays, sands and gravels.

The troughs of the Hampshire Basin and its peaks of great sheets of chalk have come about because of the folding and faulting (the squeezing up) of the Earth's surface in southern England. It's likely that the chalk was laid down in fairly level sheets over millions of years, but pressure caused by movements in the Earth's tectonic plates has caused the folds and faults in the surface.

Glorious Mud

Around 55 million years ago, seas once again spread into the Hampshire Basin, and mud – called Reading Clay and London Clay – was deposited. Reading Clay lies below and round the edges of the London Clay which dominates. As with the chalk deposits, this settling of the clay took millions of years. London Clay – so called because the same type of clay lies beneath our capital – is about 100 metres thick in Portsmouth and there's a lump of it in Purbrook too. The clay in some parts of Hampshire has been covered by a thin veneer of sands and gravels and they are evident around Purbrook – our particular variety is known as Bagshot Sands. The village of Purbrook owes much to these sands and, what's more, without them it's unlikely that cricket would have found a home at Purbrook Heath.

Our Isolated Eminence

Back to the folding and squeezing up of Hampshire's lands for a moment. One major outcome is the South Downs and another is our own "isolated eminence," Portsdown Hill. Nearly seven miles long and one mile wide, the hill in its present form evolved about 25 million years ago when Africa, forever moving northwards, squashed up the Alps and the ripple effect led to the arching of a rib of chalk over Portsdown. Since then the soft chalk rock of the hill has eroded, leaving today's resistant slab standing defiantly in the centre of the fold, its highest point more than 380 feet above sea level.

But, if this was the ancient background of southern Hampshire, what was it that enabled Purbrook to bubble into life, when all to the north was forest and the land between Purbrook and Horndean unsuitable for habitation? The answer is water, plus Purbrook's particular mix of sands and gravels that brought it dribbling to the surface.

Exposed chalk on Portsdown Hill

Chapter 2

The Ground Beneath Your Feet

The ground beneath Purbrook Heath is layered. A thick band of chalk is down there but, as many local cricketers know, it's not this porous, soft white rock you find beneath the green sward, but clumps of clogging clay. There are sands and gravels tucked in too. Along Portsdown Hill's northern slopes, above Purbrook's domain, chalk remains uppermost and dominant. Way down at the bottom of this hill slope, Purbrook's mixture is different. The chalk here has been overlaid with clays, sands and gravels, and you would have to dig deep to find it.

Down Under

The ground beneath south Hampshire consists mainly of:

• Chalk;

• London Clay and Reading Clay;

• Sands and Gravels.

In the South Downs area, on places like Butser Hill and Harting Down, the chalk is exposed and nearest the surface. It's just the same on our own solitary, resistant rib, Portsdown Hill. Chalk – trillions of compacted shells of tiny sea creatures – was laid down first, then came the clay, and after that the sands and gravels. Not quite as neatly as that, but it's a fair summary. Whereas Portsea Island is a mix of clay, gravel, brick earth and estuary mud, and Portsdown Hill is chalky downland, Purbrook is a different mixture.

Purbrook sits on a foundation of chalk because, like all this region, it was under the sea for millions of years. The chalk dips down from Portsdown and forms a trough. Over time this trough has been partially filled by two layers of clay. The upper layer is London Clay which provides the subsoil for much of Purbrook. Lying underneath the London Clay, and also around its edges, is the other belt of clay: Reading Clay, which is a redder soil and occurs in narrow belts. Interspersed with Purbrook's two sorts of clay are streaks and stretches of sands and gravels.

Water, Water, Everywhere

Every time rain falls on the South Downs it sinks through the porous chalk, which acts like a sponge. Gradually this water permeates all the chalk areas but, because layers of thick clay sit above the chalk in much of southern Hampshire (notably from Horndean through to the borders of Purbrook) water is sealed in the chalk below the clay.

Rain also falls directly onto clay-topped areas, where it can't sink in. Here gravity takes a hand and the water runs along surface ditches that might be full or dry, depending on recent weather. And all the while, the ever present "South Downs water" is trapped in chalk below thick clay seams. Fortune smiled on ancient Purbrook, because right here was a chink in the geological armour and several factors helped its watery cause.

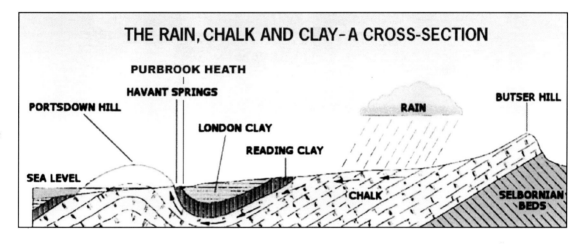

Diagram of the land around Purbrook

By kind permission of Portsmouth Water

Springing To Life

South of the clay lands of the Forest of Bere, the vital spot where water could escape from being trapped beneath the clay was at Purbrook. A fracture zone in the chalk (a junction of the chalk and clay) in the Bedhampton area encouraged springs to form. And streaked into Purbrook's surface were sands and gravels, in particular what are known as Bagshot Sands, allowing rain that fell on the heathland to sink in and then bubble to the surface here and there through springs.

(This fracture zone enables the city of Portsmouth to obtain much of its water supply from 29 springs at Havant and Bedhampton, situated in a line east to west about half a mile long. What seeps out is the drained rainfall from 100 square kilometres of chalk from the South Downs of Butser, Harting and all around. This groundwater is high quality because it's been filtered through the chalk).

The River Runs By

The sands and gravels and a nearby fracture zone gave Purbrook its springs. Water collecting in the Bagshot Sands seeped out to join the surface rainwater ditches. The Pur brook provides our local evidence. Nowadays, most of the brook's journey through Purbrook is hidden by culverts...but it's there, although many residents don't know it. The water emerges 30 metres west of the old A3 London Road adjacent to Purbrook Heath Road, and then saunters across the edge of Purbrook Heath on its journey west.

You can trace the brook's progress along the southern boundary of Purbrook Heath. Since the excavation for new sports pitches in 1953, the stream runs along the bed of a small ravine, caused by the levelling of the ground.

This Pur brook never dries up, even in the hottest summer, but I can't claim that it's a stirring sight as it meanders west across farmland in a healthy dribble before joining another tributary from the Sheepwash direction and heading for Southwick Park lake. Soon after this, near Walton Heath, the enlarged stream is accorded a name by Ordnance Survey: the Wallington River. These waters, some of which have gently tacked along from Purbrook's springs, begin to encounter the sea-salty stuff south of the village of Wallington. Their destination is Fareham Creek at the top of Portsmouth Harbour.

Pass The Source

Having traced the stream to the sea, let's paddle back to its source in Purbrook, reflecting that the old name Pokebroc meant a brook haunted by a goblin. There were several springs in Purbrook that seeped into rainwater ditches bringing water through Purbrook towards "the Bog" east of the bridge.

These springs are now piped and hidden, including one by Woodlands Grove, one in Stakes Road, one at Fielder's Park and another by Valley Close in Widley. There used to be several springs (pools) visible just east of Crookhorn Lane, feeding water west towards Purbrook. In years past there was a pond in front of Crookhorn Farm and another beside Gauntlett's Dairy Farm in Stakes Road. More ponds were once in evidence south west of Waterlooville near Hambledon Road. And wells featured regularly in Purbrook's yesteryears; they were dug to extract water sealed in the chalk below the clay.

In Purbrook today, storm drains and natural ditches feed in spring-water plus surface rainwater from the hillside and adjacent areas. The manmade lake set between Woodlands Grove and Shaftesbury Avenue has two inlet culverts at its eastern end. One brings water from the direction of Elizabeth Road/Stakes Hill, and the other collects water from the general direction of Crookhorn. At the opposite end of this latter-day Lake Louise (perhaps not – I should've gone to Specsavers!) there is one outlet culvert through which our brook (the River Pur) begins its westerly journey.

At the start it's subterranean. The route cuts underneath Westbrook Grove alongside Ivy Court, and across Stakes Road where it emerges for the first time into public view. But, after a bit more than a cricket-pitch-length, it ducks below the surface once more, veers across, and then runs parallel with Penjar Avenue, finally coming up for air west of the London Road, alongside Purbrook Heath Road. From here it's plain sailing (not literally) to the Wallington River.

You Can Take A Horse To Water...

As tracks over Portsdown Hill developed in olden days, there was always a place at the brook where horses could be watered and refreshed. Later, as the dockyard grew, the track from London to Portsmouth began to

Purbrook's manmade lake

be used by travellers using horse-drawn wagons. Around Purbrook's watering hole for animals a watering hole for humans grew up, in the form of coaching inns and stables. In the 1700s and 1800s, though still a sleepy backwater, a small village started to develop alongside the road from London at the southern edge of the Forest of Bere.

By contrast, the area between Horndean and Purbrook had no reliable access to water. The clay soil ensured that it was no place for human habitation, and the area remained forest until a building or two, in particular the Heroes of Waterloo, sprang up after 1815 at a crossing of the tracks now known as Waterlooville. (The exception that proves the rule is the Hermitage Stream, which bubbles up from a gravelly area by the Queen's Inclosure in Cowplain and flows all year. But the Hermitage flowed too far east of the London Road to be useful, and ran parallel whereas the Purbrook stream cut across the road at right angles. The Hermitage Stream flows due south to Langstone Harbour).

Our Fading Lowland Heath

The mix of Bagshot Sands, gravels and London and Reading Clays, all seated on top of a thick seam of buried chalk, provided the environment for the heathland that characterised Purbrook. Heathland occurs where poor soil combines with a cool, moist climate and most of Britain's lowland heaths are found within a band from Cornwall through to Norfolk. Purbrook Heath is one such lowland heath, situated about 150 feet above sea level.

Farming was introduced into Britain around 4,400 BC, and early communities cleared woodlands and burned forests to encourage animal grazing. These heathlands became populated by wild plants, and in its prime Purbrook Heath was home to hazel, holly, bramble, hogweed, silver birch and gorse. The bank of our humble River Pur was lined with oaks, while further west it hosted patches of watercress and a very occasional otter. The oaks are still there, with a faint sprinkling of fallow deer in nearby fields for company.

Purbrook's heathland was squeezed between the downland of Portsdown to the south and the heavier clays of Bere Forest to the north. In this space between down and forest the changeover from clay to sand can occur at short intervals, sometimes within the same field. The deposits of sand around Purbrook Heath are as white and fine as any on the beach at Hayling and they give rise to some unexpected natural

The River Pur
begins its
journey west

ponds. Less than half a mile from Purbrook Heath there is a thriving pond beyond Newlands Farm.

Purbrook Heath's two makeovers (the first for its sports ground in 1953 and the second for its bowling green three decades later in 1982) signalled the end for our local heathland.

In today's Purbrook it survives only at the margins. Once upon a time it was wild and rural, and its relative uselessness agriculturally was a major reason behind its longevity. Our good fortune is that this scrap of land was laid on one side and left. Proximity to easily worked adjacent land meant it was never considered for anything more profitable than pasture for animals, and kindling for the solitary inhabitants of yesteryear.

The Common Touch

Purbrook Heath is also known as Purbrook Common, so what's the link? Back in the mists of medieval England it became customary for stretches of non-arable land belonging to the lord or squire or church, to be set aside for villagers to utilise, even though they weren't the owners. These areas were called Commons and local people enjoyed common rights over them; they could use the land as pasture for their cattle and pigs. Early maps of Purbrook Heath show an animal pound in the south

21

west corner, where grazers could be kept secure overnight or lost animals kept safe until claimed by their owners.

Common Rights existed in Purbrook well into the 19th century. When Purbrook House was sold in 1830, the advertisement confirmed "about fourteen acres of meadow land with Right of Common on Purbrook West Common." And in 1843 the sales pitch for seven-bedroomed Portsdown Cottage on the brow of the Hill (now Christ Church Gardens) highlighted good stables, a coach-house, a small meadow, beautiful views and "rights on Purbrook Common."

Tithe maps drawn at the beginning of the 19th century referred to the area east of London Road - covered today by Park Farm Road, Shaftesbury Avenue and the manmade lake - as "Purbrook East Common." The area west of London Road that we call Purbrook Heath was referred to as "Purbrook Heath Common."

Up On The Downland

Rising gently from the southern edge of Purbrook's heathland is the chalk downland of Portsdown Hill. It has received more protection than the heath and is in better nick agriculturally. The chalk forming the hill produces light, easily worked soils. The subsoil is flint and chalk and on top of this, though it varies a good deal, is a thin mixture of clay, sand and loam.

One muddy autumn Monday I threaded warily round the golf course perimeter on the northern slopes of Portsdown Hill to check on the variety of surfaces: chalk, clay, flint, sand and gravel. What surprised me was that so many of the fairways are clay, when I expected to find only chalk near the hilltop. Red in colour, I guess it's Reading Clay. Stepping off the fairway, just 150 yards further on, the surface was entirely different, predominantly chalk. Then, half a mile to the west, still on the northern slopes of Portsdown in a farmer's field, the ploughed earth was heavily infiltrated with chalk and flint; altogether a much lighter density of soil.

These northern slopes of Portsdown shelter farms that reach to the edge of Purbrook Heath. They have been here for centuries and reveal open fields, hedges and small clumps of trees. Their fields are used for grazing cattle, and the farmers' crops include wheat, maize and barley. Most of this agricultural land is managed by tenant farmers; the owner is Southwick Estate.

Down In The Forest

If you head north on country roads past Portsdown Hill and the Heath, you come to the third type of countryside around Purbrook: the ancient forest, or what little remains of it. It was about 11,500 years ago that the ice of the last glacial period receded far enough for trees and plants to begin to colonise Britain once again. Ice had not extended south of the Thames, but the severely cold conditions had put a block on vegetation. Following the retreat of the ice, Britain became a land mostly covered by forest, although this process took several thousand years to evolve.

Locally, the first trees to dominate were birch, giving way to thickets of hazel, and then to oak, beech and elm. This mix formed the basis of our southern forest from about 5,000 BC on. By the time the Romans invaded in AD 43, a forest (Anderida) stretched from east Kent as far as Dorset, and covered almost the entire area between the North and South Downs. From Roman through Saxon times parts of this wooded landscape provided grazing for pigs, cattle and oxen. After the Norman invasion in 1066, our local forest became known as the Forest of Bere (meaning swine pasture) which, at its peak, stretched over a huge arc encompassing Hursley, Eastleigh, Bishops Waltham, Denmead, through to Rowlands Castle in the east.

And So To Bed

Time to take stock. The survey of soils and springs is complete. My geological jaunt has been undertaken with a newcomer's enthusiasm as well as a layman's limitations because, despite great expectations, that's all I claim to be. Having said that, I'll put Purbrook's soils and springs to bed with the following expert summary, exactly as relayed to me when I was gathering information for this chapter:

"The core area of Bere Forest is really that zone separating the chalk pericline of Portsdown Hill from the dip-slopes of the secondary escarpment of the South Downs.

It's a major synclinal vale filled with erosionally unresistant early Tertiary clays, loams, sands and gravels. The London Clay of the Hampshire Basin gives rise to wet land with heavy soils, as exemplified by Bere."

So now you know, folks!

Chapter 3

The Road To Civilisation

And then came the Romans! The first invader was Julius Caesar in 55BC. But he met more resistance than anticipated, and within a few weeks he was back in Gaul. At this time Belgic tribes ruled the roost in south east Britain. They had migrated northwards from Gaul and were well established. A year later Julius had another go, and invaded again. His Roman army attacked the Belgic militias in their stronghold north of the Thames. The tribal King eventually made peace and agreed annual payments to Rome. Caesar seemed satisfied with this arrangement and hit the road for home.

I, Claudius

All was quiet on this island outpost for another hundred years. In 43AD Claudius was Emperor of Rome and was looking to enhance his reputation. One sure way was to make some foreign conquests, so his army under Aulus Plautius invaded Britain, the main force landing at Richborough in Kent. There were four legions: 2nd, 9th, 14th and 20th. The legion was the main fighting unit of the Roman army, comprising 5,000 men, including cavalry, and led by 60 centurions. The major group battled north, crossing the Thames and setting up base at Colchester. Emperor Claudius trekked across and joined them there, staying a fortnight before heading home, content that his invasion was on the way to being hosed down and polished.

The success of the first stage depended on a secure left flank. This was provided partly by the dense forest of the Kent and Sussex Weald, and partly by a friendly tribe, the Regni, who ruled an area around what later became Chich-

"Give me two legs please, Umpire."

ester. It was the second stage of the invasion that embroiled southern Hampshire in the Roman occupation. The conquest of the West Country was entrusted to Vespasian, commanding officer of the 2nd Legion. He was a high-flier, destined to become Emperor of Rome a quarter of a century on (69AD to 79AD), thereby establishing the Flavian Dynasty. Vespasian's 2nd Legion was due to head west and landed at several points along the south coast, including the natural harbours in our region.

Vespasian needed a strong supply network and one of his initial bases was at Fishbourne. He didn't hang around. Vespasian subdued the Isle of Wight (some say it's been subdued ever since!) and his troops headed west as far as Exeter. The southernmost land route – the marching route for troops – was probably along the line Fishbourne : Wickham : Winchester. Road building was a priority to maintain troops and supplies, but obviously roads couldn't precede the first push west, although the troops' long slog helped identify preferred routes for later roadways.

In these early days of the invasion, 43AD, Fishbourne was a useful harbour, but the Army didn't stay here long. As they pushed west and consolidated, Fishbourne was soon abandoned, only to develop through the next 30 years as a trading settlement. Around 75AD work began on Fishbourne Palace which was in its prime by the end of the century. If you visit Fishbourne Palace today, you can view the earliest of the mosaic floors, an impressive black and white chequer board.

Vespasian was a man on a mission. After breezing through the Isle of Wight, he quashed 20 fortified Belgic strongholds in Dorset, Wiltshire and Somerset, and by 44AD was back in Rome being honoured for his successes. All told, by 47AD the Romans had conquered most of southern England and had established a frontier along the line Lincoln : Cirencester : Exeter.

Getting Connected

But what has this Roman Conquest to do with Purbrook Heath? The answer is a top-notch Roman road. Before the Conquest in 43AD, roads in Britain were just broad pathways connecting domestic centres of trade. There was an ancient trackway along the ridge of Portsdown, and some rudimentary tracks north-south over Portsdown, linking isolated farming communities. To the north lay the daunting forest much later known as the royal Forest of Bere, and in these early times nothing much penetrated that.

With the coming of the Romans, Britain received the trappings of civilisation, including the Roman road system. It happened something like this: the rendezvous for the Roman invasion in 43AD was Colchester, from where the Legions spread north, west, and south west. Some of Vespasian's troops were already heading along the south coast, having landed at suitable harbours here. After the Legions came the road engineers. Roman roads were supply routes bringing troops, food and goods to the Roman forts being established along the way. The original roads spread out like spokes in a wheel from the new HQ of London. Later on, roads became increasingly important for trade.

The first road ran from Richborough in Kent through London and on to Warwickshire, where it crossed the Severn east of Shrewsbury. This was Watling Street.

The second road headed north from London, through Lincoln and on to York. This was Ermine Street.

The third road started from London, crossed the Thames at Staines, and headed west through Silchester to Winchester and on through Dorset. It is this third Roman road that, together with the establishment of Fishbourne and the emergence of Novio Magus (Chichester), begins to connect Purbrook Heath with the major Roman road network.

A Date On The Roman Road

The Roman occupation lasted from 43AD to 410AD and at some point a major road link was built from Chichester across Purbrook Heath to Winchester, thereby linking to London via Silchester and across the Thames at Staines. This was no minor roadway; its dimensions signify that it was a major route. Precisely when the road builders strained across the northern boundary of Purbrook Heath is uncertain.

It's likely to have been in situ by 200AD, because this Chichester : Wickham : Winchester : Silchester : London road was included in a register of Roman roads known as the Antonine Itinerary, believed (although this is uncertain) to have been drawn up on the orders of Antoninus Augustus (Antoninus Pius), who was Emperor of Rome from 138AD to 161AD. Our route was described in Itinerary VII.

If the first push west along the coast by Vespasian's troops was promptly followed by the road builders, then our road must have been built much earlier than that. The principal routes may have been in place shortly after the Conquest, probably by 47AD. But a 1981 discovery of

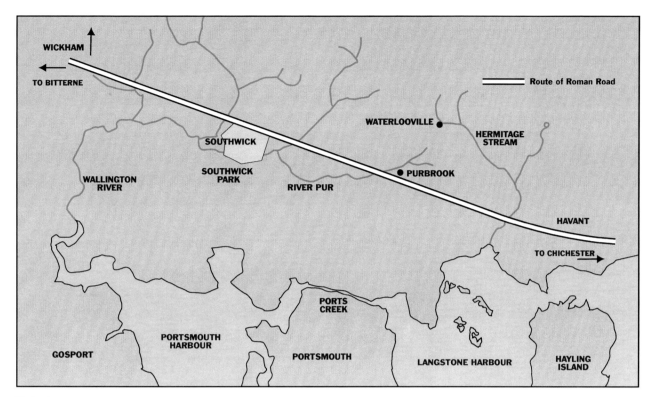

The local route of our Roman road

200 Roman silver coins in a field close to the Roman road at Purbrook Heath House was dated at around 272AD by the British Museum, so is this close to the birth date of the road? The possibilities seem to be: a) between 43 and 47AD; b) mid 2nd century; or c) around 272AD. We know that there was a considerable Roman presence in our district: there were brick kilns at Crookhorn with a villa nearby, and Roman farmsteads between the Heath and Plant Farm.

Roman Roads enthusiast GM Hughes held the view (in 1905) that, because Stane Street (Chichester to London across The Weald) was not included in the Antonine Itinerary, whereas Chichester : (Purbrook) : Winchester : London was, our route must precede the famous Stane Street. Hughes believed strongly that the Chichester : Winchester road was laid as a main military road soon after the Roman invasion in 43AD and at that time provided the only route from Chichester to London.

So, mid first century through to late third century for Purbrook's Roman road? I go for the early military road choice...but I wasn't there at the time! What is clear, however, is that although the Roman road network was ultimately comprehensive in its coverage of Britain, the number of major routes was limited. To have one arrowing across the Common at Purbrook is quite a coup. A bit sad that so few people know about it. Until well into my crisis years, I knew little of it myself.

The Fort Of The Saxon Shore

There is a streaky (but undeniable) link between the vast Roman fortress at Portchester and cricket at Purbrook Heath. The explanation gathers pace in chapter five, but a swift dab of information hereabouts will smooth my story along. The fort at Portchester was not on the route of the Chichester : Winchester Roman road because it wasn't built until the end of the third century, when Saxon incursions threatened the region. Portchester was one of several Roman forts (Saxon Shore Forts) erected along the south coast to repel these sea-borne invaders. Because the road network was set up before the fort existed, the engineers kept well to the north, cutting across Purbrook Heath.

The impressive eastern wall of Portchester's Roman fort

The Portchester fort was built between 285AD and 290AD. Roman naval commander Marcus Aurelius Carausius oversaw its construction, proclaiming himself Emperor of Britain and northern France in 286AD. The Roman army used the fort mainly in times of conflict, but it was also populated by local people who built their timber houses and workshops within its protective walls, keeping their animals and their rubbish heaps and cesspits close at hand too.

Portchester has the best preserved Roman walls in northern Europe.

These Roman builders used locally sourced materials - the flint quarries of Portsdown provided the main material for the walls and an estimated 15,000 cartloads of materials were used in the construction. Chalk was also brought to the site from Portsdown to make lime for the mortar, and limestone was shipped over from the Isle of Wight in single-masted ships.

This water gate in the eastern wall of Portchester's Roman fort is late Saxon

(By the end of the 18th century, the owners of the manor of Portchester, including the Norman castle built inside the Roman walls, were the rich Thistlethwayte family, the same Southwick Park Squires who owned Purbrook Heath. In 1926 they placed Portchester Castle in the guardianship of the nation and in 1936 they sold Purbrook Heath to the local Council).

Where Did Our Roman Road Roam?

The Roman road across Purbrook Heath was no second rate mud slide. It was set between ditches and raised up on an embankment which was cambered to allow rainwater to drain into the ditches. The base of the roadway was made of sizeable stones with gravel, flints and small stones pressed down on top. This compacted surface above the larger stone base was a few inches deep at each side, building to a foot or more in the centre of the road.

The width of Roman roads varied considerably. Fifteen to eighteen feet was typical for minor roads, but on the important roads a width of 24 feet was common, with 30 feet being the maximum. The width of the Roman road just west of Purbrook Heath has been estimated at about 27 feet. Between Southwick Park and Wickham the road was approximately 24 feet wide. Clearly, this road across Purbrook Heath was a major Roman thoroughfare.

Purbrook Heath's Roman road in its 21st century clothing

Our Roman road starts at Chichester, then passes through Fishbourne, Southbourne, Emsworth, Havant, Bedhampton, Crookhorn, Purbrook, and on to Wickham. There the road splits, a south westerly fork heading for the Roman seaport at Bitterne, and a northerly fork heading to Winchester. After that, the road heads for London via Silchester and Staines. (Another branch heads west). In Purbrook's neck of the woods much of the Roman road has been built over, but the exact route is known. From the end of Hulbert Road at Bedhampton, the road tracks north of Portsdown Hill Road towards Purbrook, crossing Sandy Brow and heading towards Alameda Road, cutting across the sharp bend near the end of the Crescent.

After this, trekking up Purbrook Heath Road to the cricket ground and beyond, we are travelling on the Roman route in its 21st century clothing. The Roman road continues in a straight line to the northern boundary of Southwick Park (HMS Dryad), and then it joins the Wickham Road which it follows in an unerring line for a mile.

Back at Bedhampton, the initial choice for the Roman engineers had been whether to head west using the ancient ridgeway along Portsdown Hill or pick a different option. They preferred the lower route across the fields from Bedhampton through Purbrook, cutting along the extreme southern boundary of the forest (of Bere) at Purbrook Heath.

The Roman Army had its own surveyors and engineers. Troops did some of the road building, with forced labour from local tribes doing much of the heavy work. As the Roman occupation settled down, the road became increasingly used as a trade link to ports such as Bitterne, and as a connection between centres of population such as Chichester and Winchester.

The importance of Purbrook Heath's Roman road faded once Roman governance of Britain ended in 410AD. Most organised Roman life had ebbed away by 450AD as the Saxon raiders gradually became settlers. They had little need for a road network because they didn't use market centres at first. Consequently the great Roman road system fell into disrepair and disuse in rural spots like Purbrook.

And so the Roman Empire shrank from these shores. The Saxon raiders turned their hands to farming and nothing much stirred down at the forest edge for several hundred years. It wasn't until the second millennium was into its stride that the next dose of trouble started to brew.

Chapter 4

The Domesday Scenario

In 1066 all hell broke loose. William, Duke of Normandy, poked Harold II firmly in the eye at Hastings and conquered England. He was crowned King and promptly engineered a widespread land-grab. Most of the lands belonging to the English nobility were confiscated and granted to followers of the Norman Conqueror. These days rewards are peerages and patronage. Back then it was land.

The Conqueror's Land-Grab

The Conquest was the work of a small power group of strong and ruthless men. The Norman occupiers probably numbered no more than 20,000, yet they lorded it over two million English. King William learned very quickly that he couldn't count on support from the English aristocracy, so he took their land and bought enduring loyalty from his principal 200 or so northern French followers by assigning the land to them in return for rent and/or military service. They knew their privileged place; they were in essence tenants-in-chief of the King's land.

Previously, in Saxon times the men of England could own their land. Under William, the King owned it and parcelled it out to his noblemen and to the Church, in return for services to the monarch (called a fief). The Conqueror's Norman followers swallowed up half the land, and the Church a quarter via favoured archbishops and bishops who were in many cases French. Almost all the rest was retained directly by the King.

William and his henchmen torched countless villages on their initial rampage through the countryside. Thousands were killed and thousands more starved, ensuring that this invading force of French noblemen was loathed and feared. After tearing down the thatch and timber dwellings of the locals, they built impressive castles and cathedrals high into the air, to emphasise their dominance. At first they built in wood for speed, but thereafter they built in stone for power and eternity. The language of England changed too. Latin continued in the churches and English prevailed in the countryside, but in the corridors of power Norman French became the new language of influence.

Hunting For A Forest

William relished a good battle, but he was also fanatical about hunting. He loved the chase and he loved the venison. Soon after the invasion, he and his gang were on the lookout for suitable hunting grounds. High on their list was the place they soon named the New Forest, but the Forest of Bere also fitted the bill. It had the requisite natural features for hunting deer and boar, and had been used for that purpose by the Saxons. From Roman times people living in and around Bere Forest enjoyed free grazing for their pigs and cattle and free use of forest timber for fuel and building. But there were no rights to hunt or fish.

Durham Cathedral provides evidence of the Normans' power and influence

Purbrook Heath was at the very edge of this vast forest. The line of the once-mighty Roman road could have doubled as its front gate and picket fence. Because of widespread grazing, parts of Bere Forest were open pasture, while other areas were fenced or coppiced to protect woodland from the animals. But the Normans saw all this as hunting territory and William simply acquired the land as spoils of conquest.

Much of it had once belonged to Harold II who perished at Hastings in 1066. As Harold Godwinson, he had dispossessed two tenants and incorporated their manors, including Chalton, Meonstoke and Soberton into his holdings. Bere became a royal forest, and the Conqueror was severe on anyone caught poaching deer. Retribution got even worse under his son William II – a poacher caught in the act might expect blinding, mutilation or execution.

The Forest of Bere was officially taken outside common law and put under Forest Law in 1086, in order to stop people other the King and those sanctioned by him from hunting and killing game, especially deer. Forest Law also made it illegal to cultivate land and to fell trees. People living within the forest risked being kicked out of their homes, thereby losing their livelihoods for good measure.

A patch of what remains of the Forest of Bere, near Rowlands Castle

William the Conqueror established 21 royal forests during his reign, and this grew to 80 by the 1150s, covering 30 per cent of England. But the Forest of Bere was never popular with the Crown, although King John came a-hunting in Bere in 1214. Royalty preferred the New Forest and Bere slipped into mismanagement and neglect, despite the establishment in 1306 of a Verderers' Court to enforce Forest Law. Although most locals toed the line, poaching was never cut out completely. Forest Law may have been dear to the hearts (or deer to the harts!) of the Kings, but it was seen as brutal and arbitrary by people living on the fringes of the Forest.

Even in its pomp the Forest of Bere didn't belong entirely to the Crown, with bits of it remaining in private ownership. Bere was a patchwork of woodland, chases, heathland, and farmland. As the Kings lost interest in this hunting forest, illegal encroachments grew, and despite wardens, verderers and keepers, the Forest became worth little, except where it had been cultivated. And by the time Charles I became the last monarch to hunt here in 1628, the Forest was more important for providing timber for ships than for providing land for hunting deer. It was now the worst kept royal forest in England, and had shrunk from hundreds of square miles to just 25.

Shires, Sheriffs, Squires and Serfs

But back to the Normans, because it was their Conquest that set in train the events that delivered Purbrook Heath to us. When William invaded in 1066, he found England structured like this:

• ancient Shires subdivided into Hundreds, with the King keeping tabs on the Shires through local Sheriffs;

• these Hundreds assessed in numbers of Hides and taxed accordingly.

The Conqueror wanted to be seen as the legitimate monarch, so it made sense to retain the administrative fabric of Shires and Sheriffs and County Courts too. It also enabled him to tax his new subjects until their pips squeaked.

Our southern area was an agricultural economy – few towns but a fair number of manors, villages and hamlets. In Saxon times before the Norman Conquest, peasants were free men, although they were dependent upon the lord of the manor. They were bound to work many days of each year on their lord's land and make payments of their own hard-earned crops to him. In return, workers were given tools to use on their allotted strips of land and utensils to use in their tiny houses. When a peasant finally curled up his toes, the lord took charge of what remained. But never mind these hardships, during his lifetime the Saxon peasant called himself a free man.

Under the Normans this free man became a serf, a bondsman. He could be bought and sold along with his family. All land had a lord, and all land was held on behalf of the King. The serf was at the bottom of the pile, with few rights and privileges and no access to the courts. At the top end of Norman society strode the King and his lordly tenants-in-chief. Reinforcing their authority were Knights, and aspiring knights called Squires.

This was a warrior class – the sons of lords and sons of other knights. From as young as seven, an "apprentice" knight would live in another lord's house as a page, learning to ride, to use a sword and a bow. By 21 he could be a fully fledged knight, bringing power and protection to his lord. England was the King's land held by his chosen elite, and it remained in their firm stranglehold. The peasants had to put up with it.

Records In Their Hundreds

You didn't cross the Conqueror; he was a tough cookie. But on the credit side he set in motion a priceless eleventh century snapshot of the country. Almost 20 years after his 1066 conquest, William determined to get a better grip on the value of his new land and how much tax he could extract from it. He sent men all over England to record what land and livestock each landowner had and what it was worth. The information was collected in Winchester and became the Domesday Book. But William I died in 1087, so the main beneficiary of this mass of information was his son William II.

The Hundreds described in the Domesday Book were the administrative, judicial and taxation units of their day. There was no Purbrook in 1086 – it was simply a place where the brook flowed – but the villages round about were included in the Portsdown Hundred. There were several major landowners, ie tenants-in-chief. The Domesday Book records that the King himself owned land at Wymering, Cosham and Portchester, and Hugh de Port from Bayeux held land at Bedhampton and Cosham. Land was often sub-let too.

The Portsdown Hundred incorporated Bedhampton, Boarhunt, Buckland, Copnor, Cosham, Fratton, Portchester, and Wymering. Villages were tiny: Wymering comprised sixteen villagers, six smallholders, two serfs, and five pigs. The ancient Saxon parish of Farlington was part of

These days the wild old Forest of Bere has been softened and sanitised

Portsdown Hundred. It contained two royal manors, with land being leased by the King to various tenants.

The parish was about five miles long and one mile wide, stretching into part of what we know today as Purbrook, at the Stakes/Crookhorn end. Farlington parish boundary was (using today's place names) Drayton Lane to the west, Rectory Avenue (approx) to the east, Farlington Marshes to the south and Waterlooville crossroads to the north.

The Way We Were

Imagine our section of the Portsdown Hundred around the environs of Portsdown Hill in 1086. The parishes, manors and villages of Bedhampton, Cosham, Farlington, Portchester and Wymering are all living, breathing communities at the time of the Domesday Book. Hovering in the wings, but not yet on stage, are the hamlets of Crookhorn (Creuquer), Stakes (Frendstaple), Drayton and Southwick. As for Purbrook and Waterlooville, their lines aren't due to be written for a long time yet.

So the Saxon Dusk makes way for this Norman Dawn and, in the county of Hantescire as the Domesday Book calls it, powerful Norman landowners control many of the big estates with lords of the manor running the smaller ones. The Church holds vast tracts of land too. There are a few towns here and there such as Winchester, Chichester and Southampton. The island of Portsea is mostly marsh with a handful of settlements and farms dotted about, plus a hint of commerce in its south west corner.

In the countryside there are parishes, manors, villages and hamlets, and the peasants who live out their tired lives in these tiny districts rise early and go to bed knackered. They are hard grafters, bound to the soil. No Human Rights Act for them! The Forest of Bere has become a hunting preserve for royalty, though a second rate one. Across our Common the brook flows quietly west and forest filters into heath. Buried underground, a forlorn Roman road has lost sight of its vibrant past.

Over at Portchester the towering walls of the old Roman fort still dominate. In one corner of the ancient site are the murmurings of a Norman castle. In another corner by the southern wall, something else is stirring. There's a parade of black canons, although these canons can't be fired. But Purbrook Heath is definitely within their range.

Chapter 5

A Prior Engagement

Developments down by the southern wall of Portchester's Roman fortress had a vital knock-on effect for Purbrook Heath. The establishment of an order of pious, god-fearing canons – monks to you and me – in the far corner of the grounds was a stepping stone to cricket being played hundreds of years later on Purbrook Heath. A good yarn admittedly, but it happens to be true.

We must return to the powerhouse days of William the Conqueror to pick up the thread. He assigned Portchester to one of his influential supporters, William Mauduit. By 1120 both Mauduit and his son Robert had died, and the building and land (land that included Southwick) passed to another Norman noble, William Pont de l'Arche. By now there was a walled area within the old fort, and Pont de l'Arche added a tower.

The Priory Church of St. Mary at Portchester

Canons To The Right Of Them, Canons To The Left

William Pont de l'Arche probably started building a church within the grounds of the fort *before* any monks were brought over from Normandy to be based at the site. A few years later it was Pont de l'Arche who gave orders to set up the priory of Augustinian canons. Building the church had started around 1128 and the popular date for founding the Priory is 1133. It was a "royal foundation" because Henry I granted the Priory a charter in 1133, which provided the canons with land, timber and tithes. Portchester's new canons were a disciplined bunch, even if they were the original hoodies. They wore black cassocks, sleeved surplices, cloaks with hoods, and square, black caps. The man in charge was the Prior.

Their Portchester priory was set within the south east corner of the Roman walls, with cloisters, dormitory and dining hall set around the southern side of the church. The latrines on the first floor of the building, sometimes referred to as the lavatorium or the garderobe (but never the bogs!) comprised nine holes in the old Roman wall that discharged the sweet monks' effluent straight into the harbour. Today the Priory Church of St Mary stands alone with its graveyard; the other Priory buildings have gone. Around the graves you can trace the outline of the

The monks' lavatorium viewed from the outside

40

cloisters, see where the cooking range was and view, in all their glory, the 900-year-old bogs – nine holes in the wall. Mind where you walk the dog, missus!

Settling For Southwick

Within a decade of setting up, the canons decided that their priory within the grounds of a fort was not the right environment for prayer and piety. It was certainly no place for peace and quiet, as a township had also grown up within the walls of the fort. The Priory's endowments put the canons in a privileged position, because Henry I had assigned them a hide of land way over that hilltop they could see from their Portchester base. The hill was Portsdown, and the land was at Southwick. It included a wood, a mill, a meadow and pasture.

Between 1145 and 1153 they quit Portchester and set themselves up in the area that nowadays comprises much of Southwick Park. Before long their new countryside home boasted a guest house and a church (dedicated in 1181-2). Outside the gates they had an almshouse built and another church, St James Without the Priory Gates which, in remodelled 1566 guise, stands on the same site today. All this was achieved by the grit and determination of one Prior and about a dozen canons.

The Priory's land at Southwick was added to considerably in the 1200s and 1300s and became the manor of Southwick. It was a centre of Christianity and the Prior became rector of the church and lord of the manor, to a large extent running the business of the village. Monks from Augustinian orders made a point of involving themselves with village life, and so it was at Southwick. The canons even took part in summer-time plays staged on the green. Now thoroughly settled in Southwick, the Priory benefited from subsequent royal grants of land and possessions. And over several centuries the Priory busily added to its estates through gifts, purchases and exchanges (though it never became enormously wealthy). At its peak the Priory owned a vast amount of land in our tiny corner of the globe.

Give And Take

One lucrative way that the Priory added to its stock of land required little effort by the canons. A custom of the time was for local men of means to offer parcels of their land as gifts to the Priory who then took on responsibility for collecting tithes and rent from tenants. But such gifts were not wholly altruistic from the land-givers' point of view. The wording that accompanied these grants made it pretty clear that a landowner's primary motive was to achieve some brownie points in the eyes of the Almighty and to broker a good deal for both landowner and family in the life hereafter. Such gifts of land often took effect on the death of the particular dignitary, and the monks were then bound to pray for his soul.

The ancient Cartularies (registers) of Southwick Priory record several local pieces of land being given to the Priory. Sometime between 1153 and 1163, Matthew de Scurys made:

"a Gift in free alms" of his chapel at Widley to Southwick Priory, complete with "the full tithe of all things from the demesne of his manor of Widley; also land called Sheepwash."

De Scurys made this gift: "for the salvation and welfare of himself and his (family)."

Sheepwash Farm still exists; it's part of the Southwick Estate and is barely a mile north west of Purbrook Heath. "In free alms" signified a charitable deed by de Scurys, and "with the full tithe of all things from the demesne of his manor of Widley" meant that all revenue raised from his Widley and Sheepwash estates would in future go to the Priory. A gift is a gift, but in de Scurys' eyes it warranted some heavenly recognition in return. That's why he made his gift to the Priory "for the salvation and welfare of himself and his (family)."

St. James without the Priory Gates, Southwick

These ancient Priory records tell us more about the lands around ancient Widley. At some date between 1185 and 1210, Roger de Scurys (son of Walter de Scurys) also made a gift to the Priory:

"for the love of God.....and for the salvation of himself and his (family) as endowment for the church of Widley, of all the land of the fee (meaning a grant of land in return for money) of Ralph de Plais which adjoins Planta, and which he holds of Adam de Portesia by charter."

At Southwick Priory's request, de Scurys gave this land at Planta in exchange for sixteen acres near Widley church. Land at Planta is the area known much later as Plant Farm, immediately north of Purbrook.

Take A Patch Of Purbrook Heath Too

So the 900-year-old registers of Southwick Priory refer to Plant Farm, Sheepwash Farm, and Widley. And they also make reference to the area we know as Purbrook Heath. They describe:

"a Gift in free alms, by Hugh de Pageham – for his salvation and that of his wife Margaret, his children and all his friends – to Southwick Priory of half a virgate, of which five acres lie south of Newlands Grange in one close, and the rest near the forest next to the land of Blakeman de Porteswalde." (Half a virgate is approximately 15 acres).

This land south of Newlands Grange, half a mile south of Newlands Farm, is present-day Purbrook Heath, or at least a patch of it. Hugh de Pageham had been granted this land in return for grain and money by Adam de Pokebroc, the original owner. Hugh gave the land to the Priory with Adam de Pokebroc's full support, and the Priory agreed to pay Adam two shillings per year in return, whereas Hugh de Pageham received one pound of cumin each year in acknowledgement of his gift of land to the Priory. The Priory received Hugh into full brotherhood and promised to record his name in their martyrology after his death. Let's hope it worked for him.

This gift of land at Purbrook Heath took place between 1213 and 1215. Not much else is known about benefactors Hugh de Pageham or Adam de Pokebroc. There is an archive reference to a William de Pageham who was a Knight in the 1240s, and there is a local association with the surname, because Pageham crops up again a century later in 1361, when Laurence de Pageham dies and the new manor of Drayton passes to his young grandson John. The Pagehams held Drayton manor until 1442, when it passed to a cousin.

Of Adam de Pokebroc, even less is known. Because of his name, he seems to be the local man, a landowner well connected with the Normans. In confirming Hugh de Pageham's gift to Southwick Priory, Adam was likewise keen to polish up his CV and safeguard his family's pathway through the afterlife. The registers say: "Confirmation....by Adam de Pokebroc - for the salvation of his soul and those of all his (family) both living and dead – to Southwick Priory, of Hugh de Pageham's gift...."

Local Knowledge

Adam's surname was the Old English name for the spot that ultimately morphed into today's village of Purbrook, ie Pokebroc or Pukebrok. This means goblin's brook or brook of the water sprite. Today's name, Purbrook, probably has a much simpler meaning – pure brook – referring to the clear springwater eddying through.

There are other medieval references to lands nearby. In 1215 or thereabouts, William de Merlay made a gift to Southwick Priory of St Andrew's Church Farlington, plus its tithes, lands and pastures. We know something of Widley too. Originally called Widelia or Widelya, it means Wood Clearing or Wooded Place. Before the 1066 Norman Conquest, Widley was an estate of approximately 240 acres owned by Bricsmar. It fell to the Normans after their invasion and by the time of the 1086 Domesday survey landowner Hugh de Port from Normandy had sub-let a part of Cosham that probably evolved as the manor of Widley, to a man recorded simply as Geoffrey.

In 1248 Roger de Merlay granted one and a half carucates of land in Farlington to William, son of Alan Stake. And so we have the link with our hamlet of Stakes (also known as Frendstaple). Around 1320, a man called John de Upton petitioned the King for the return of land he claimed had been seized from his father Roger by the Crown. The places in question were the small manor of Creuquer (Crookhorn), the hamlet of Frendstaple (Stakes), and the royal manor of Farlington which the King leased in parts to various tenants.

At the start of the 1340s, Southwick canons had reason to be grateful to King Edward III, because he made the Priory a gift of his Crookhorn and Farlington manor, which helped them get their finances back in the black. Farlington manor remained in the hands of the Priory until King Henry VIII's Dissolution in 1538, after which it was sold to William Pound of Beaumonds. After much buying and selling through the ages, by 1857 some of it ended up in the hands of Purbrook's Squire and benefactor John Deverell.

All told, a fair bit of medieval giving and taking around Portsdown's slopes. But what was in store for Purbrook Heath, a slice of which now belonged to Southwick Priory? Much of it farmland but the rest – the genuine heathland – consisting of a boggy marsh hidden by undergrowth and gorse. OK for grazing animals on the drier bits (though sheep were always excluded), but suitable for nowt else. It turned out that the good men of the Priory kept their land safe and sound for over 300 years until the dawn of their own demise in the 1530s. It was then that they suffered the wrath of Henry VIII and became canon fodder.

"Cut the sledging Bruv, the bishop's opening their batting."

Chapter 6

Dissolution Desolation

By the early 1500s Southwick Priory had grown into a sizeable land-owner in Hampshire and beyond, but still struggled at times to keep a healthy balance between income and expenditure. Building projects and a penchant for hospitality cost it dear. Through it all the Priory survived, and at times even prospered.

By 1538, however, the bell was tolling for the Priory, and hundreds of years of service and devotion were about to come crashing down. There were six Augustinian priories established in Hampshire, with Southwick the second largest after Christchurch. Other monastic orders had spread across the county too, such as Cistercians and Benedictines, but the end was nigh for the lot of them.

Trouble And Strife

King Henry VIII broke with Rome in 1532, and the constitutional independence of the Church in England was overthrown. Henry became controller of both Church and State. Reasons behind the fall-out with Rome are aired in numerous history books. For our Purbrook Heath Story, it's enough to say that the Pope resisted Henry VIII's attempts to annul his marriage to Catherine of Aragon and wed Ann Boleyn. The split came when Henry married mistress Ann anyway and by so doing violated holy law.

Throughout this holy dispute Henry relied on ruthless Thomas Cromwell for advice. The Crown was short of funds because of Henry's obsession for building palaces and the high cost of wars and spats with France, so monastic properties provided a gold-plated answer to Henry's prayers. Chief minister Cromwell saw a financial lifeline for the Crown through the sale of monastic lands, and the King's land-grab began. It was a one-off sale of stolen capital assets.

On April 7th 1538, the dissolution of the monasteries reached Southwick Priory's front gate. The Prior was William Noxton and he was in charge of twelve canons. He signed on the dotted line, surrendering his Priory to notorious Government agent Layton. Southwick had escaped the net two years earlier, when all Hampshire's smaller monasteries had bitten the dust – its grand income of more than £200 a year had delayed the chop. Prior Noxton gave up peaceably and received a goodly pension of £66 13s 4d for his pains. He probably didn't realise that his opposite number in charge at wealthier Christchurch Priory received twice as much!

Opportunist Number One

Young Thomas Wriothesley (pronounced Rizzley) served in royal government and was slick enough to spot an opportunity, his chance coming when he was required to act as liaison between Henry and minister Thomas Cromwell. Born in 1505, Thomas Wriothesley was full of self importance, and an opportunist right down to his boots. By 1544, and still in his late 30s, he had climbed the greasy pole to become Baron Wriothesley of Titchfield and Lord Chancellor of England.

Earlier, in the 1530s, there were winners and losers in the King's monastery land-grab. Primary losers were the 800 religious houses shut down nationwide, causing 5,000 monks, 2,000 nuns and 1,600 friars to lose their livelihoods. The principal winner in Hampshire was Thomas Wriothesley, who collared a massive 22% of the county's monastic manors, including Southwick Priory.

All through his life the primary reason he climbed out of bed each morning was to make himself richer and more powerful. If this was achieved at someone else's expense, so what? He loved all the perks, bribes and patronage that his position brought. When Thomas Cromwell confiscated all the monastic lands and properties between 1536 and 1540 and sold them off, Wriothesley's eyes were popping at the front of the queue. With liberal doses of smarm and charm, he ended up acquiring more of Hampshire's monastic lands than anyone else. Not bad for an outsider.

In 1537 he grabbed the Isle of Wight's Quarr Abbey. By November 1537 he had his hands on Titchfield Abbey and, within days of its surrender, had builders knocking it about to transform it into his grandiose main residence, whilst demolishing its church in favour of a gateway. This eyecatching Titchfield country house was constructed using the old abbey walls as the shell. He called his new pride and joy Place House.

Wriothesley converted Titchfield Abbey into his main residence, Place House

But this wasn't the end of the affair; Wriothesley was now on a roll. In 1538 he paid £1,350 6s 8d for Beaulieu's Cistercian Abbey. On the premise of removing superstitious religious objects, he ramraided Hampshire, stripping statues and shrines and taking objects of value from religious buildings. Wriothesley was a thieving menace; he removed Winchester Cathedral's impressive shrine to St. Swithun and pinched the supposedly idolatrous treasures at Hyde Abbey and St. Mary's Abbey, Winchester. Closer to home, Southwick Priory landed in Wriothesley's hamper too.

Opportunist Number Two

By the end of his Dissolution devastation, King Henry VIII had piled up a fortune of one and a half million pounds through the sale or lease of much of England's monastic property. And in one quiet corner of Hampshire, twelve black-hooded canons and their leader William Noxton moved out, bringing to an end 400 years of service at Southwick Priory.

Thomas Wriothesley was the cat who got the cream. But you can have too much of a good thing, and he was disposed to dispose of Southwick. A certain John White from Havant was in his good books, because White had eased through the transfer formalities of Wriothesley's religious acquisitions in Hampshire while working in the service of the King as Steward (today we would call him Recorder) of Portsmouth.

In 1546 Wriothesley offered to sell him the Priory and creepy-crawly White snapped it up for the weighty sum of £914.

But it was a good deal because the sale included the Priory, Southwick parish church and 46 acres of land, Widley church and the entire manor of Newlands at Purbrook Heath. Piled on top of this was a massive potential income from the rents and profits of dozens of farms, fisheries, fairs, markets, hamlets and rectories within his sprawling estate.

John White already had his hand in Southwick's pockets, because in 1537 he had acquired a 99-year lease of Priory land. From all this he could look forward to rental income of £257 per year. White set himself up in the Priory buildings, pulled down the church and still had the bile to complain about the meagre furnishings.

Family Affairs

Southwick's new owner John White married three times, his first wife Catherine providing his only son, Edward. In turn, Edward and his wife Mary produced one son, John. This second John (grandson of the Priory's purchaser) and wife Frances produced a daughter who, in 1606, married well-breeched Sir Daniel Norton.

The Purbrook Heath Story won't benefit from trawling through the entire lineage of Southwick from 1606 to the present day. For us, a few key connections will suffice. The well-breeched Sir Daniel Norton

All that is left of Southwick Priory today

(owner through marriage of the old Southwick Priory lands) was a king's man, but his son and heir Richard Norton was an active supporter of Oliver Cromwell in the Civil War, fighting gallantly in the local battle at Cheriton, which was a bloody affair.

Richard Norton died in 1692 and the Estate passed to his grandson Richard (Mad Dick) Norton, so called because he was! Mad Dick was the last of the Norton line and died mad as a hatter in 1732. His nephew Francis Thistlethwayte immediately took over Southwick Park. And so the Thistlethwayte name took hold and, via one or two skirmishes, owns Southwick to this day.

The neighbouring manor of Widley (in its old location behind Purbrook Heath) fronted up to what we know as Southwick Park. Widley has passed through many hands since Geoffrey held Cosham at the time of the Domesday Book in 1086. By 1823 the Woodrow and Maidment families owned the manor and they sold Widley to the Thistlethwayte dynasty who already owned Southwick Park Estate which included Purbrook Heath.

The Thistlethwaytes were established landowners not just in Hampshire, but in Scotland and London as well, notably as trustees of the extensive Paddington estate. Many years later, in 1936, the Thistlethwayte Squires surprisingly sold Purbrook Heath to Havant & Waterloo Urban District Council, although they still own much of the surrounding land today.

Its Secretive Self

Back in Southwick, from the time that the Priory was booted out in 1538, things were never the same. But for the next several centuries we can safely leave the place to its secretive self. On the old patch at Purbrook Heath the grasses grew, the animals chewed and the stream flowed much as before. But 300 yards to the east, our goblin's brook was about to encounter years that would change the nature of Purbrook, bringing it from nowhere to somewhere.

The emergence of Purbrook village was dependent to a huge degree on the growth of Portsmouth, that small town gathering itself at the south west tip of Portsea Island. To appreciate our Purbrook Heath story, we need to spend some time in Portsmouth, our next port of call.

Southwick House

The first mansion at Southwick was built after the 1538 dissolution of the village's Augustinian priory. Thomas Wriothesley acquired the ex-priory estate from Henry VIII and in 1546 sold the park and buildings to his retainer John White, who used some of the old priory materials in constructing his grand house.

Although White died in 1567, the Southwick estate prospered in the hands of son Edward and grandson John. By the latter's death in 1607 the centrepiece of the grand estate was an impressive Jacobean mansion with extensive gardens.

The house burned down in 1750 and was replaced in 1812 by a two storey mansion on a new site. Another fire in 1840 destroyed the splendid mansion although much of the furniture and effects were saved. Squire Thomas Thistlethwayte decided to rebuild Southwick House along similar lines to the fire ravaged building, with the addition of a third storey. Sydney Howell of London was the architect and the new mansion (the present one) was completed in 1841. Of course many of the humbler dwellings in the village are much older than 1841 Southwick House.

At the outbreak of World War 2 in 1939, Southwick House was home to the Squire, Colonel Evelyn Thistlethwayte. He owned an extensive Southwick Park Estate that, with one or two twists, had been in the hands of the Thistlethwayte family for hundreds of years. The Colonel had served in the King's Royal Rifles, fighting for his country in the Boer War.

He became Squire in 1924 on the death of his older brothers (Alexander died in 1915 and Arthur in 1924).

To his eternal cost, Evelyn Thistlethwayte became friendly with Admiral William James, Naval Commander-in-Chief, Portsmouth. The Colonel was in the habit of inviting guests to join him in a favourite pastime, his Southwick Park "shoots" and on a number of occasions he "offered a gun" to Admiral James.

By 1940 the Admiral had urgent matters on his mind as Portsmouth Dockyard became a regular target for German bombers from July onwards, and he decided that Naval training establishments must move from Portsmouth – it was not a good learning environment! James persuaded the Colonel to allow officer pupils from the RN School of Navigation to spend their nights in the relative peace of Southwick House. A foot in the door.

After heavy bombing of the Dockyard during 1941, Admiral James took advantage of Evelyn Thistlethwayte's kindness and requisitioned the House. From September 1941 it became the new home for the RN School of Navigation and the Colonel was turfed out. From that moment Southwick House and its lake and gardens belonged to the military. The Squire of Southwick was forced to move to smaller premises on his estate, first to Bridge House and then to Broomfield House. Bachelor Evelyn died in November 1943 and the estate (minus Southwick House) passed to nephew Hugh Borthwick.

Meanwhile Southwick House became the HQ for Operation Overlord, leading to the D-Day invasion of Normandy in June 1944. It was a hive of military activity in the months prior to June 6th and for a whole month afterwards. A vast wooden wall map displayed the latest position of naval ships in the Channel and the disposition of allied troops on the French coast.

In 1946 the RN School of Navigation resumed its tenancy. Despite the new Squire (Hugh Borthwick Norton) seeking to recover the lost mansion and grounds, the Royal Navy took steps to compulsorily purchase Southwick House and in 1948 they finally bought the mansion and 295 acres from a distraught Squire Hugh. The price was a derisory £40,000.

Southwick House became HMS Dryad and a topsy collection of offices, accommodation blocks and sport facilities grew up around the mansion in the second half of the 20th century.

Through all this development the splendid house, lake and gardens survived. In 2006 came a change of use. The Royal Military Police decamped from Chichester and established their training HQ in Southwick Park. The sign by the front gate reads: "The Defence College Of Policing And Guarding."

Chapter 7

Harbouring Grand Designs

When Richard I gave Portsmouth its first royal charter in 1194, the island of Portsea was pretty much a nonentity. Open land, with just a few dwellings dotted here and there. If you lived on Portsea Island, you lived in an isolated environment. Access from the mainland was by boat across Ports Creek, or by a causeway at low tide. The first bridge spanning the creek was cobbled together as dusk settled on the old century, and this helped Portsmouth to come in from the cold – one small step in the direction of civilisation.

Lionhearted Geezers

Most of the Island was marsh, but there were some farms, and three tiny manors at Copnor, Fratton and Buckland. Around 1170, a wealthy Norman from Gisors (halfway between Paris and Rouen), bought Buckland from the de Port family. The purchaser was Jean de Gisors, a landowner and shipowner who had spotted the potential for trade between Normandy and southern England. His newly acquired Buckland manor included land at the south west tip of Portsea Island, and it was here in about 1180 that de Gisors established a small town settlement.

Not long afterwards he gave Southwick Priory some land to build a

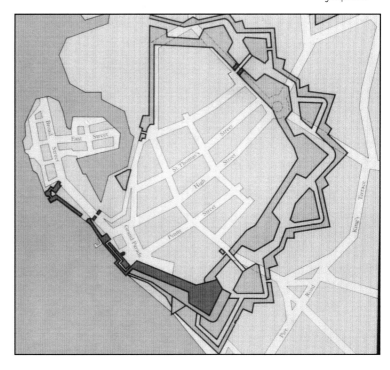

Portsmouth's fortified town in 1800 (plan shown here) evolved from Jean de Gisors' 12th century grid pattern

53

chapel – now Portsmouth Cathedral. Jean de Gisors' footprint was on Portsmouth from the start, with chapel and market and high street and side streets all planned, in grid formation – the area we know as Old Portsmouth. Despite its founder's personal wealth, the small town was backward and poor when royalty rode in during May 1194.

King Richard was there with a great army and a hundred ships awaiting favourable weather so that he could head for Normandy. He wanted to secure Portsmouth as a royal town, because it was a convenient embarkation point for France, and a safe haven for ships.

Consequently, before leaving these shores on May 12th 1194, Richard the Lionheart granted Portsmouth its charter, pocketing some readies in exchange, as was the way with Kings. He was never to walk upon England's green and pleasant land again; in 1199 he was struck by a French arrow and the wound turned gangrenous.

Portsmouth has had 24 royal charters in the past 800 years but this first one was the most significant. King Richard's 1194 Charter of Liberties, drawn up in Latin, granted townsmen an annual fair and a market, although it denied them the big prize of collecting and administering the King's dues. The lights went out on Jean de Gisors' expansive plans in this same year of 1194. Jean took the side of Richard's brother John in a rebellion that never got off the ground, and King Richard confiscated all de Gisors' English possessions.

Prince John had better luck and bounced back, succeeding his older brother as King in 1199. The new King, keen to re-conquer the recently lost lands of Normandy and Anjou, set in motion a large naval build-up, constructing a stone-walled base for his fighting ships in Portsmouth. Although King John generally receives a poor press, he was pivotal in establishing shipbuilding in this primitive south coast town. His galley ships required oarsmen, not a popular occupation, so "pressed men" were forced into service on the King's galleys by tough Pompey bailiffs. These galley crews kept half of whatever they captured from the enemy.

After King John's time, the tiny town began developing through ships and trade and fishing, thanks primarily to its great natural harbour. But right through to the 1500s Portsmouth remained small and insignificant. Only in times of war did it prosper, and even then there were setbacks like the disaster of 1338 when the French stormed in and burnt the town down.

The Protection Racket

Henry VII (King from 1485-1509) saw potential in the small, unsophisticated dockyard and bolstered defences against the threat from France. He made Portsmouth a royal dockyard, protected by a resident garrison. In 1494 the Square Tower was built to protect the sea approaches to the harbour, together with a blockhouse on the Gosport side. In 1495 Henry VII built the world's first dry dock in Portsmouth; it was an excavated ditch into which ships could be floated and repaired. At low tide the dock was sealed with mud walls and gates acting like a dam, with a rudimentary pump to get rid of water seeping in.

Henry Tudor's son Henry VIII (King from 1509-1547) needed ships with their home port in the right location for ongoing battles with France. Two significant 60–gun warships, Mary Rose (500 tons) and Peter Pomegranate (450 tons) were built at Portsmouth, and in 1512 Henry VIII ordered the 25 ships of his fleet to assemble here, riding down in person to review them.

In his first ten years as monarch, seventeen front line Men of War were built and twelve more naval ships were constructed or requisitioned. Naval men were now in the King's pay, and Henry's monastic sell-off provided funds to develop Portsmouth as a naval base. He built fortifications along the south coast, Southsea Castle (1544) being prominent among them. A protective ring was built around the small town and in 1544 the northern edge of Portsea Island was protected for the first time, guarding against attack from the mainland. By the time of the Civil War a hundred years later, this had grown into Portsea Bridge Fort, located on the Cosham side of Ports Creek.

By 1685 (Old) Portsmouth was protected by walls, bastions, a moat and triangular ravelins, all designed by Sir Bernard de Gomme, chief military engineer to Charles II. The remains of these 1680s defences (updated through the years) are visible today: the Moat, Long Curtain, King's Bastion, and Spur Redoubt. Fort Blockhouse on Gosport's waterfront was upgraded too, and Portsmouth became England's strongest fortress.

A Peep At Pepys

In the second half of the 1600s Samuel Pepys, best known for his ten-year diary, became heavily involved in naval matters. By age 37 (1669) he was the driving force in the Navy Office, helping Charles II build a powerful navy. Pepys rose to become Secretary of the newborn Admiralty in 1673, then resigned in 1679 but was back in the service of the King (Charles II and then James II) as Secretary for the Affairs of the Admiralty, in 1684.

During his gap in service the Navy sank into decay, but Pepys turned things round and the Navy took a stranglehold on world trade routes, which aided Portsmouth's development. This in turn helped the growth of road connections with London and one major beneficiary was the direct route via Purbrook and Horndean.

Serving The Services

The dockyard town of Portsmouth was also home to a major army garrison which brought a measure of prosperity to traders and publicans – and to prostitutes, although much of their trade was carried on outside the town at Point. Back inside the walls, foreign dignitaries became frequent visitors. The town was making its mark, boasting bake-houses, brew-houses and store-houses.

Defensive Insecurities

The Navy became the biggest industrial organisation in Europe and by mid 18th century the dockyard was like a separate town with docks, basins, houses, offices, storehouses and workshops. The workforce numbered 2,000 men, increasing by another 500 in times of war. A new town called Portsea grew from the mire to accommodate workers and their families. Portsmouth Common became Portsea by Act of Parliament in 1792.

The moat formed part of Portsmouth's defences from the 1680s

Because of the fear of invasion via Langstone Harbour, John Desmaretz was appointed to build a star-shaped fort on farmland by the harbour entrance at Eastney. Fort Cumberland was fully operational by 1750 and, at the same time, two gun batteries were placed along the shore to protect a vulnerable area at Eastney and at Lumps Farm (Lumps Fort).

In 1746 at the northern end of the Island, Portsea Bridge Fort (through which the London road passed) was strengthened to house six-pounder guns. But any part of the Creek could still be forded at low tide, making all Portsea Island vulnerable. So in 1757 Desmaretz built a moat, earth ramparts and gun batteries close to the southern bank of Ports Creek. A century later Palmerston's stouter defences on the same site became Hilsea Lines. At the mouth of Langstone Harbour a second version of Fort Cumberland was completed in 1810, built of Portland Stone a few yards north of the original site.

Hard Times

Portsmouth wasn't visitor-friendly in the 1750s. Having already forked out to pay tolls at turnpikes along the highway, travellers had to shuffle slowly through Portsea Bridge Fort and put up with checks by armed

Landport Gate was the main entrance to Portsmouth town. The present gate was built in 1760. Beyond the gate was the moat

guards at drawbridges between Hilsea and the town. On reaching the town gate there was yet another check before the nod came to enter. And if weary visitors rolled up later than 9pm they were out of luck. They found the gates slammed shut for the night!

And if visitors found things tough, life for the inhabitants of Portsmouth and Portsea Island wasn't all buttercups and daisies either. Dockyard workers remained poor and there were hideous slums. Returning sailors had a tough time too, having to wait until their ships were paid off to get their dues. Worst of all, in times of war the Navy boosted its manpower levels by sending press gangs around the streets of Portsmouth and Gosport to hoover up likely males for service in the Navy. They would be unlikely to see their wives or girlfriends for many a long year. A heavy price to pay for a night out on the town!

Commercial Break

In tandem with the dockyard's growing influence, the port was developing in other ways. During the 1700s England's most powerful trading organisation, the East India Company, made Portsmouth its major provincial depot. East India Company bigwigs, plus military personnel and other passengers, became a familiar sight travelling down the notorious Portsmouth Road (or one of its alternatives), then waiting in town for a ship ready for the long sea voyage to the Indies.

The East India vessels were sleek and fully armed. There was plenty of work maintaining, supporting and supplying them, and Portsmouth's economy benefited. Agents and messengers were needed, and local traders sold wares and services to East India officials and passengers. Often cargoes were loaded in Portsmouth and shipments from the east arrived here too, although most incoming bulk was unloaded in London. The Company's trade included sugar, spices, furs, silk, precious stones and porcelain.

Come The Revolution

The Industrial Revolution had a big impact on the dockyard. In 1799 Samuel Bentham (Inspector-General of Naval Works) introduced steam pumps, and French engineer Marc Brunel (Isambard's dad) was recruited by Bentham to design a factory in the yard, mass-producing pulley blocks using steam power. Demand was huge; the rigging operation of a 75-gun sailing ship required 1,400 blocks. The dockyard was leading edge in the 1800s, and from 1815 the Royal Navy could claim it ruled the waves for a hundred years.

Warships morphed from wooden sailing ships into iron-hulls, and then into brutish, coal-fired, battleships sporting fifteen-inch guns. Many ships were built at Portsmouth and Chatham dockyards (and elsewhere too).

- In 1891 the battleship of the day was the Royal Sovereign. At 15,585 tons and made of steel, she was the biggest ship built in Portsmouth so far.

- The battleship Dreadnought knocked Royal Sovereign off her perch in 1906. Powered by turbines and weighing 17,900 tons, she was now the biggest ship built in Portsmouth....but

- By 1915 Portsmouth had completed the two largest vessels its dockyard ever built: the battleships Queen Elizabeth (1913) and another Royal Sovereign (1915), both displacing 27,500 tons.

Industrial Heritage

Portsmouth dockyard built 150 warships during a productive nineteenth century. The new town of Portsea accommodated many dockyard families as did its eastern extension, Landport, which also boasted a few middle class streets like Commercial Road. Southsea established itself as a fashionable place where the families of Army and Navy officers liked to live. Architect Thomas Ellis Owen designed many of its elegant streets.

Much of Southsea Common remained marsh until gentrification started around 1831. A Great Morass stretched from the environs of Southsea Castle to what became Marmion Road and Albert Road. A marshy pond at Craneswater was transformed into the Canoe Lake, and a more attractive seafront promenade was constructed in 1848. It was Southsea's good fortune that its Common was strategically important for the Army and hence was never built on.

In 1841 dockyard workers numbered 2,227 and by 1911 there were 10,439 workers in the yard. Pay remained low and the houses and streets were cramped and unhygienic. The dockyard was a male environment; war meant work and troughs of peace meant lay-offs. Consequently many women needed to earn money to make ends meet.

So, while the naval yard employed men in shipbuilding, metalworking and engineering, another industry bloomed – the Dress sector. From the mid 1800s the female population (and males too) worked as milliners, dressmakers, shirtmakers, seamstresses, tailors and shoemakers. The numbers were amazing. By 1911 there were 10,373 workers in the Dress sector – within a rivet or a hatpin of the numbers in the dockyard.

Portsmouth's other 19th century industries included commercial ship-building, brewing, confectionery, baking and milling. A harbour inlet called Mill Pond extended as far as today's Park Road sports grounds. Until 1868 there was a flour mill at the edge of Mill Pond, powered by the tide.

Another Brick In The Wall

Politicians continued to fret about a French invasion. In February 1860 a royal commission recommended building a series of granite forts out in the Solent. By 1880 four had been constructed on stone and concrete foundation rings on the seabed: Spit Bank, St Helens, Horse Sand, and Nomansland - the most expensive at £242,000.

At the northern end of Portsea Island, by 1871 Hilsea Lines had been built at a cost of £269,000 - a mile and a half of walls, bastions, case-mates and ammunition stores. Ports Creek needed to be accessible to our gunboats, so a new Portsbridge was built. This ingenious piece of engineering rolled back to a central pier, leaving a clear channel; it cost only £5,000 and survived until 1927.

The next pieces in Portsmouth's defensive jigsaw have a strong

Spit Bank Fort is one of four granite forts built in the Solent, all completed by 1880

Purbrook connection. The forts on Portsdown Hill were built to guard against landward attack. They were sanctioned in 1863 after much lobbying by Prime Minister Palmerston. Preliminary work had already started and by March 1861 the folks who lived on the hill had received notices to quit.

Most of the land was owned by the same country Squire who owned Purbrook Heath, Thomas Thistlethwayte of Southwick Park. Nine hundred acres of his land were compulsorily purchased to build the forts and the Squire also felled hundreds of trees on another thousand acres north of the hilltop, to provide clear lines of fire from Fort Southwick and Fort Widley. In 1862 the Squire received £95,200 compensation. Similarly, east of the Portsmouth Road Squire Deverell of Purbrook Park was forced to sell 188 acres and trees were felled right down to today's Park Road to ensure clear lines of fire from Fort Purbrook.

By 1868 five forts had been completed along the summit of Portsdown. From east to west: Forts Purbrook, Widley, Southwick, Nelson, and Wallington. There were brickworks nearby at Wallington, Fareham and Swanwick, so the forts were brick-built in English bond style, with walls up to five feet thick. The scale of defence installations around

Fort Purbrook was built on Portsdown Hill in the 1860s to guard against landward attack

Portsmouth was staggering: more than 25 forts plus numerous batteries and bastions. By 1874 Fort Purbrook housed 165 soldiers and six officers, and Fort Widley was home to 175 soldiers and seven officers.

Nothing Stays The Same

It took the best part of a thousand years for Portsea Island to evolve from marsh to macadam, from farmland to fortress, from empty to full. The town became a city in 1926 and started to spread its residential cloak beyond Ports Creek. By the outbreak of World War Two in 1939, the city's population had peaked at more than 250,000. This level of density was unsustainable, and when peace returned a family tide began to flow to the satellites and suburbs of south Hampshire. One of the destinations was Purbrook; its time as a snug and sleepy village in the lee of Portsdown was well and truly up.

By 1871 the northern reaches of Portsea Island were protected by bastions and casemates like this one at Hilsea

Chapter 8

From Nowhere To Somewhere

At the beginning of the 1500s, Pokebroc (Purbrook) didn't have much of a past, but there were signs that the goblin's brook might possibly have a future. The factors that helped its cause were: 1) an eternal supply of springwater; 2) its location at the southern edge of the Forest of Bere; and 3) rough tracks into the Forest that would ultimately provide a link between Portsmouth and London.

Through the 1500s and 1600s the dockyard town on Portsea Island endured a spurts 'n' lulls growth. There had been only a limited need for people to travel between London and Portsmouth but, as warships increasingly used the protected harbour and naval administrators established a local base, tracks between the capital and its dockyard began to echo to the patter of hooves.

Making Tracks

In 1500 the way from London to Portsmouth was *not* over Butser, nor through the Forest of Bere, nor on through Purbrook. The very few travellers of that time would have copied local traffic, heading from Petersfield to Buriton, then around the edge of the Forest via Rowlands Castle and Havant. They would have returned the same way.

That's not to suggest there weren't any tracks through the Forest of Bere in the 1500s, but they were pretty much hit and miss. Leaving Portsea Island up and over Portsdown, odds and ends of pathways veered north towards Bere Forest at right angles from the ancient, east-west ridgeways. Once over Portsdown's crest, lanes sought the easiest route down the northern side through the woods. And from the opposite end of the Forest, heading south from Horndean and Blendworth, lanes dipped into Bere's nether regions...and strangers using them frequently dipped out! If your luck was in, you hoped to meet a lane venturing from the other end.

In time, Wait Lane (also spelt Waight or Wheat) became one of several tracks that looped up or around Portsdown, heading north. It ended at Forest Gate and there was no road onwards through the Forest. Ruts and trampled grasses signalled a way forward and, with a bit of good fortune, you made it through. The Wait family owned land here, at the southern edge of what is now Waterlooville, close to Mill Road.

Pigeon House Lane on Portsdown Hill

The area nearby is still called Forest End. On the downland that rolls from the top of Portsdown Hill towards Southwick and Potwell and Purbrook, a number of country lanes survive to this day, such as Crooked Walk Lane, Pity Moor Lane, Pigeon House Lane, Mill Lane, Widley Walk (Widley Lane), Drayton Lane and Crookhorn Lane.

But back in the year 1500 there was no village of Purbrook. The tiny parishes, manors and hamlets of Farlington, Stakes, Crookhorn and Widley were on the map, although Widley – comprising manor house, church, windmill, cottages and farmland – was located half a mile west of where it is now. The water sprite of Pokebroc was morphing into the watering hole of Purbrook, but so far it was just a brook where water flowed across the common, south of Bere Forest.

Then gradually, as the 1600s arrived and traffic opted for a more direct route to and from the capital, this brook took on some faint significance because of the availability of fresh water for horses. And for travellers heading towards London, it was the last recognised point of safety before encountering the Forest's mazy tracks and crazy robbers.

By the 1670s Purbrook was literally on the map. Ogilby's wonderful 1675 strip map showed every stretch of the direct route from London to Portsmouth. Purbrook had clearly arrived, nestling between the hill of Portsdown and the forest of Bere. One surprise is that Ogilby called it Purbeck Heath, just like those wild-bill-hillocks of Dorset. Other contemporary mapmakers called it Purbeck too, so perhaps they were right and we've been wrong all these years!

The map's accompanying narrative says: "...through Bere-Forest and over Purbeck-Heath and Portsey-Down, you come to Cosham, thence to Portsey-Bridge over an Arm of the Sea, guarded by a Fort." Ogilby was fully aware of the dangers of this direct route, warning travellers to be careful of backward turns and to "take the broad middle way through the forest."

Dangerous Liaisons

Samuel Pepys at the Admiralty was instrumental in building up the 17th century Navy, which helped the growth of Purbrook. A strong Navy demanded better connections between London and Portsmouth, and steadily the meandering tracks began to straighten out and trace a route south, even if the state of the tracks remained diabolical – muddy, dangerous, often impassable.

Pepys wrote about his journeys to Portsmouth. He liked the town, but rarely took the direct route through the Forest, via Horndean and Purbrook. When he did so, he made sure that he was properly accompanied. In the mid 1600s, tracking through Bere Forest was an adventure few cared to face without an escort. Guides could be recruited at either Horndean or Purbrook.

Pepys records that, in 1662, he hired a conveyance at Petersfield together with a man to guide them to Havant, to avoid going through the forest.....and they were carried well out of their way. The guide was ducking and diving because of the persistent fear of highwaymen and lost his way among the tortuous tracks. They reached Portsmouth as the town gates were about to close.

In August 1668, Pepys made the journey south accompanied by his wife Elizabeth. This time their coach lost its way over Hindhead and didn't arrive at The Royal Anchor in Liphook until 10pm. They were "exceedingly tremulous about highwaymen" and had hired an old man as a guide. On another trip south in 1671 he slept

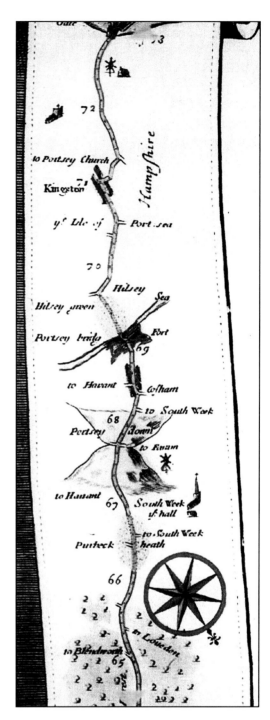

Ogiby's 1675 map of the Portsmouth Road at Purbrook

By kind permission of J and M Norgate: Old Hampshire Mapped

65

overnight at Guildford; Portsmouth was a long slog in those days.

The alternative routes from London to Portsmouth through to the late 1600s were several. One option was way-out-west along the Meon Valley, through Alton and Fareham. The direct route was through Guildford and Petersfield, over Butser to Horndean, and through the Forest of Bere to Purbrook, and then over Portsdown. Another route (referred to already) went through Petersfield, turned left to Buriton and followed the valleys through Finchdean and Rowlands Castle to Havant, keeping to the eastern boundary of Bere Forest. (Today's railway line follows a similar route).

There were pros and cons for each route. Hazards that the traveller tried to avoid were:
• the long drag over Hindhead, which could be avoided by heading through Guildford and then making for Godalming, to Haslemere, and then Liphook;
• the treacherous climb over Butser – at this time there was no V-shaped cutting, and the track was a greasy mudslide for much of the year;
• the Forest of Bere, with a genuine fear of getting lost;
• the threat of highwaymen waiting in the hills and open country around Butser, and lurking by the tracks in the four miles of the Forest of Bere between Horndean and Purbrook.

Post Early For Purbrook

From way back in the 1500s royal (government) mail had been transported along the great roads from London. In Henry VIII's time (1509-1547) royal post to the naval dockyard at Portsmouth was usually taken along the Meon Valley route. During Queen Mary's reign (1553-1558) royal post used the Guildford and Petersfield route for the first time, mostly via Buriton and Rowlands Castle.

From 1635 the royal posts were made available to Joe Public and general mail was carried by post-boys on horseback along the main post roads in addition to their royal mail duties. They rode from inn to inn, and had to put up with second rate horses, third rate roads, and first rate highwaymen!

Road To Ruin

From about 1670, Stage Coaches with fixed routes and timetables offered people the means to travel around the country. One early Stage

Coach route from London started in Stones End, Borough, but the paved roadway soon ended and the boneshaking coaches sucked and wallowed their way along muddy tracks all the way to Pompey.

Goods were transported by road on hulking Stage Wagons rather than Stage Coaches; the wagons had nine-inch-wide wheels and teams of eight pack horses to haul commodities around. They sometimes carried people too, but it was a rough way to travel, dawdling along at four miles per hour.

Through the 1500s and 1600s each parish through which a road passed was legally bound to provide labour and supervision to maintain it. Not surprisingly the roads were a mess. Coaches got stuck, wheels came off and vehicles overturned. The worst section on the Portsmouth Road was south of Petersfield where the track climbed forever and a day up Butser Hill. The parishioners of Weston, Buriton and Nursted were leaned-on to keep this part of the road in good repair, but they couldn't cope. Another ruinous section was through Bere Forest between Horndean and Purbrook, where the heavy clay could trap coach wheels in its gunge.

Turning To The Turnpikes

Salvation was eventually at hand. The bad old Portsmouth Road took a turn for the better with the introduction of the 1711 Portsmouth and Sheet Turnpike Act. A petition in 1710 had pointed out that the road from Petersfield to Butser was "almost impassable for at least nine months in every year." Resulting from the 1711 Act, the section of road between Portsmouth and Sheet was placed in the hands of trustees who charged road users a toll, collected at toll gates along the route. Toll revenue was used to repair and re-surface the road. The initial scale of charges included:

"One penny for every horse; one shilling for every Stage or Hackney Coach drawn by four or more horses."

Our local section of highway benefited straightaway, because in January 1712 the Turnpike commissioners instructed their surveyors to "amend the road through Purbeck Heath and Waight Lane, the same road being very ruinous and dangerous to Her Majesty's subjects passing and repassing with horses, carts and carriages...."

Two toll gates were set up between Sheet and Portsmouth. Literally gates across the road, they were located at Sheet Bridge and at Portsbridge which soon moved to the bottom of Cosham High Street. In

1772 two more toll gates were added: the Horndean gate where the toll-keeper's cottage was at the north end of the village, and the Purbrook gate on the east side of the roadway near today's Portsmouth boundary stone at Widley. Cosham toll gate was the real breadwinner: at its peak in 1810 it collected more than £1,071 for the year. In the same period, Purbrook gate took £632.

Surveyors were hired by the Turnpike trustees to repair particular sections of the route, and local men were taken on as labourers. Repairs usually consisted of filling ruts and layering the surface with gravel, stones, flint and chalk. In 1718 another section of the road, between Southwark and Kingston On Thames, was turnpiked. Finally, in 1749 a turnpike was completed between Kingston and Sheet Bridge and at last the entire route from London to Portsmouth was regulated. The Portsmouth and Sheet Turnpike Trust remained in force for a remarkable 160 years; it was finally wound up in 1871.

Travails And Triumphs Of Travel

The first Stage Coaches (late 1600s/early 1700s) were pioneers on the rumbustious highways in our patch of countryside. Without them and their rattling forays through the Forest of Bere, Purbrook might be the

The Portsmouth Coach approaches Hindhead

A painting by Brian Browne

place that never was. The Stage Coach was a plodder with few restrictions – fifteen people might be crammed inside and out. It was slow going, even after the introduction of the turnpikes. By 1770 it still took a whole day for the Stage to travel 73 miles from London to Portsmouth. And this combination of ponderous travel and bleak roads encouraged highwaymen.

The introduction of sleek Royal Mail coaches from 1784 improved speeds considerably. They were lighter, smarter and always had the best horses. Stage Coaches competed with them for passenger business but Mail Coaches, though expensive, were quicker with fewer people on board.... and they didn't have to pay turnpike tolls. The Post Office supplied each Mail Coach with a red-coated guard who carried a blunderbuss, two horse pistols and ammunition, plus his horn and timepiece.

Leaving Portsmouth at 7pm the Mail Coach would reach London by 6am next morning. Regulations on the Mail Coaches were specific: they were permitted to carry four passengers inside, plus one (later increased to two) outside. The boot under the coachman's seat held parcels and a locked mailbox sat underneath the guard.

Have The Decency To Wear A Mask!

Throughout the 1700s highwaymen were a menace, not only in the hideaways of the Forest but also along the deserted commons that fronted the isolated road from London to Portsmouth. In their dreaded "Stand and deliver!" glory days there was "no road so wild and lonely as the Portsmouth Road," despite Turnpike Trusts improving roads markedly by the end of the century. Three Trusts regulated the entire highway from London by 1749 but not until the early years of the 1800s did the threat of highwaymen disappear.

So much of the long Portsmouth road was bleak. Hindhead hill was described as one of "the wildest bits of scenery to be found in England." The chalk downs were "bare, barren, windy expanses." Closer to home, the green by the bridge at Ports Creek was termed "the coldest spot between Portsmouth and London." Murders were part and parcel of travelling the Portsmouth Road and it witnessed gloomier scenes than any of the other great thoroughfares out of London.

Even the supposedly safer way via Buriton and Rowlands Castle, around the eastern edge of Bere Forest, was dicey. The whole region was in the comfort zone of a long line of notorious bandits – villains such as Black Jim, Jack Lumley, Jack the Gunman, and Butser Dick, who plagued the area that gave him his nickname. (He ended up on the gallows at Winchester).

South of Purbrook lay the village of Cosham, handy for smugglers as it was tucked away from the prying eyes of Customs men aboard their cutters patrolling the Solent or checking the narrow entrances to Langstone and Portsmouth harbours. The smugglers' booty was typically wine or spirits or tobacco or tea or coffee or French silks, and rewards could be substantial.

Villains stole in at dead of night with their contraband and flogged brandy to the innkeepers, who watered it down and sold it on. One gang heading the other way were the Portsdown Owlers, who exported woollen fleeces to France with the help of many a farmer. The export of wool was, at different times, either banned or heavily taxed.

Anyone For A Bere?

The Forest of Bere had lost much of its best timber by this time. In 1810 it was removed from Forest Law and the Crown sold off parcels of land to new owners who could do what they liked with their prize. The forgotten forest had been infiltrated by speculators for years anyway. Bere had been under Forest Law for 744 years and was the last of the royal forests to be sorted out. The Crown wished it a regal good riddance. Our once-mighty forest had by now been reduced from a primetime 90,000 acres to a miserable 16,000. When it was ultimately taken over by the Forestry Commission in 1923, Bere Forest had only 1,450 acres of woodland left, split into three parts.

The Stage Coach takes a day off

All The World's A Stage

The improved surface and better repair of the Portsmouth Road, together with the receding Forest of Bere, gave an enormous shot in the arm to the travel business and, from 1784, sleek new Mail Coaches gave transport a further boost. Improved design helped the lumbering

Stage Coaches too – they even boasted springs. In the same timeframe the naval base at Portsmouth was growing in size and importance.

Stage Coaches had once taken three days to reach London, with passengers lodging overnight at coaching inns along the way. In 1770 the quickest Stage Coach took sixteen hours. By 1805 the Mail Coaches had it down to nine hours. Numbers were up too: by 1820 there were 1200 travellers and 100 coaches every week, leaving at half-hourly intervals. The fare was 12s 6d outside and £1 1s inside.

Competition for passengers between Portsmouth and London was intense. In the years after 1810, a typical slice of the timetable looked like this:

- The George Hotel in High Street, Portsmouth was the 9am start point for "The Regulator" heading for the Bull-in-Mouth in the City. Thirty minutes later "The Royal Mail" departed for Piccadilly, Fleet Street and Fetter Lane.
- At 10am at the High Street's Fountain Hotel, "The Independent" set off for Charing Cross and Gracechurch Street. Its route was round-the-houses, via Havant, Emsworth, Chichester, Petworth, Godalming and Ripley. "The Tantivy" was a summertime-only Stage Coach using the Fountain as its starting point. "The Star of Brunswick" was a night coach, leaving the Fountain at 8.30pm bound for the City's Bolt-in-Tun and Bull-in-Mouth.
- The company operating "The Rocket" and "The Night Rocket" had Portsmouth offices at 61 High Street. At 10am "The Rocket" headed for Piccadilly and Ludgate Hill and "The Night Rocket" made the same journey at 9pm on weekdays.
- "The Times" coach made the journey at noon from Portsmouth's Blue Posts in Broad Street, bound for Snow Hill and Piccadilly.
- Another regular was "The Royal Blue" which set off from the Globe in Oyster Street at 8am on Mondays, Wednesdays, and Fridays in summer, heading for Cheapside.

London wasn't the only destination. There were Coaches bound for Bristol (via Southampton, Romsey and Salisbury); for Winchester; for Chichester; and for Oxford. Another destination was Brighton, with "The Defiance" making its first change of horses at Havant's Dolphin or Bear Inn.

Efficient changing of horses was important. The Royal Mail Coach from Portsmouth to London made a change every ten to twelve miles at places like Waterlooville (after 1815), Petersfield, Liphook, Hindhead, Godalming and Guildford – depending on the route taken. The quickest journey ever recorded took seven hours fifty minutes and involved seven changes of horses.

But even during this boom time bad weather could mangle both highways and timetables. On January 28th 1814, heavy snow caused mud slides along the route, causing "Evening Coaches" bound for London to set off early, around three in the afternoon. The tracks were so bad that coachmen refused to attempt the climb over Butser in the dark.

Peak time for the coaching bonanza on the Portsmouth Road was between 1810 and 1840. From 1815 on, John MacAdam's compacted stone road surfaces made a startling difference to journey times. Two more improvements helped: by 1820 a cutting at the top of Portsdown Hill lowered the road, making the climb less arduous, and in 1827 the first major cutting through Butser Hill was attempted. The old route was a high level crawl. The new V-shaped cleft was "the largest and most spectacular road-cutting in England." It took more than 50 men seven years to complete.

Inns And Outs

Travelling by coach was still an achy-braky graft for passengers, but at least there were some chipper local inns vying to raise travellers' spirits. "The George Inn" on Portsdown Hill was built around 1780 and became a favourite spot to sup ale and take in the view. It had its own well outside, drilled into the chalk.

"The Woodman" was a cornerstone of Purbrook's emerging village. It started life around 1730 as a lodge for Purbrook Park Estate on the corner of London Road and Chalky Road (Stakes Road). In time the lodge became a beer house after the 1830 Beer House Act permitted the sale of beer with few of the licensing restrictions endured by inns that sold spirits. The Woodman was a haunt for bewigged dandies travelling the Portsmouth Road and for posh Portsmuthians on their days out in the country. Much later, in 1937, The Woodman relocated 100 yards south.

"The Leopard Inn" was opposite the original Woodman, but a little further up the street. It obtained its first licence in 1783. The London Stage changed horses twice daily at The Leopard whose coach-house facilities included stables and an ample garden. They say that cock-fighting took place in the loft, and also that in 1807 gunman Jack Pitt

The Stage Coaches may have vanished but The George lingers on

drank here with butcher Pescett from Horndean, before taking him to Liberty Firs near the crossroads at lonely Waterloo and relieving him of his wealth. The Leopard Inn was rebuilt in 1940.

"The White Hart Inn" was a stone's throw from The Leopard. It was a popular coaching inn, with a water pump and horse trough at the front and stables round the side. Apparently cock-fighting took place here too, right up till 1900. Obviously Purbrook wasn't simply bluebells and a babbling brook! The White Hart was eventually demolished and replaced by new premises in 1923.

At a quiet crossroads barely a mile to the north, an inn was built around the time of the Battle of Waterloo. The district was virtually unpopulated but a sale of land by the Forestry Commission in 1815 led to the birth of this solitary inn – "The Heroes of Waterloo." The dapper Royal Mail Coach made its last change of horses there at 9pm each evening on the journey down from London and many other coaches used it too. From such isolated beginnings grew cottages and shops and a village called Waterloo. Later, around 1854, "ville" was added to the name.

The End Of The Road

In 1842 along came the railways and spoilt it all! The London and South Western Railway started the rot. They completed a route to Southampton in May 1840, which by itself might not have killed off the coaches on the Portsmouth Road. But in 1842 a branch line from Eastleigh to Gosport was opened and a round-the-houses rail route from London to Portsmouth became a reality. Gosport terminus was half a mile from the floating bridge/chain ferry linking the town to Portsmouth.

For the Stage Coach companies it didn't just rain, it poured. A second rail option was made possible in 1847 when the London, Brighton and South Coast Railway opened a route from London via Chichester. Once Royal Mail began using railways from 1847 it was the knacker's yard for horses.

Coachmen were put out of work, as well as porters, grooms, ostlers, blacksmiths, wheelwrights, innkeepers, waiters, servants and chambermaids. A thriving industry died, and from 1850 to 1900 the Portsmouth Road hibernated, kept alive only by the carts and wagons of local carriers.

In 1875 there was a forlorn attempt to rekindle the Coaching Age along the pining Portsmouth Road. "The Rocket" was back in operation between Portsmouth High Street and London's Piccadilly on Mondays, Wednesdays and Fridays, but this revival was short lived. In August 1878 the Portsmouth Evening News reported that "The Rocket" had been pulled by its four horses for the last time.

The ill-fated service had 55 horses in total, and they were sold at Tattersall's within a fortnight of closure. Several of the prime roadsters fetched over 60 guineas and were bought for hunting. This signalled the end of the Coaching Age on the Portsmouth Road and we can respectfully roll the credits.

Manor House Purbrook 1898   Photographer CHT Marshall   from the Steve Pethybridge Collection

The main road to London in 1898, viewed from the bridge at Purbrook

By kind permission of Steve Pethybridge

Chapter 9

Squirearchy Malarkey

Purbrook people were thin on the ground when the name Purbeck Heath appeared on Ogilby's strip map in 1675. It was a point on the map rather than a place of habitation. By comparison, soporific Southwick and tiddly Widley were centres of sophistication.

Fifteen hundred years before, a vital Roman road had cut across Purbrook's empty spaces, linking Chichester to Winchester to London. After the Romans left in the 5th century, the Saxons gradually settled the area and by the late stages of the 8th century a parish system incorporated villages like Boarhunt, Corhampton, Fareham, Soberton, Titchfield and Warblington - but there was nothing at Purbrook. The Saxons and then the Normans developed Hundreds and Manors, and places like Farlington, Southwick and Widley came into their own.

Manors Maketh Man

Following Henry VIII's dissolution of the monasteries and their subsequent sell-off from 1536, the district around Portsdown Hill had several owners through the next 350 years. In 1540 there were two main players: 1) William Pound of Beaumonds bought Farlington and Cosham for £317 8s 4d; and 2) John White became owner of Southwick Park which included Newlands, part of Purbrook Heath and Sheepwash.

Jumping forward to Ogilby's mapmaking in 1675, Hearth Tax returns suggest that only about 20 households lived in the greater Purbrook area. Not many when you consider that this same timeframe saw Portsmouth grow as a base for the Royal Navy, with Stage Coaches starting to use the direct London to Portsmouth route through Purbrook.

The 1711 Portsmouth & Sheet Turnpike Act helped popularise this direct route and a community began to develop along the roadside. In 1684, Captain Thomas Smith became Lord of the same Farlington Manor owned in the century before by William Pound. Captain Smith bought the Manor from Nathaniel Hunt, and boosted Purbrook's cause by switching his centre of operations (his Manor House) to the district. Its probable location was near today's Park Road.

By 1720 Captain Smith's Manor was in financial trouble, because his son Thomas had lost his shirt in an investment con called the South Sea Bubble. Captain Smith was forced to mortgage most of the estate and it took until 1742 to pay off all the debts. Farlington Manor remained in the hands of the Smith family until 1764, when Peter Taylor bought the estate. Taylor had made a fortune in some dodgy dealings in Germany during the Seven Years' War, and came home to spend his money. He built a classically-styled villa, with 21 bedrooms, on high ground adjacent to where Purbrook Park School is today, converting the old Manor House down the hill into the estate dairy.

Next he cleared woodland to create a park and set about cultivating his land on Farlington Marshes, but a plan to fence and cultivate 75 acres in Purbrook upset newly-wed Jervoise Clarke who lived in Crookhorn Lane – it would deny access from Crookhorn to the London Road. Jervoise Clarke took legal action and Chalky Road (Stakes Road) was kept open. Jervoise moved on to Chalton and, in 1789, to Blendworth (Idsworth House).

Peter Taylor's Purbrook Park mansion was completed in 1770

From a drawing by Brian Browne

In 1774 Purbrook's Peter Taylor became MP for Portsmouth, but his parliamentary contribution amounted to diddly-squat. After thirteen years as Squire, Taylor died in 1777 and his youngest son Charles inherited the Purbrook Park Estate. Its development was unfinished and troubles were brewing. A 1797 Act of Parliament settled outstanding debts, vesting the estate in trustees. By 1800 Charles Taylor had commissioned London's fashionable architect, John Nash, to design a new home for him at Hollycombe near Liphook. He let his Purbrook Park estate to a succession of tenants.

Although now resident at Hollycombe House, Charles Taylor was still selling off remnants of his real estate in Farlington and Purbrook as late as 1810. He sold Drayton Farm for £24,000, Wheatlane (Waitlane) Farm for £6,580, and Kentidge Farm for £3,500. The sales took place at The George Inn on Portsdown Hill, which was also the venue three years later for the sale of what remained of his land in Farlington and Drayton - bought by Admiral Lord Keith.

A Tidy Pile

Within the first couple of years of the new 19th century, Purbrook Park Estate had been sold for £22,000 to Lord Ennismore whose priority was to stop hunters and poachers from destroying his stock of game. Just a few years later, in 1806, he sold to Admiral Lord Keith (once a Royal Navy rival of Nelson) who bought Purbrook Park in readiness for his marriage to Miss Hester Thrale in January 1808. Lord Keith concentrated on bringing the classical villa up to scratch – by 1814 it was enthusiastically described as "a handsome building, with detached wings and offices, advantageously situated in a spacious park."

The handsome villa and its influential owner were grand enough to attract the toffs. The Duke of Clarence (the future King William IV) popped in for tea and cakes during December 1815, and the following year the Marchioness de Bourbel visited with family in tow. Admiral Keith's wife marked the occasion by inviting neighbouring nobility to an elegant ball and supper.

In 1818 Viscount Keith sold his Purbrook Park Estate for £43,000. The sales blurb described it as a "splendid mansion, seated in a fine park....and upwards of 830 acres of rich pastures, meadow, arable, and woodlands; extensive manors, abounding with game strictly preserved, and manorial rights."

The purchaser was John Walker, son of a Liverpool shipping merchant. Walker mismanaged Purbrook Park from afar, running up a long list of creditors through the 1820s. By 1829 the situation was so dire that the estate's assets were divided up and sold to pay off debts. These assets included the furniture, the wine cellar and many acres of land. By the end of the decade the house had been torn down and sold off in lots at knockdown prices.

A New Broom

A seminal moment in the history of the village came in December 1837 when Purbrook Park's remaining 600 acres were bought by John Deverell, a 37 year-old married man living at Park Place, Wickham. He also purchased adjacent land on the northern slopes of Portsdown, and owned some land in Widley too. Deverell oversaw his village of Purbrook with a benevolent, determined hand for the next 43 years.

John Deverell acquired a considerable Purbrook Park Estate with farms, tenants, workers, park lodges and other buildings, but he couldn't reside in a ruined villa. Straightaway he set about building a new mansion suitable for Squire and family adjacent to the ruined classical villa. By 1840 the imposing new house was ready for occupation, complete with its four Ionic columns.

The League Of Gentlemen

John Deverell bought into a changed climate in 1837. Alongside the break-up and sale of the larger Purbrook Park Estate back in 1829,

Purbrook Park House (1840) has been a school since 1924

politics and power in Farlington Manor had shifted and shuddered. Squire John still regulated the heartbeat of the locality, but there were now farmers who had bought parcels of land, and micro-squires and landlords who resided in neighbouring country houses and farms. People like William Taylor who had bought Stakes Farm for £5,020 back in 1820.

Just up the road, John Spice Hulbert (1778-1844) purchased the hamlet of Stakes Hill. Mr Hulbert, who also had a residence at 3 High Street, Portsmouth, built Stakes Hill Lodge in 1820. His gentrified pile covered 400 acres including the surrounding woods. JSH became the Squire of newly-emerging Waterloo village. (The Hulbert heirs maintained their dignified status until the 1970s when the surviving family sold the land. At the same time they mysteriously decided to demolish Stakes Hill Lodge....and then it burned down!)

Along the lane towards Crookhorn stood impressive Oaklands, resplendent with corner turret and standing in 80 acres. This was undoubtedly "a fine house," the home of General Charles Napier (1782-1853) a famous soldier who had fought against Napoleon. The worthy General is buried in Old Portsmouth's Garrison Church. When Napier graced Oaklands, Stakes Hill Road was no more than a country lane venturing south to Crookhorn Lane.

Another stately residence was Purbrook Heath House beyond the Common. Built in the late 1790s, it was owned throughout Squire Deverell's time by William Harvey. Another person splendidly housed was the Rector of Farlington parish, Edward Tew Richards, whose rectory was at the bottom of Portsdown Hill, next to his Farlington church. He enjoyed an impressively long spell in office, from 1824 to 1887.

The undisputed champion of the heavyweight division of local landowners was Squire Thistlethwayte of Southwick, monarch of practically everything he surveyed west of the main Portsmouth Road. In this region of Hampshire, he was the Squire of Squires.

But not everyone loved the landowning superstar; Squire T felt his timbers rudely shivered by an anonymous letter posted to him in 1830. The sender threatened to set Southwick House alight unless the Squire lowered his labourers' rents and increased their wages. Squire Thistlethwayte hastily summoned a meaty band of local constables to patrol Southwick until the threat faded away.

The Great Divide

If the goblin by the brook at Purbrook read his tea leaves, he would have known that the Farlington Rector (Richards) and the Purbrook Squire (Deverell) would never see eye to eye. Rector Edward Tew Richards (I'll call him ET) had a vision to save his dutiful Purbrook parishioners the slog of attending church at faraway St Andrew's Farlington. It was a tidy trek along Crookhorn Lane and over Portsdown. Even the newborn hamlet of Waterloo had managed to build itself a church (St George's) in 1831. But at Purbrook there was nothing. ET planned a chapel of ease there, to make the lives of his Purbrook folk that bit more congenial.

Building St John's took a while because Rector Richards had to provide most of the funding

Squire Deverell was in favour of a church and a schoolroom too, and offered £400 to help. Building started in 1843, on land donated by Reverend Allen who lived at Purbrook House between The Leopard and The White Hart. But Squire Deverell soon fell out with ET over what he saw as the Rector's high-church, Catholic, leanings. The Squire strongly favoured an Evangelical low-church approach and upped sticks, refusing to worship at the Rector's Farlington church, preferring St George's Waterloo and St Mary Magdalene Widley instead.

ET ended up funding most of the £1,500 project himself, completing Purbrook Church in 1850 and the schoolroom next door one year later. Because of the dispute between Rector and Squire, the Bishop of Winchester didn't consecrate St John's Purbrook until eight years after its completion. Reverend Alfred Poole was installed as curate and his income (£50 per annum) was provided by ET.

But Squire Deverell wasn't happy and defiantly opened a chapel (at Fir Lodge) on his own land in 1859. It was known as Christ Church Purbrook and still survives as part of a private dwelling at the junction of Park Avenue and Stakes Road. It was registered as an estate church, and was a kick in the shins for the Rector because all Purbrook Park Estate workers were expected to worship there rather than St John's. They knew better than to cross the boss! John Deverell installed Reverend Thomas Roberts as minister, a position he held until Christ Church Purbrook finally shut its doors on December 11th 1870.

The Low Church High On The Hill

National politics stirred up this ecclesiastical indigestion even more. Palmerston's Tory Government set about building a series of forts along

St John's schoolroom next to the church is a private dwelling these days

the top of Portsdown Hill, and by 1868 there were hundreds of soldiers garrisoned there, notably in Fort Purbrook and Fort Widley. John Deverell proposed to the Bishop of Winchester that a new church be built at Portsdown to meet the spiritual needs of the troops. ET objected, but Deverell won the day. The Bishop granted approval in 1870 and Christ Church Portsdown was consecrated in 1874, with a new district being carved out of the parishes of Farlington, Widley, and Purbrook.

The Portsdown church was strictly Evangelical, with Squire Deverell as its patron. It cost him £5,000, with an additional £150 per year for the Vicar's endowment. Not surprisingly, the vicarage for Christ Church Portsdown was located on the Squire's Purbrook Park Estate. Though sold in 1926, it's still there today.... the "Old Vic."

Man On A Mission

John Deverell was a benevolent patrician. As well as Christ Church Portsdown (which a century later gave birth to a cricket club close to my heart), back in 1844 he built a school for 30 girls in Purbrook village – April Cottage. Later, in 1853, he converted it to a reading room, open on weekday evenings from October to April and stocked with newspapers, books and games. Its regular 20 to 30 members paid one penny per week.

He also provided land near the junction of Chalky Road and Stakes Hill for an Industrial School for 70 boys to be built. The Industrial School opened in 1868, maintained by grants from Government and County education authorities. It took boys from Hampshire and surrounding counties, and a few from London too.

It was an institution for "destitute boys who have been exposed to vicious influences," where training was given in "tailoring, shoemaking, baking, farm and garden work, gymnastics and swimming...." The regime was tough, but they had their own brass band....and a cricket pitch! Although Squire Deverell died in 1880, his Industrial School grew to accommodate 95 boys by 1900.

In 1912 son William Deverell of Stockbridge made a gift of the Industrial School to Hampshire County Council, who took over its administration. At that time there were ten staff, including a matron and a bandmaster cum gym instructor.

John Deverell pulled out the stops for his Estate workers, setting up night schools for working men and boys in the 1860s, so that they could improve themselves. The local press reported that one evening Squire Deverell and Reverend Roberts from the estate church visited the night school in Stakes, laying on a roast dinner for the 41 workers attending. Quite a treat in 1866. Naturally enough, the Squire grasped this opportunity to address his well-fed audience, urging them to be the best that they could be.

Squire Deverell enjoyed his place at the top of the pile and did more than his share in looking after the spiritual, social and educational needs of his flock. His annual party for local schoolchildren was a case in point. For the "do" held in September 1862, no less than 130 of the little blossoms bowled along to Purbrook Park! They wore themselves out sampling sports and games before a prize-giving session rounded off their day in the footlights.

For Whom The Bell Tolls

John Deverell had a soft spot for the Methodists, and he helped them build a chapel in 1879....right next door to ET's Anglican Church! But the establishment of St John's Church Purbrook, Christ Church Portsdown and the Methodist Chapel, all in the space of twenty years or so,

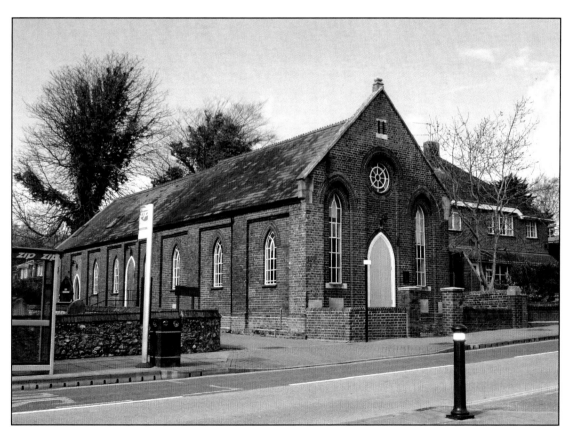

Purbrook Methodists' first chapel was built next door to St John's

proved to be the epilogue for St Mary Magdalene, tucked away behind Purbrook Heath in Widley. Though rebuilt in 1849 (architect John Colson of Winchester also designed Christ Church Portsdown), the church became surplus to requirements as Widley's population steadily decamped eastwards and settled closer to the London Road.

St Mary Magdalene withered on the vine. In 1919 services were discontinued, but faithful volunteers continued to dust down the interior right through until 1937. Young Trevor Harfield (see later connection with Widley Cricket Club) lived nearby and sometimes helped his grandmother clean the church during the 1930s, Mill Farm providing the hot water. Ultimately, Widley's church suffered as all abandoned buildings do, and St Mary Magdalene was demolished in 1953.

Family Fortunes

Although the Portsmouth Road sparked Purbrook village into life, it was the succession of Purbrook Squires who shaped the land and workforce. In particular, Squire Deverell placed an indelible thumbprint on the character of the village. Purbrook's benefactor died in 1880, but the Purbrook Park Estate remained with the Deverells for another 39 years.

When John Deverell's widow (his second wife) Sarah died in 1895, daughter Frances let the mansion and in 1897 moved to her newly built Purbrook Grange (the Red House) in Stakes Road next to the grounds of the Industrial School. Eventually the Estate's upkeep became a major problem and rents from tenants took a nosedive too. By the end of the First World War the decision to quit became inevitable and Purbrook Park Estate was auctioned at St. George's Hall, Waterlooville in June 1919.

A glance at the auction handbills shows how much of Purbrook village was owned by the Deverells. Up for sale were:
- Purbrook Park Estate, complete with mansion, lodges, keepers' cottages, stables, and 230 acres;
- five compact farms – Chalk Farm, Crookhorn Farm, Dairy Farm, Flint Farm, and Park Farm;
- ten building plots;
- an assortment of houses and cottages and garden plots.

The Estate's tenant workers and tenant farmers were invited to purchase their homes and livelihoods. George Gauntlett bought his dairy farm (as well as shelling out £6,200 for 196 acres of neighbouring Crookhorn Farm) and Ted Miles bought the house he was already living in for £200, which he considered a snip. Some of the land was bought by Portsmouth businessmen and then sold for development over the ensuing years.

The mansion didn't reach its reserve price and was not sold straight-away. Ultimately it was purchased by Hampshire County in 1924 with three acres of land, for £11,000. In September 1924 it opened its doors as Purbrook Park County High School.

The section of Estate land fronting the A3 London Road south of the "Old Vic" had been let to tenants (copyhold) throughout the Deverells' reign and remained an open space after the sale. It became Purbrook Allotments after World War Two, at a time when Government were encouraging people to grow their own crops. Purbrook Horticultural Society made the land their home as long ago as 1949.

As for the rest of the Estate, the fall of the Deverell dynasty triggered development in Purbrook. Before too long there were new arrivals on new doorsteps and the old parishioners sensed their traditional way of life slipping away, whether they liked it or not.

St Mary Magdalene's congregation faded away as (old) Widley's inhabitants moved out.

Chapter 10

The Butcher, The Baker...

So much for the tiffs and triumphs of Purbrook's landed gentry. But what about the Ordinary Joes? As the Portsmouth Road turnpiked and the Dockyard industrialised, what stirred village people into life down by the brook?

Downhill Struggle

In the hundred years that followed the first Portsmouth & Sheet Bridge Turnpike Act of 1711, a sleepy village yawned into existence alongside the Portsmouth Road, to meet the needs of the carts and carriages that careered down the long hill to the pure brook. A blacksmith and a wheelwright were primary requirements because the brook was at the bottom of a long descent that tested the skill of the coachmen and the durability of the wagons.

Coaches in those early days of travel had a high centre of gravity and were prone to accidents on hills. They could easily lose a wheel or turn over. The churned-up passengers needed looking after too, hence the emergence of coaching inns. By the later years of the 18th century notable local inns were The Leopard and The White Hart, plus The George at the hilltop.

Aside from Purbrook's country mansions and churches, old buildings that survive are thin on the ground. The White Hart Inn hung on until 1923 when it was demolished and rebuilt, and The Leopard Inn was re-hashed in 1940. A few steps south, an early 19th century terraced house lives on at 27 London Road, and several precious old cottages known as Van Dieman's Row still cluster together in the heart of the village. Local legend has it that the cottages were erected by prisoners held at Portchester Castle some 250 years ago, but it seems more likely that they saw the light of day around the same time as neighbouring April Cottage (1844).

19th century elegance near The Leopard Inn

A Grain Of Sense

Before 1800 there was no great demand for grain, fruit or vegetables from the inhabitants of that small, walled town of Portsmouth but now a different picture was emerging. By 1801 Portsmouth's numbers had swollen to 7,839, traffic on the Portsmouth Road had grown from a trickle to a flood, and the 1810 Act to enclose the Forest of Bere – allowing many of the trees to be felled – encouraged farmers to cultivate more land and produce more food.

The people of Portsmouth needed fresh food and countryside farms proved invaluable. Although there were a number of farms and market gardens on Portsea Island itself, the energetic suburbs of Portsea, Landport and Southsea had voracious appetites. Portsmouth's market operated on Tuesdays, Thursdays and Saturdays, selling meat, poultry, vegetables, fruit and fish.

Out-of-town Portsdown held its own annual Fair until 1861. It was a busy three-day event at the end of July which attracted upwards of 30,000 people and was an important outlet for farms of the locality, selling horses and cattle as well as agricultural produce.

The farms stretching down both sides of Portsdown Hill had lighter, better soil than the lowland farms of Portsea Island. The chalky down-

87

land above Purbrook produced the best corn for miles around and in 1823 William Cobbett, popular editor and champion of rural society, passed this way heading west.

One of the objects of his journey was to see the state of the corn on the slopes of Portsdown Hill. In his view this was the best and earliest corn in the whole of England, from Bedhampton all the way to Fareham. He was heartily impressed on this trip and sang the praises of both wheat and barley.

A Stable Environment

Horse-drawn traffic along the Portsmouth Road through Purbrook reached its peak in the first half of the 19th century, before the railways steamed in and ended a romance. Travelling down from London, some of the competing Stage Coach companies made their last change of horses at the top of the village, at The White Hart Inn or The Leopard run by John Webb. Favoured alternatives were The Heroes of Waterloo up the road – used by Royal Mail Coaches after 1815 - or Billetts Stables further up, or the old Spotted Cow at Cowplain which was closer to the road than today's successor.

Long Day's Journey Into Night

Are you ready to have your bones barbecued? Hitch up your strides and clamber aboard the famous Rocket, one of the toll-paying Portsmouth Stage Coaches as it thunders down from Butser. The guard takes a blast on his horn 250 yards short of the Horndean turnpike gate, the pikeman grudgingly shuffles out ready to open up, dues are paid and the coach rattles through.

Next the coachman coaxes his four horses through what remains of the once-dreaded Forest of Bere, passes the crossroads at tiny Waterloo, parades past Waitlane End Farm and Plant Farm, climbs past lofty Purbrook Windmill off to the left of the carriageway and, after another 400 yards, spies The White Hart in the distance. At this point the guard blows his horn to warn workers at the inn and stables that the coach is approaching.

The White Hart is a welcome sight, especially for the poor sods whose seats are on top of the windswept coach, next to coachman and guard. By comparison, those crammed inside are shaken and stirred, but not so shiveringly cold. Petersfield, the previous stop, seems a lifetime ago.

Enclosure

In 1700 about one third of England was common land and village people enjoyed long-held rights to use these commons to graze their animals, even though property rights remained with the landowners (lord of the manor, church etc).

By 1800 landowners had reclaimed huge tracts of land, fencing and hedging them for their own use. This process of Enclosure was achieved by a mixture of Acts of Parliament, formal agreements, and informal action. In Hampshire between 1700 and 1900, there were 192 Enclosures brought about by Acts of Parliament alone.

Enclosure was about optimum farmland use, productivity, better drainage and crop rotation. Prior to Enclosure, as well as open commons on which they grazed their animals, peasants were allocated strips of land in their lord's open fields which they cultivated.

But Enclosure handed absolute property rights to landowners, and tenants had to stump up cash if they wanted to carry on. Commoners saw Enclosure as another word for theft.

In 1810 an Act of Parliament enclosed the Forest of Bere, which resulted in most of the wood pasture being cleared and replaced by fields and paddocks. Commissioners were appointed to consider claims to "rights of common" but, as most villagers couldn't read the notices that were displayed, very few claims resulted.

Four hundred landowners benefited from the Forest of Bere's enclosure. Principal beneficiary was Southwick Squire Thomas Thistlethwayte, who was allotted 517 acres.

Locally, 76 acres of forest adjacent to the turnpike at Purbrook were auctioned at the Golden Lion in Southwick. Five men bought the seven lots for £3,244. James White of Purbrook village was one of the buyers. A further Act in 1812 (effective in 1815) saw 74 acres in Widley Field enclosed.

But Purbrook Heath, also known as Purbrook Common, always avoided enclosure. As part of the Southwick Estate it remained common land/common waste.

Fields replaced woods in the Forest of Bere

Busiest man at The White Hart is the ostler who detaches the four horses who have dragged the coach from Petersfield and leads them to the stables. Next the final team of fresh horses are manoeuvred into position at the head of the coach.

Inside the cosy White Hart passengers stretch aching limbs and maybe swallow a mug of Hampshire ale. One cooped-up passenger opts for a brief stroll instead, past Purbrook House - its three storeys of white brick hosting nine bedrooms, then The Leopard Inn, then The Woodman on the corner, then the smithy and the wheelwright. Just out of earshot the village's innovative steam-powered corn mill is grinding away.

All too soon the coachman is ready to roll and everyone climbs back on board. In anticipation of 250 yards of potentially dodgy descent to the brook, the drag plate is lowered. Meanwhile, down at the brook a lad waits dutifully to replace the drag shoe in readiness for the pull up to

Purbrook House stands serene by London Road

the summit of Portsdown. The boy's reward is a free trip on the coach as far as Highbank dairy. With its fresh team of horses the coach negotiates the turnpike gate at the brow of the Hill and rattles over the crest.

Beyond the long descent stretch the farm strips of Portsea Island, and somewhere in the distance lies our destination in Portsmouth High Street. Still five miles to go, a precarious downhill gradient to negotiate, another turnpike gate to be encountered before the Creek...and we should be enjoying the comforts of the Fountain Hotel before nightfall. By then, the start of our journey at Piccadilly's White Bear Inn will have been a bonecrushing eleven hours ago!

A Self-Sufficient Lot

As the 19th century matures, so does Purbrook. From mid-century on, the heart of this small community gains St John's church, a schoolroom, a chimney sweep, a carpenter, a builder or two and a joiner. South of the village a building of mid 18th century origin (the Old Vic) will soon be home to the Vicar of Christ Church Portsdown, once the church has been consecrated.

On the brow of the hill, partially hidden by trees to the right, is Portsdown Lodge – home to Jane Austen's brother, Francis William Austen. This grand old man was Admiral of the Fleet in his time. Sir Francis survived at Portsdown Lodge until 1865, his 92nd year. On the eastern side of the highway Christ Church will open its doors in 1874, and on Portsdown's summit beside the sunken road hewn through the chalk around 1820, stands The George Inn.

By 1867 Purbrook's population has grown to 335. The village boasts shoemaker Edward Knight, draper James Webber, bakers James Banting and James Phillips, butcher Elizabeth Kent, plus two grocers and a tailor. George Miles is the blacksmith in London Road and Frank Miles is one of three carpenters in the village. Reuben Clear is the local builder and Richard Leaver doubles up as postmaster and bookseller. Very soon James Ford will be in charge of the Post Office opposite The Leopard.

Squire Deverell still presides at Purbrook Park House where grand carriageways (Park Avenue) sweep up to his impressive front door. The Squire shepherds his human flock with a benevolent hand and the villagers know their place. Many of them work on the Estate or at neighbouring farms, and are dependent on the gentry for their livelihood and accommodation.

Far From The Madding Crowd

Good things have a habit of coming to an end and down in the village the boom has already bust. Stage Coaches and Mail Coaches disappeared by 1850 as people, post and parcels defected to the railways. London can be reached by steam train in just three hours.

Traffic on the roads is now entirely local, reduced to horse-drawn omnibuses, farmers' carts and tradesmen, plus carriers transporting wares and produce. Prominent among these are Mays of Hambledon and Greenaway & Sylvester from Waterlooville. In the dry days of summer a solitary soul with a water cart wanders the main street, spraying the surface to keep down the dust. Life goes on, but life is duller than it was. The Coaching Ways that brought revenue to Purbrook have scarpered.

Over The Hills And Far Away

Purbrook has little choice but to adapt, its inhabitants providing most of the services their community requires. In the 1870s Purbrook welcomes a horse omnibus from Petersfield en route to Portsmouth on Tuesdays, Thursdays and Saturdays, the bus completing a return trip on the same day. More regular is the daily horse bus from Waterlooville that passes through Purbrook at 9.30am on its way to Portsmouth, heading back from town at 4pm. Portsea Island remains a self-contained unit with none of its boundaries coming north of the Creek.

Chalk Farm
viewed from
Stakes Road

*Picture
courtesy of
Ted Lamont*

In the 1880s Purbrook was still considered out in the sticks. In 1884 the Hampshire Telegraph remarked that, for "those fond of seclusion and quiet pastoral scenes, the country to the north of Portsdown Hill will afford the greatest pleasure...(you) only hear the birds and insects on the wing and the sheep bells from the neighbouring fields...a rural aspect."

In Purbrook butchers, bakers, barbers, blacksmiths, builders, drapers, grocers and tailors toiled away. Other locals worked in the market gardens and farms that ensured food for country tables. These farms also helped provide food for the 100,000 people who by now were packed onto Portsea Island. Purbrook farmers traded at Portsmouth market on Tuesdays, Thursdays and Saturdays. This meant setting off from home as early as 2am with loaded carts pulled by two horses, to be sure of getting their various wares to market in good time.

Ordnance Survey's 1897 map of Purbrook lends support to the importance of Portsmouth's food basket over the Hill. The local map reveals Pigeon House Farm, Mill Farm, Widley Farm, Purbrook Farm, Plant Farm, Waitlane End Farm, Chalk Farm, Dairy Farm (Gauntlett's from 1901), Stakes Farm, Crookhorn Farm, plus the Purbrook Park Estate smallholdings.

In this rural outpost called Purbrook, not everyone was angelic. There was poaching, there was theft, there were punch-ups, there was an occasional murder, and there were accidents even on these quiet roads and byways. Nevertheless, in the latter years of the century one policeman served the whole of Purbrook, Waterlooville and Cowplain.

Last Days In The Countryside

A biting draught of technology was preparing to blow through Purbrook's tranquil main street. A harbinger would be the first motor car driving through an excited village around 1900. By this time the horse bus was a meaty double-decker pulled by three horses. With their eye to business these buses made regular calls at the local train station in Cosham. For the devilish climb to the summit of Portsdown, a trace horse was added to the normal complement of three, to tow the bus to the hilltop. Just a few years after Purbrook's sighting of its first motor car came its first tram – the inaugural "green car" jogged through the village in 1903.

At the beginning of the 1900s Purbrook remained a country village, where Christopher Miles (having succeeded his father George who died in 1883) made horseshoes at the forge and Frank Miles ran the carpenter's shop nearby. The Miles blacksmith's shop was a busy place; horseshoes were fashioned and hung up all around the shop in readiness for shaping and fitting.

The most prominent shop in Purbrook was Blackman's opposite The Leopard, run by George Blackman. It was a bakery, a grocery, a confectionery and much else besides. Distinctive wrought iron railings highlighted the balcony immediately above the shop. Mr Blackman's wife ran a similar store in Waterlooville, and between the two villages lay open land.

Stretching south along Purbrook's main highway, chestnut trees guarded the roadside beyond St John's schoolroom, while six oil lamps hung morbidly from tall posts. One man's important job in winter months was to carry a ladder to the posts, clamber up to the lamps, oil them up and then light them at 5 or 6pm. Religiously at 10pm he would repeat the communion to put them out. There was no other light but the moon.

The village had little gas or electricity until 1920, but in 1900 this was not considered a hardship, and neighbours generally mucked in and helped each other. The business up and down the main street comprised

Van Dieman's cottages in the heart of the village

carters delivering coal, wood, oil and household goods, and wagons full of hay and straw being hauled towards Portsmouth.

In the village an assortment of door-to-door salesmen paraded their wares – anything from tin plates to brushes to combs to buttons to laces. And all the while kids played marbles along London Road and Chalky Road, only occasionally having to stand aside to let horse-drawn traffic plod through.

On Mondays Cosham had a cattle market and Purbrook's flock of farmers were regular traders. Cows were herded along the main road with a farmhand walking slowly at the front of the small procession. Pigs and chickens were taken in carts. Pony carts clattered through from Denmead and Clanfield every Friday, on their way to Portsmouth with eggs and butter.

Despite the Age Of The Stage having long since disappeared, there were still working horses everywhere, widely used on farms. Horse manure decorated the streets and tweaked the nostrils. Mind you, Mrs Fortescue had a wonderful display of roses!

Breaking Up Is Hard To Do

Although Squire Deverell died in 1880, the ways of Purbrook people changed but slowly during the years preceding the First World War. From 1918 onwards, however, change became a more constant companion. Signposts of change were the appearance of the motor car, the coming of the Portsdown & Horndean Light Railway, and the break up of Deverell's Purbrook Park Estate in 1919.

Before the Estate's 1919 sale, Purbrook village looked like this:

- North to south, a ribbon of intermittent development along the main road, from The White Hart at one end to the Old Vicarage at the other.

- West of Purbrook village below Marrelsmoor Coppice was the byway to Purbrook Heath and Potwell, dotted with substantial dwellings such as Woodside House, Purbrook Lodge and Purbrook Heath House. There was money west of the bridge!

- East of the village, Chalky Road (Stakes Road) ploughed a lonely furrow past April Cottage, Chalk Farm, Fir Lodge, Fir Coppice, Deverell's stables, the Dairy Farm, the Grange/Red House, and on towards Morelands – an elegant country house with glass conservatories that stood near Crookhorn corner.

- South east of the village, the Deverell family's Purbrook Park House was enthroned on top of a rise. Much of the area was open land where cowslips bloomed in springtime. From the House you could peer through the trees and see meadows all around. (It would all disappear one day, evolving into Fir Copse Road, Frances Road, Lone Valley, Privett Road, Serpentine Road and so on).
- Back in the village south of Chalky Road, the terrain was very much wetter. There was a "Fish Pond" and an area called "The Bog."

The Bog

The Bog (roughly occupying the latitude of Ladybridge Road today) was wet, wet, wet. It was the meeting place for water spilling from Purbrook's springs and ditches. After socialising in The Bog, the water identified itself as the brook and headed west past Purbrook Heath to the Wallington River and ultimately to the sea.

The Bog was surrounded by abundant flowers and bird life. Osiers – a type of willow tree – flourished in the wet conditions, and The Bog was sufficiently deep in places for a Stakes Road resident to own a rowing boat. A man from Cosham village used to harvest the osiers each autumn. He would row or wade out to the trees, cut their branches, tie them in bundles, stand them in the water to keep them supple and, in due course, weave the green branches into bushel baskets or cross handle baskets and sell them.

The shorn osier stumps were commandeered by moorhens for their nests. Other birds made their homes in the coppices and meadows all around The Bog. There were plovers, rooks, lapwings, nightingales, blackbirds, thrushes and cuckoos. The nearby fields and woods were full of partridges and pheasants.

Up Chalky Road the fir copse provided a perfect rookery nook and annual rook-shoots in springtime did their best to trim the numbers of these raucous birds. There were three flocks of sheep close by – one on Deverell's estate farm, one on Gauntlett's dairy farm, and one north of Purbrook village. There were plenty of foxes too.

The Bog squelched on through the 20th century, hidden behind the advertising hoardings of London Road. In icy 1940s winters there was sufficient water hereabouts for bold youngsters to skate precariously across the frozen "willy beds" on rickety blades. The Bog was eventually drained, its water piped underground as far as the bridge.

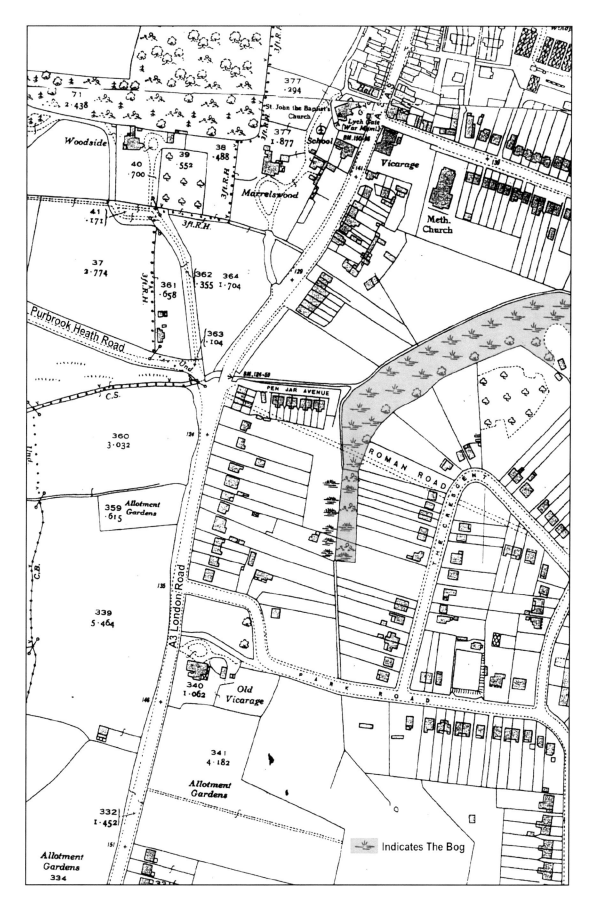

The Bog was the meeting place for Purbrook's water

Reproduced from 1937 OS map with the kind permission of Ordnance Survey

Indicates The Bog

The Estate We're In

Bricks and mortar waited patiently in the wings until Deverell's Estate was sold off. Then roads and their attendant houses or bungalows began springing up. Grand carriageways that had once led to the mansion (Park Avenue) became roadways where rows of homes with neat gardens sallied up to the kerb stones.

Nearby, small housing estates bloomed in areas like Park Farm, Queen's Grove, Westbrook Grove and Shaftesbury Avenue, all built in the late 1920s and 1930s by local builder Mr West who lived at the top of Westbrook Grove and ran a tree nursery at the bottom. Top house price for Westy's best was £450. His family firm built almost 300 homes in Purbrook.

In the heart of the village, Stakes Road had a new landmark in 1929 when the Methodists purchased land for £320 and built a new church for £6,287. Many local families such as the Browns, Fielders, Murrants, Taylors and Windebanks were supporters of the non-conformist Methodists. Their old chapel next to St John's was sold to the Anglicans for £1,500.

(St John's Vicarage on the corner of Stakes Road became headquarters for local haulier Battman's by the 1960s. Today part of the flint Vicarage survives but all its residential grandeur has drained away. The Vicarage once shared its generous lawn with a mighty oak, but the garden was killed off and the venerable tree disappeared up a dozen local chimneys).

Country Comes To Town

For working folk it was now possible to live in Purbrook and work in Portsmouth. A favoured few drove to and fro. Others cycled there and back and many more hopped aboard the double-decker green cars of the Portsdown & Horndean Light Railway. When the trams stopped in 1935, Southdown's petrol buses made daily commuting even easier. Purbrook's population reached 2,000 by the mid 1930s. Country had come to town.

Chapter 11

An Appealing Game

Our rollercoaster ride through Purbrook's past now switches back to the 19th century, whose early years witnessed some special events in southern Hampshire – and beyond.

- In 1805 Admiral Nelson left Portsmouth aboard Victory. He won the Battle of Trafalgar but didn't live to tell the tale.
- In 1806 the wife of a great engineer gave birth to an even greater engineer in Britain Street Portsea. The father was Marc; the son was Isambard; the surname was Brunel.
- In 1812 naval pay clerk John Dickens and wife Elizabeth became proud parents of a newborn son whilst living in Landport. They named him Charles.
- In 1815 Wellington and his allies finally nailed Napoleon at the Battle of Waterloo. A by-product of this famous victory was the naming of a new inn at a lonely crossroads one mile north of Purbrook. In tribute to the returning troops, the inn was called The Heroes of Waterloo.

The Battle Of Ealward's Plain

In addition to Belgium's Waterloo there was another battle in 1815, a much more local affair that I've called The Battle of Ealward's Plain. Nobody died, nor was there any rape and pillage. The firepower was leather and willow. On September 16th 1815 the Hampshire Telegraph recorded the first written evidence of a cricket team representing the village of Purbrook. The report described:

"a return match at cricket between eleven gentlemen of Denmead and Ervills and eleven of Purbrook, commenced playing on Monday last, on Ealward's Plain."

A "return" match signifies that Purbrook cricket must have existed before this fixture, but there is no trace of when the very first Purbrook ball was under-armed.

So, Monday September 11th 1815 is as near as dammit Purbrook's birthday innings, but their absolute "big bang" was probably a bit earlier.

The match was a tetchy affair, with Purbrook embroiled in controversy. It was a two-innings game, with low scores all round. Denmead reached just eighteen in their first knock and followed up with 33 all out in the second. Purbrook totalled 31 first time round, and were twelve for six wickets in the final innings when red mist descended.

The Hampshire Telegraph reported Purbrook's second innings in measured tones: "Twelve, and six wickets down; when, in consequence of a ball being struck to the booth, a dispute arose between the parties what number of runs should be allowed for such booth ball; the striker, considering the ball as dead, left his wicket, when one of the opposition party obtained it and put the striker's wicket down. The decision of the Umpires was asked, and the gentlemen in the booth, who pronounced him not out. This caused a further dispute, and the match was undecided."

Home From Home

Purbrook Common was used by other teams as well as Purbrook. In fact the two earliest references do not involve a team called Purbrook at all. On the first occasion, a notice in the press read:

"I'd give my right arm to be batting at Purbrook Heath."

"A match of cricket is to be played between eleven gentlemen of the parish of Hambledon and eleven of the parish of Farlington on Tuesday the 5th of September 1815, on Purbrook Common for eleven guineas. Refreshments on the ground or at The Leopard Inn, Purbrook."

Less than a week later, Farlington played another match at Purbrook Common, this time against Denmead and Ervills, which Farlington won by 22 runs. First mention of the

Common as Purbrook's home ground came in 1817. On Tuesday July 8th ten gentlemen from Purbrook plus a ringer plucked from Horndean's ranks, took on eleven gentlemen of Havant, "the wickets to be pitched at 10 o'clock precisely." There was a last line to the promotional patter: "Good accommodation on the ground, or at The Leopard." The good news ended there, because Havant won the game.

Purbrook Common became a popular cricketing venue, teams usually comprising local landowners, their gentrified pals and athletic farm-hands and labourers called upon by the Squire. Hence matches were frequently played in midweek, and you can bet your last sovereign that there was usually a gentlemen's wager on the result.

Betting On Batting

Wagers for matches on Purbrook Common were tidy sums, although affluent parts of the county displayed more extravagance. In June 1813, for example, a match at Twyford Down was advertised as "a grand match of cricket on Tuesday between eleven gentlemen of Farnham Club and eleven of Winchester, for fifty guineas a side, pay or play. Wickets to be pitched precisely at 10 o'clock."

Betting at Purbrook Common was down a notch from Twyford Down's high rollers; in September 1836 a local advertisement read as follows:

"A match of that manly and truly English game will be played on Purbrook Common on Tuesday the 6th of September, between the parishes of Farlington and Southwick, for twenty two sovereigns. Wickets to be pitched at half past ten."

To general delight, Mr Edney from The Leopard Inn was on site by half past one, to ensure that everyone slaked their thirst and stoked up with grub. Southwick won by seven wickets. It was normal practice for the villagers in a team to be rewarded for their winning efforts, and sometimes they would receive a share of the spoils (the wager).

Cricket Around And About

Purbrook Common was high in the popularity stakes, but where were the other cricketing hotspots in our neck of the woods? Southsea Common – adjacent to the old Cricketers' Tavern near the Queen's Hotel - often played host to the gentlemen of Portsmouth & Portsea in the early 1800s. A good deal of betting accompanied their games, with odds quoted not only at the start of play, but again at the close of the first innings.

Portsmouth & Portsea's regular opponents included Horndean, with return matches taking place at Bulls Copse Corner. A report on their game in September 1811 included the worthy phrase: "the play produced in the spectators the vicissitude of opinion...." Not your typical tabloid hack, obviously!

Hambledon's great days as slayers of All England were well and truly past, but the village still played regularly and their opponents included Portsmouth & Portsea. In 1815 a July encounter between the two was played on a Tuesday at Southsea Common, with the return at Windmill Down the following Monday. Both matches began early at 9am.

Havant were another well established team and in August 1815 they took on Hambledon at Havant. The game started at 10am and was played on a Tuesday. Naturally there was a wager on the result: 22 guineas. I've already mentioned Denmead, Farlington and Southwick, and other local cricketing villages playing prior to 1820 were Compton, Droxford, Fareham and Rowlands Castle, as well as Clanfield who sometimes bolstered Horndean's ranks.

The Bat and Ball was Hambledon's HQ before they moved to Windmill Down

Game For A Change

When wickets were first pitched on Purbrook Common during the 19th century's teenage years, the Laws demanded three stumps and two bails. But in the previous century wickets had originally been two stumps a foot high and a single bail across the top. At that time the ball was rolled under-arm along the ground, and bats were shaped a bit like hockey sticks to counter this. During the 1770s under-arm "length" bowling became popular – the ball was lobbed through the air and bounced near the batsman. Straighter bats were more effective, so their shape changed. They were made from one piece of willow with no splice.

Purbrook Common's emergence as a cricket field of substance from 1815/1820 came on the cusp of a new fashion – round-arm bowling, where the bowler's arm was horizontal and he released the ball with a slinging action, frequently from round the wicket (and sometimes with both umpires positioned at square leg at their respective ends). It was formally legalised in 1828 and under-arm and round-arm vied for supremacy.

Under-arm had the edge in cunning and subtlety, but round-arm was wilder and faster. As a consequence batsmen everywhere, even on self effacing Purbrook Common, began to protect themselves with rudimentary pads and gloves, and learned to move their feet to the pitch of the ball.

By 1851 Lillywhites of London were advertising leg guards stuffed with horsehair, tied up with string and tapes. A decade later buckles and straps existed, although such trendy gear took time to permeate down to Purbrook's rustic cricketers. And it wasn't only the methods and styles of playing that were altering. Through the early years of Victoria's long reign, the nature of local cricket was changing. The gentry still played and gambled on results, but village cricket attracted local supporters loyal to their own amateur participants.

A rumpus blew up during the 1850s. Bowlers started experimenting with "over-hand" deliveries which were immediately outlawed, although some trial matches allowed them. Over-arm bowling wasn't a new invention; it had been tried long before and abandoned as illegal. Now this wind of change proved unstoppable, its exponents showing that it led to straighter, quicker bowling. Eventually, in 1884, over-arm bowling was made legal.

On The Common And In The Park

Taking changes and challenges on the chin, cricket at Purbrook was in a healthy state. In May 1858 there was a Saturday match in the village between Purbrook and the newly formed United Borough (Portsmouth) Club. Spectators were impressed by the batting of Borough's Smith and Martin who stayed together for an hour! Borough's fielding was praised as well, especially wicketkeeper Keys who conceded only eight byes, although long-stop Martin had to work his socks off. Borough won the two-innings game by eight wickets. Purbrook scored 44 and 26; Borough scored 63 and nine for two wickets.

Thomas Lord founded Lords Cricket Ground in 1814. He is buried in West Meon churchyard

Cricket on the Common carried through until the end of September and Purbrook's last home game in season 1858 was against Horndean. The match was played on a Tuesday and was notable for Mr G Gale of Horndean scoring 25 in the first innings. George Gale had taken over The Ship and Bell from his father five years before. Now he was busy developing Gales Brewery, which flourished for 150 years. In 2005 it was sold for £82 million.

Late in the following season, September 1859, Purbrook's team had a new benefactor. By kind permission of Squire John Deverell, their match against East Hants Club took place in the verdant grounds of his Purbrook Park estate. In such beautiful surroundings, the game drew a large crowd for a Wednesday. The ladies and gents who sashayed into the Park may have been enticed by the "sumptuous refreshments provided for them," as well as the opportunity to mooch around the mansion which was thrown open for the occasion by its "liberal-hearted and universally respected owner."

East Hants were a posh outfit, and their team sheet boasted one lord (Cecil) and plenty of Navy gold braid. Their generous home ground in Southsea incorporated a clubhouse and a hotel. It was situated just north of Clarendon Road, but poshness didn't save it. Club and ground were sold at auction in 1885 and residential development soon swallowed it up.

Back in 1859 at Purbrook Park, East Hants were still vibrant and savouring the match. Squire Deverell entered into the spirit of the occasion. To the "manor" born the 59 year-old donned gloves and pads and marched out to bat last man for Purbrook. Number eleven proved to be his rightful spot – the Squire hit his own wicket and was dismissed for nought. His son William batted higher at number six, but fared no better – he was clean bowled for a duck! Neither Deverell was required to bat second time around. Alas, with Purbrook about to clinch victory, stumps were drawn.

September 1859 proved quite a festival of cricket on John Deverell's Purbrook Park estate. The benevolent

There's a duck behind you, Squire. And when you go out to bat we'll see another one!

Squire set aside a recreation day for his labourers, their wives and children. Squire Deverell was all for a bit of piety before a party, so everyone trooped to church at 11.30am for a sermon by Reverend Roberts on family duty. Service over, the jolly-up followed. A horde of more than 40 workers plus their families legged it to the Park, where they tucked into lunch.

Later in the afternoon the Squire organised a cricket match, one team representing his Purbrook Park estate, the other representing his estate land in Bedhampton. The Purbrook bunch, overawed and overfed, suffered an indigestible defeat. But tea and supper dulled their pain, putting them in good humour for Squire John's inevitable speech, which brought the day to an end. Pastoral care in full bloom. And cricket in the Park.

A Punch-Up, Then A Carve-Up

A rural idyll? Eternal peace and harmony down Purbrook way? Not quite. At 7am on the morning of September 29th 1862, two horse-drawn cabs followed by several carts rattled conspicuously over Portsbridge and out of town. Up and over Portsdown they went, down into Purbrook's vale, then left past the Common to a nearby meadow in Newlands Lane. Here the quaint caravan stopped.

Although it was still early, a crowd of 200 people had gathered, and in the midst of them was a ring, staked and roped for a fight. Into the lion's den clambered William Littlejohn and Michael Rees, both of them bareknuckled and sweating hard. Queensbury rules were still five years into the future and this was primitive, illegal, prizefighting – untimed rounds ended only by a knockdown. After brief ceremony, Purbrook's own prize fight was about to burst into grisly action.

Regrettably for the baying crowd, Police Constable French chose this moment to appear ringside. He had spotted the dodgy posse at Portsbridge and followed them all the way to the meadow. Earnestly he did his duty, stepping into the ring and arresting the two pugilists. The fight was over before it had begun, and the crowd slunk away. Prize-fighters Littlejohn and Rees came up before the Beak three weeks later at Fareham Petty Sessions. Guilty as charged!

Another "situation" happened the following year – 1863. Not quite so shocking, but causing longer-term distress. This time it was on the Common, where the cricket ground had been chewed up. By now Purbrook Cricket Club had been joined at the Heath by Purbrook United CC, both clubs sharing the preparation of the ground. During winter months the two clubs toiled to improve both pitch and outfield.

Together they raised the considerable sum of £10 12s 6d; the volunteers grafted hard, using materials to the value of £9 19s 6d, leaving a healthy balance of thirteen shillings. At the conclusion of their close-season endeavours, it was generally agreed that Purbrook Common, "when properly rolled, bids fair to be worthy of the name of a good Cricket ground."

When they reported for duty on the Common the following week, these faithful volunteers were distraught to find that their carefully manicured cricket pitch had been cut to pieces by a school from "a neighbouring village," who played on it when it was far too wet. The school left it in a dreadful state, and the grafters from Purbrook and Purbrook United were spitting bullets.

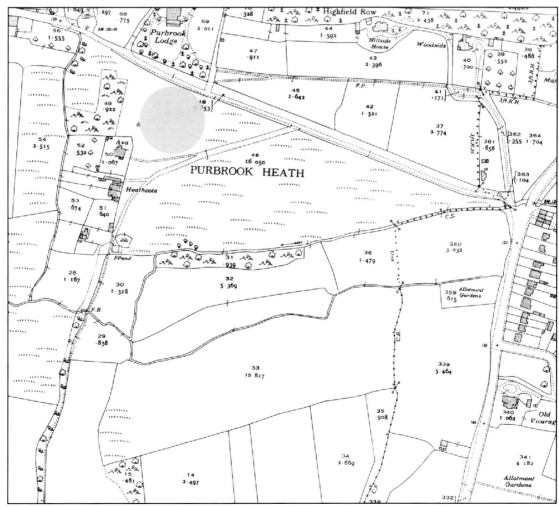

Purbrook's first cricket ground was located on the driest part of the Heath

Reproduced from 1937 OS map with the kind permission of Ordnance Survey

The trouble arose because the Common was considered a public ground, and generally available for use. Purbrook United's leading lights complained in the next issue of the parish magazine. Their appeal was to those using the Heath "who haven't shared in that expense and who are not immediately connected with the locality, not to take advantage of its being public ground, so as to deprive the two local clubs of the benefit of the outlay."

An Established Club And Ground

Purbrook CC attracted prestigious opponents. On Whit Monday 1863, they entertained The Royal Engineers. Scores were low in the two-innings game, and Purbrook won comfortably. Purbrook totalled 77 and 53, while The Royal Engineers responded with 45 in each innings.

Conspicuous in Purbrook's batting line-up was GJ White who top-scored, contributing eighteen and then 23. He had been turning out for the village since the 1850s and his influence continued right through to the next century. Purbrook cricket has enjoyed many larger-than-life characters in its 200 years, but George Joyce White – cricketer, wrestler, dairy farmer, publican – was among the largest.

Monday was a popular choice for cricket, and on Monday June 15th 1863 Purbrook took on rivals Horndean. George White was among the wickets, taking four in Horndean's first knock of 62. Horndean's brewer, George Gale, scored eleven first time around, and reached 22 in Horndean's second total of 95. Purbrook's scores were 65 in their first innings and 35 for two wickets in their second.

The match report said "the game was not played out (ie not completed) and therefore, according to custom, Purbrook claim the victory on the first innings, having exceeded their opponents by three runs." In other words, Purbrook won even though their total scores were 100 whereas Horndean amassed 157.

United At The Heath

Newcomers Purbrook United were enthusiastic, even publishing the team's "averages" for the previous season (1862) in the parish magazine. As yet, they didn't have many fixtures but eagerly sought new members and set aside Tuesday and Friday evenings for practice. They knew a thing or two about diplomacy too, respectfully referring to their long-lived partners as "the Purbrook Senior Cricket Club."

Purbrook United played half a dozen games during 1863 season, usually on Mondays with a 10am start. They struggled to win matches but were encouraged by "a very marked improvement on the part of several members of the Club in the style of their batting." Watched over by enthusiastic Club captain Frank Miles, United began running a Junior XI. By the end of the 1865 season, Club members were so impressed at the effort put in by Frank Miles that they presented him with a tea service. Frank was not the only Miles on the local cricketing scene; Christopher (blacksmith, chimney sweep and son of George) was a cricket enthusiast too.

Cricket was approaching its golden age, widely played in schools, universities and in the military. The Duke of Wellington's command back in 1841 promoted the game throughout the army. As Commander in Chief he ordered that "Cricket grounds be laid out at each end of the barrack stations throughout the United Kingdom for the use of officers and privates." Purbrook cricket was chugging along nicely too. The Common was a respected venue and, although it was too early for a pavilion to be considered, there was always a tent or two on site, serving the same purpose.

A Singular Passion

In 1878 a celebrated Single Wicket match was earmarked for the Common. Mr Ricardo travelled all the way from Devon to compete against a local tradesman from Landport. Betting played its part and the two rivals weren't there just for the sandwiches! The match was scheduled for the evening of July 8th, starting at half past six. Ricardo was a well respected cricketer back home amongst the clotted cream and his foray east included several matches designed to send him back with a heavy wallet.

Purbrook's Single Wicket match was a rare event because this format was falling out of favour. With its own set of quaint Laws, it was a battle between one batsman and one bowler, two innings each. After the first one-to-one contest finished, the next one would begin. Single Wicket matches could involve one per side as in the Ricardo v Landport affair, or more.

Frozen Asset

Purbrook United's efforts to provide cricket for youngsters was a nudge in the ribs for Purbrook Common's senior club. It had the right effect, because they too began to encourage juniors to join them. And by the 1880s Purbrook CC had an established Junior section.

If you know the Heath, you know that Easter Monday in late March is a ludicrously optimistic starting date for Purbrook Juniors' cricket season. But in 1883 the topside of the Common was not too boggy for the Juniors' game against Cosham. Mums and dads rolled up to watch and everyone was remarkably enthusiastic. They were also remarkably cold! The temperature was way down and a bitter wind was whipping snow flurries across the pitch.

The organisers should have known better, but the kids stuck at it and won the game. Best part of the day was supper in the cosy Leopard Inn, supplied by Club stalwart George White. Purbrook Juniors also won the return game at shivering Cosham, both matches being washed and ironed before the senior members had even elected their captain for the approaching season.

Purbrook and Waterloo United

Purbrook's 1883 AGM was a longwinded affair, taking place over two Monday evenings in April at The Leopard Inn. Duly elected President was a grandee of the Southwick Estate family, Mr F Thistlethwayte. He wasn't the Squire (that was Thomas Thistlethwayte) but he nevertheless provided a tad of clout. Mr Nash was voted in as Secretary and The Leopard's George White was elected to two posts – Captain and Treasurer.

By the second Monday meeting, Treasurer White produced a financial statement showing a balance of 12s 10d. Members' subscriptions collected on the night brought the healthy figure up to £6. Other members elected onto the Committee for 1883 were

They said: "Join Purbrook and you get free travel to every match!"

Messrs Barfoot, Clear, Kitchen, Knight, Lawson, Simmons and Webb. President Thistlethwayte and his committee had high hopes that local gentry, especially Squire Thomas, would support the Club during the season.

Purbrook CC's catchment area incorporated the neighbouring village of Waterlooville and the cricket club began calling itself Purbrook and Waterloo United. Waterlooville was still a small rural community, coming to life during summer weekends when townies flocked in to fill their lungs with pure country air.

Two decades later, in 1904, Waterlooville's population had topped 600 and Purbrook's northern neighbour felt mature enough to form its own cricket team so, understandably, came the parting of the ways. The Heath continued to prosper but, though Purbrook's sportsmen didn't know it, cricket's golden age was slipping carelessly away.

For the moment it was boom time. The game had become a popular spectator sport, particularly since the introduction of a County Championship in 1873. At the top of the heap strode WG Grace, a cult figure and the biggest draw on the circuit. The glitter fluttered down to village cricket too. The pitch at Purbrook Heath was in its pomp; tended, respected and enjoyed. The best it would ever be in its slot on the topside of the Common.

The Worst Of Times

The dark cloud hanging over these mellow summers was Germany's growing belligerence. But the severity of an impending Great War was unsuspected by most citizens of Britain. In June 1914 the County Championship shuddered to a halt with Surrey declared early winners, and village cricket seized up as enthusiastic young men volunteered for the fray.

The word on the street was that it would be over before it had begun: home for Christmas. Four years on and the folks at home sang to a different, melancholy tune. In a scene that would be repeated only 20 years down the line, Purbrook Common's cricket lawn surrendered to creeping undergrowth and gorse. When they picked up the cricketing pieces in 1919, the best of times were but a memory.

Chapter 12

A Transport Of Delight, 1903-1935

When the emerald green cars of the Portsdown & Horndean Light Railway first came to call, road surfaces around Purbrook incorporated a generous helping of stones and flints. These were collected from the downs by female workers for a shilling a day and then carted to the main roads and dumped in heaps. In Purbrook there was a flinty pile just before The White Hart, another at the bottom of the village by the bridge, and another further along by the Old Vic. Stakes Road was considered worthy of a stony heap too.

The Flintstones

As and when sections of road became rutted, men decked out in face masks appeared with rakes and hammers to repair the highway. They selected a quantity of stones and flints from the heap, broke them into smaller pieces and measured them. Once they considered the broken bits to be the right size, the men watered the road, laid the stones on top and rolled them into the surface until they were compacted.

Although pneumatic tyres were starting to ride over the horizon, these were still the days of solid tyres on motor vehicles; no bad thing, as rolled-in flints could retain sharp edges. Over time, unforgiving iron tyres on the wheel rims of horse-drawn wagons, plus metal horseshoes, ground the surfaces to dust. Replacement stones, flints and gravel were vital. Steep hills remained vulnerable after heavy rainstorms, and over Portsdown the combination of water, chalk, grit and manure was so lethal that bundles of sticks had to be laid across the roadway to make it passable.

Horses For Courses

Before trams, the only public transport in and out of Purbrook was the horse omnibus. These double-deckers linked Portsmouth to the villages over Portsdown Hill, including Denmead and Waterlooville. There was even a service that tackled the hazardous journey to Petersfield through the Butser cutting, operating three times a week. In Portsmouth, transport was a notch more sophisticated and horse trams existed from as early as 1865, when the first horse-drawn tramway in Britain began running between South Western station (Portsmouth and Southsea) and Southsea Pier (Clarence Pier).

Horse trams moved along rails sunk into the roadway, which made things easier for the horses (sometimes one horse but usually two). In contrast, out in the country north of Portsdown, it took three horses to drag each omnibus along the unrailed road surfaces, the condition of which might range from solid to slippery to sodden.

No Stopping The Trams

My tale of the Portsdown & Horndean Light Railway concentrates on how it affected Purbrook. There are several publications that recount the full glory of the Light Railway – mine is a limited edition.

Portsmouth Corporation took over Provincial Tramways in 1900 and began replacing horse trams with electrified tramcars. Before long, passengers could hop aboard Corporation tramcars and be transported in some style beyond the confines of Portsea Island. The Provincial Company moved on, but a subsidiary company called Hampshire Light Railways had been hived off in 1897. This off-shoot had an ambitious manager in Mr AW White who had plans to run a service out to Horndean.

London Road Purbrook in the days of the tram

By kind permission of Steve Pethybridge

113

On July 6th, 1898, an august body called the Light Railway Commissioners undertook a local enquiry at Cosham – its two Commissioners were the Earl of Jersey and Colonel Boughey. Promoters of the Light Railway claimed 1) that it would open up a large agricultural district, and 2) that it would develop suburban traffic. Among those opposing the scheme was Southwick's Squire Thistlethwayte, who owned 8,000 acres locally, including land at Portsdown upon which the track would intrude.

The Squire was an influential opponent, so it was significant that the might of the War Department favoured the cause of the tramway, because of their plan to build Queen Alexandra Military Hospital on Portsdown Hill. The upshot of the Commissioners' five hours of deliberation was a Light Railway Order, which approved a scheme to run an electric tramway for six miles and 2.9 chains, all the way from Cosham to Horndean.

By this time AW White had been busy selling the idea to local communities through which the proposed Light Railway would run. On June 11th, 1898 a well attended meeting at Purbrook heard Manager White explain details of the scheme. The meeting resolved that "the introduction of a light railway from Cosham through Purbrook will be of great advantage to the ratepayers of Farlington (parish)." Just three people voted against, including Vicar Spyers who felt the trams might divert his congregation from church.

The Light Railway Leaves Town

The Commissioners' positive decision was good news for the aspirational AW White, and there was more joy for his new organisation when they were authorised by the Board of Trade to construct the light railway along the roadway from Cosham to Horndean. Work started in January 1902, using a gauge of 4 feet 7¾ inches for the rail track.

Mr White's boys didn't hang about. On March 2nd 1903 the Portsdown & Horndean Light Railway began operations. Their timetable was a far cry from the infrequent horse omnibus. The first tram into town left Horndean at 7.50am, the next followed at 8.40am, and after that there was one every 20 minutes. In the opposite direction, the first green car left Cosham heading for Portsdown Hill at 8.35am, then 9.15am, and every 20 minutes thereafter.

Mr White's timetable enabled businessmen to catch the early tram and connect with the 8.21 train to Southampton or the 8.26 train

Horses outside
The George. And
tram lines too!

*Picture courtesy
of Ted Lamont*

to Portsmouth. At the late end of the day, a train from Portsmouth arrived at Cosham at 10.48pm, connecting with a tram that departed at 11.05pm.

At a stroke the shops and markets of Portsmouth became accessible to country folk from over the Hill, and although the leisurely start times of morning trams were not yet set up to meet the start times of Portsmouth's factories and dockyard, at least travelling to work by tram became a gleam in the eye for country folk.

There was also a gleam in the eye of families trapped in back-to-back houses in grimy parts of Portsmouth. This mechanised transport link between town and country promoted the possibility of moving out to the villages and commuting back in. For this to become reality there needed to be sufficient, affordable, housing stock north of Portsdown Hill. From the 1920s and '30s, development of Purbrook's former Deverell estate and competition from motor buses made all these aspirations achievable.

As the Light Railway matured, morning departures moved into line with workers' requirements. By 1923 the early morning tram heading for Portsmouth rattled

TRAM FARES IN 1903	
Cosham and George Inn	Twopence
Downs and Purbrook White Hart	Twopence
Purbrook Common and Waterloo	Twopence
Waterloo and Park Lane	Twopence
Park Lane and Horndean	Twopence
Cosham and Purbrook White Hart	Threepence
Downs and Waterloo	Threepence
Purbrook Common and Park Lane	Threepence
Waterloo and Hornsdean	Threepence
Cosham and Park Lane	Fourpence
Purbrook Common and Horndean	Fourpence
Cosham and Horndean	Sixpence

through Purbrook soon after 7am, and the first tram heading towards Waterlooville passed through Purbrook village before 8 o'clock. Efforts to boost trade included workmen's cheap return tickets valid on all cars setting out from Horndean by 8.05am, day return tickets between Horndean and Cosham, and tickets for school children.

Up And Over

The Light Railway adventure connected villages along its route more systematically than before and gave country people access to town. And for Portsmouth's urban warriors it offered trips to the countryside, something outside their normal routine in those isolated days. In the early years of the service, five additional cars were added to the initial nine and the frequency of trams was improved in summertime.

Purbrook Heath, with its country walks, trees and birds (not forgetting its cricket!) became a desirable destination. Hopping off the tram at Purbrook Common, the byway across the Heath took ramblers past swaying grasses and gorse bushes, then headed north to Sheepwash (farmed by the Westbrooks and later on by the Windebanks). Beyond the farm at Furzeley Corner, they could rest up and buy a pot of tea at Mrs Warren's cottage.

When AW White's country service began, there was an overlap en route. Portsmouth Corporation trams ran up Portsdown Hill too, but

Emerald green and heavy metal at Purbrook bridge

A painting by Brian Browne, from a CHT Marshall photograph

they terminated halfway up. The Portsdown & Horndean Light Railway started south of Cosham rail station at a junction with the Corporation track, and headed towards Portsdown Hill. The difference was that the Light Railway's green cars climbed beyond the Corporation interchange, all the way to the summit and north as far as Horndean.

The trams had their own bridge (demolished in 1953) over the railway at Cosham between the level crossing and the yet-to-be-constructed road bridge. The track ran through the line of what later became the police station and headed uphill, crossing Southwick Hill Road by means of a smart bridge. It stayed on an embankment immediately west of the highway, climbing past the Belle Vue Tea Gardens towards The George Inn, on a single track right to the top.

At the summit there was a short length of double track until - running down the northern side of the Hill – the single track took pole position down the middle of the road through Widley and Purbrook, with passing loops at the Old Vic and at the byway to Purbrook Common and near Purbrook Windmill (Mill Road). Later on, more passing loops were added – where The Hampshire Rose is now – and by The White Hart in the village.

North of Purbrook village the track headed along the centre of the road through Waterlooville where there was a short double track. Near today's roundabout at Hulbert Road, the tramlines shifted east of the highway through Cowplain, past Catherington Corner, up as far as their final resting place opposite Merchistoun Hall, short of Horndean village.

The terminus was located immediately south of a small Methodist chapel. It was an odd place to stop, some way short of the village, but this was as far north as the Light Railway ever ventured. Plans to extend the line to Petersfield were derailed. At Horndean terminus there was no need for a turntable, the driver simply changed ends, but there was need for a rudimentary waiting room, the first version being a disused horsecar box.

Contemporary descriptions of villages along the route show just how buttercups 'n' daisies it all was. 1903 Waterlooville was "hidden away on the south coast, with the unique feature of being very little known to the tourist, and altogether undiscovered by the tripper, while it is one of the most healthy resorts in the South of England."

As for end-of-the-line Horndean, it "abounds with pretty scenery among the well-wooded copses and pleasant country lanes."

1910 Purbrook was a village "where very pretty walks may be had... Down the road (Stakes Road) about 200 yards by the side of a white farm house (Chalk Farm) is a stile, and a footpath leads from thence across the fields and through the woods to Stakes Hill, coming out nearly opposite the Post Office."

The Transport Hub

The Light Railway operated with varying degrees of success until 1935. At its peak the company had eighteen green trams, of which ten were in daily use. Each tramcar had eighteen seats inside and 32 outside (top deck). There were three brakes: hand, slipper and electric, and there were automatic sand distributors that "enable the wheels to bite if necessary."

In Purbrook, adjacent to The Leopard Inn was a transformer that provided power to the line. In 1907 this was proudly upgraded and reborn as the company's own generating station, housing two diesel engines and two Brush dynamos. The Light Railway was no longer reliant on Corporation electricity at Corporation prices.

But even with the luxury of Purbrook's purpose-built generator, journeys weren't always smooth. One March morning in 1913 the 9am tram from Cosham was clambering past Queen Alexandra military hospital

Photographer C H T Marshall   from the Steve Pethybridge Collection

A tram passes through Purbrook. The (old) Woodman is on the right

By kind permission of Steve Pethybridge

when it came to an abrupt halt. Nothing would shift it. Up at Purbrook the tramcar from Horndean stuck fast as well. The seizure was down to a power failure that lasted three hours, rendering the proud electric railway totally useless until just after midday.

Especially in the early days of the green tramcars, Purbrook's country folk enjoyed the prestige attached to such modernity rattling along their main road. Numerous roadside trolley standards provided neighbourly evidence of the new-fangled tramway. A long metal arm on the top deck of each green car linked tram to power line.

Initially, the Light Railway had considered using steam engines rather than electric trams, and even tried a car running on paraffin called a LIFU (liquid fuel). This hulk of metal ended its tragic days as a booking office at Cowplain, where the Light Railway had a sizeable tram shed, complete with a pit to facilitate repairs. During the Second World War this former tram depot stored torpedoes.

End Of The Line

In its youthful years the Portsdown & Horndean Light Railway was pioneering stuff. But gradually and unerringly, competition droned in from motor cars, motor bikes, motor buses, bicycles and - in town - trains and trolley buses. In Purbrook village, what had been something to behold deteriorated into something to bemoan by the 1920s.

The track down the middle of the road became a hazard in the presence of motor cars. And the passing loops by The George, at Park Avenue, at the Old Vic, at Purbrook Common, at The White Hart and at Mill Road, caused problems. In these sidings a green car travelling in one direction had to sit and wait while a green car grunted past in the opposite direction on the single track.

Additional trams meant hold-ups for other forms of traffic; trams passing each other simply blocked the roadway. Another problem at Purbrook's narrow bridge in the 1920s was caused by steam wagons, whose drivers could snarl up the road for ten minutes at a time while filling their boilers with water from the handy brook.

There was no fun-filled roaring '20s for the Portsdown & Horndean Light Railway, and the 1930s were even worse. In town, motor buses were making inroads and trolley buses were wired up for business by 1934. The green cars were dated, their service limited. They were literally "over the hill."

On October 3rd 1934, the Light Railway Company gave notice of its intention to cease running, and the service was brought to a halt on January 9th 1935. Southdown Bus Company bought the Light Railway and replaced the emerald cars with petrol buses. Southdown proposed to run their service at seven and a half minute intervals, comparing favourably with the fifteen minute intervals of the old trams.

P & H L R, RIP

The local press reported "heartaches in Horndean, Waterlooville, Purbrook and Cosham" as the green cars ran their last journeys. Thirty years before, they had been heralded as "the last thing in transport." Equipment was swiftly removed although some of the track through Purbrook's main street was left in place for several years.

Significantly for Purbrook, the removal of six passing loops between The George at Portsdown and Mill Road near Waterlooville was hailed in the Hampshire Telegraph as "almost tantamount to a road widening scheme."

Reflecting on its thirty-year journey, the unique Portsdown & Horndean Light Railway eased Purbrook into the 20th century. It shaped the future of the village and ended its isolation. Like the Stage Coach one hundred years before, the tram had been king of the road. Now the king was deposed and on the scrap heap.

Light Railway Car 13 being restored in 1996

Picture courtesy of Bruce Oliver

Chapter 13

Between The Wars

The Great War was over at last. Fortunately, the young cricketers of Purbrook and their older patrons were a resurgent lot, able to tackle their resuscitated fixture list in 1919 with optimism. George Joyce White was still a strong supporter at 87, and the era of the Brown brothers was at hand.

Back On Track

Fourteen matches were played, with ten victories and four defeats. Reg Brown topped the batting averages and Bill Brown headed the bowlers. The membership included a backbone of village names including Brown,

Purbrook was still a country village

By kind permission of Steve Pethybridge

London Road Purbrook   Photographer C H T Marshall   from the Steve Pethybridge Collection

Clear, Cleeve and Harfield. Purbrook CC's bounce-back was confident enough for the Club to hold a Dinner at The White Hart in the run-up to Christmas. Forty tucked in and toasted "Purbrook Cricket Club."

After all the distress of war it was a hearty toast; a relief to celebrate the pleasant side of life. George White burst into song with The Island of Jersey, and other warblers soon followed, accompanied by Mrs Wright on the joanna. There was time for a report on the season by Secretary Smith who was pleased to highlight that the bank balance was almost up to £4. Mr David Cleeve (in the chair) wound up a cracking evening by asking everyone to be upstanding for the national anthem.

Things were back on track at Purbrook Cricket Club although, despite being modestly in the black, the Cricket Club needed funds to progress. Their Whist Drive and Dance at the parish schoolroom was one sure way to collect come readies. There were seven winners, one of whom, Mrs Windsor, donated her prize worth £2 3s 6d to the Club.

"Come On Over To My Place"

Conscious of the poor state of the Heath, Club members did their best in seasons 1919, 1920 and 1921 to restore their pitch to its pre-war eminence. The outcome was passable but nothing to write home about. In the early months of 1922 Purbrook Councillor George Gauntlett had an idea. On his Stakes Road dairy farm was a strip of land called Fir Copse Meadow.

Aware of the Club's problem with only Purbrook Heath to play on, the Councillor decided to lend the meadow to Purbrook CC. For their part, the Club jumped at the opportunity; they would have two grounds to choose from. From plan to reality, everything slotted quickly into place.

Fir Copse Meadow was ready for play by July 1922, and on Saturday July 8th a grand opening ceremony was organised, followed by the inaugural game against Fareham United. Adding glamour to the occasion were Colonel and Mrs Williams, Colonel and Mrs Saville, Vicar Walker and his wife, Councillor Nicholls and Mr Fielder. The Gauntlett family were there in force – Councillor Gauntlett was master of ceremonies, Mrs Gauntlett was hostess in chief, and cricket club Honorary Secretary Harold Gauntlett was hon-seccing like mad.

The weather wasn't kind, but Fir Copse Meadow was geared for a party no matter what. Peering out from the garlands of flowers, Purbrook Captain Frank Knight told the crowd that the new ground would provide an incentive for better play and would encourage "loyalty

George White receives the ceremonial first ball at Fir Copse Meadow in 1922

on the part of every member." He proposed a hearty vote of thanks to Councillor Gauntlett, which was seconded by Vice Captain Rochester. Mr Gauntlett responded, saying how glad he was to enable the Club to use his meadow.

Ninety one-year-old veteran George White entertained his audience with reminiscences of playing cricket over on the Common back in the 1850s, and at 3.20pm crowd pleaser George walked to the middle to receive the ceremonial first ball at the new ground. Then the match with Fareham began. It was a good day for the village. Purbrook declared at 100 for seven wickets (Reg Brown scoring 53 not out) and Fareham were rattled out for 27. Maybe the torrent of speeches got to them.

On this special day, a victory by 73 runs wasn't the end of the affair. There was food to be scoffed, and Mrs Gauntlett's Ladies Committee were prepared for bad weather. One of Purbrook's best ever cricket teas was served in the large marquee by the pitch. Well fed cricketers proposed hearty thanks to the good ladies, accompanied by "musical honours," which provided a good excuse to stay in the marquee and in the dry.

Two cricket balls were used in the match. The first, used only for the ceremonial first delivery, was presented to respected Vice President

Scadden. The match ball which had skittled out the opposition for just 27 runs was presented to Fareham skipper Smith ....whether he wanted it or not!

Speeches were on the order paper for the day: from Fareham's captain Smith, Purbrook's Rochester, Purbrook's Clear, and yet more earnest words. Purbrook's Honorary Secretary Gauntlett was congratulated on putting together such a great opening day and, when all syllables had been safely gathered in, the marquee and its tea tables were given over to a whist drive.

A memorable day for Purbrook cricket, shame about the weather. In the cold light of day, however, the widespread optimism proved to be sadly overcooked. The new ground at Fir Copse Meadow enjoyed a short shelf life; it wasn't really up to the job and before long all cricketing roads led to Purbrook Common again.

Deverell Hall

Elsewhere in the village the construction of Deverell Hall, in memory of Squire John and his clan, was about to start. A hall for the community beside the London Road, on land given by Lady Campbell. Local people donated £640 towards building costs of about £1,750. This was sufficient for the trustees to give builder A H Clear and Sons the go-ahead to dig foundations. Even as Deverell Hall's brickwork was being laid east of the carriageway, the ancient White Hart coaching inn opposite was being demolished in readiness for a new pub bearing the same name.

Calling Time

Cricket fan George Joyce White was now the oldest person in the village and its best known resident. He accepted that he'd had a good innings and in May 1923, after quitting as proprietor of The White Hart, he settled into retirement.

Old Father Time finally caught up with him in July 1924, and he died at York Cottage on London Road. GJ suffered a stroke in April which paralysed his left side, but he dearly wanted to see his old club play one more time on Purbrook Common. So in June his pals took him in his bath chair to the boundary edge where he watched his final game in good spirits. GJ White had survived 92 colourful years, and his life warrants a short résumé even though his best years belong in an earlier chapter.

This Is Your Life

George Joyce White was born in Purbrook in July 1831. There was neither school nor church in the village when he was a boy, and Sunday church was a long walk with dad and brothers to St Andrew's Farlington. George was only nine when he started work below stairs at a gentleman's house opposite The White Hart, where his main task was looking after the donkey. His father was landlord at The Woodman and then The Sign of the Cricketers, and it was this pub near the brook that George took over when the old boy died.

George White married in 1858 and, two years later, he closed The Sign of the Cricketers and took over The Leopard Inn which he ran for 30 years, keeping the stables busy even though Stage Coaches were in terminal decline. His fully laden wagon was a regular at race meetings where he supplied food to the refreshment booths. Another equine labour of love in the summer months was driving Purbrook cricket teams to "away" fixtures around the county.

The North End

Tea Gardens, . .

WHITE HART, PURBROOK.

TEAS at Moderate Prices.   Parties catered for.

All Spirits, Wines and Ales of the Finest
Quality—also Mineral Waters.

STABLING AND CYCLE ACCOMMODATION.

G. J. WHITE, *Proprietor.*

There were tea gardens and stables when GJ White ran The White Hart

George's natural optimism took a tumble when his wife died and he quit The Leopard in 1890. He remarried within two years and took up dairy farming on Southwick Estate land at Sheepwash. But after seven years the lure of Purbrook pubs proved too great, and he became licensee of The White Hart. This was his last business enterprise; he stayed more than twenty years.

GJ White enjoyed one love affair outside marriage, with cricket! His stint as Purbrook captain lasted a lusty 40 years. GJ was a good bat and bowled round-arm but, keen to keep one step ahead, he experimented with the new fangled over-hand method, practising this new technique up to three times a week through the summer. George also turned out for Southsea's East Hants Club and bowled against WG once, but didn't manage to get the bearded wonder out.

George White's sporting coat of many colours incorporated martial arts too. GJ boxed in the fairground booths on Portsdown Hill, and wrestled as well – it was GJ who won the last prize ever awarded at Denmead's Barn Green Revel where he fought on a raised ring carpeted with grass turfs. GJ had to cope with being stabbed by his opponent who was getting well and truly mullered at the time.

Paying Their Last Respects

With such a pedigree, George White's funeral was quite an event in the village and Purbrook Church was packed. The elm coffin was carried from York Cottage (opposite) by members of the Cricket Club. Reverend Walker met the cortege at the new lych gate and led them into the tiny church. George's widow, sons and daughters sat close to the coffin and a host of villagers squeezed into the pews. Afterwards mourners surrounded the graveside as George Joyce White was returned to the good earth of Purbrook. There were wreaths from the cricket clubs of Purbrook, Horndean and Waterlooville.

The Brothers Brown

The dominant force in Purbrook cricket circles between the two world wars was the Brown dynasty – not surprising, as there were no less than

George Joyce White was returned to the good earth of Purbrook

six brothers. There was Fred, Reg, Ernest, Bill, Richard and Frank. Sisters Annie and Emmy didn't play! Fred and Reg were the stalwarts, and Bill was a regular whenever he could be poached from his day job as game-keeper on the Southwick Estate. Richard was a useful cricketer in his own right, although there were raised eyebrows in the Brown household when he opted out of Purbrook's cause and joined Wadhams CC instead.

Urban Regeneration

The early years of the '30s witnessed the dawn of Havant & Waterloo Urban District Council, which first trod the boards on April 1st 1932. Twenty years down the line, this new authority would be the driving force behind the regeneration of Purbrook Heath as a sports ground. H&WUDC absorbed the Councils of Bedhampton, Cowplain, Havant, Hayling, Purbrook and Waterlooville.

At the time of the Urban District's formation in 1932, Purbrook was still an entirely separate entity from the big city over the hill. Portsmouth was bursting at the seams, its population now a whopping 252,712. Only a hundred years before, its residents had numbered just 46,282.

One Up To The Ville

In April 1932 Purbrook Cricket Club had urgent concerns – the lads had some cricket matches to prepare for. They were keen as mustard, buoyed by a thumpingly successful 1931 season, when they had played eighteen games and lost only one. Fred Brown presided at the AGM which elected him Skipper, with N Edney as Vice Captain. Secretary Singleton gave an upbeat report and announced a balance in hand of £3 10s.

After such an optimistic pre-season build-up, the fickle finger of fate was bound to poke Purbrook where it hurts. Sure enough, the May local derby with those Villains up the road was a disaster. Waterlooville scored a modest 69, but Purbrook went weak at the knees and managed just 50.

Following this dismal start Purbrook had a good run. They tied with Hayling Brotherhood, each side totalling 62; they battered St Pauls by 47 runs, dismissing the visitors for only eighteen - Bill Brown six for six and Edney four for eight, and they beat Denmead by seventeen runs in a two-innings game, Grayer taking seven for eighteen.

By August 1932 Purbrook had lost twice. This became thrice when Portsmouth Caledonians pipped them by two runs at the Heath – Caledonians 43, Purbrook 41. By their final match in early September, Purbrook were back to winning ways. The home side rocketed to 104 and dismissed Liss for 45. All things considered, it had been a successful season with just a handful of defeats, although the early season loss to Waterlooville took some gloss off the summer.

Reg Brown Takes The Helm

In the depths of winter Purbrook Common was dull and dreary. On the worst days it was a place to steer clear of. Even on good days a wet mist hung in the air. A place best left to its own devices during the dank winter season. The area down by the stream sank to a glutinous bog, and even the sodden green patch at the top bore little resemblance to a cricket field.

After another heavy winter, the arrival of the Cricket Club AGM in March '33 shone like a beacon of hope. Deverell Hall was the venue and Reg Brown was elected Captain. Secretary Singleton resigned his post with due gravitas. He was moving far away...to Horndean! He was proud to leave Club finances in good shape, announcing a credit balance of £3.

The Deverell Hall was popular for Purbrook Cricket Club AGMs

As the season spluttered into life, Captain Brown reported that "the pitch on the Common is in excellent condition." Take this with a pinch of salt, because within a year Purbrook were applying to play some of their games away from the Heath.

The 1933 summer ran its steady course, notable for a July revival of the local derby between Purbrook and Wadhams of Waterlooville. The clash on the Common attracted a partisan crowd. Wadhams claimed the spoils, winning by a clear-cut 26 runs. The fixture had been the first between two proud clubs for four years, and to rekindle cordial relations The Leopard Inn was chosen for a musical evening after the game.

Another local derby later in the month saw Purbrook beat Horndean in a two-innings affair. Purbrook scored 62 and 55 for five in their allotted time (Fred Brown reaching 34 not out) and Horndean responded with 49 and 45 for seven.

In Enemy Territory

The dawn of 1934 coincided with Purbrook's desire to play some of their matches at Waterlooville Recreation Ground. On the field, Reg Brown continued as Captain. Off the field, Mr Howell was President and The Leopard's Harry Friar was Secretary and Treasurer.

On the Common in early June, Purbook regained some self respect by nicking a result over Waterlooville. It wasn't all good news against local rivals; in August Purbrook made the leafy trip to Rowlands Castle and were badly turned over. Rowlands romped to 148 for seven, while Purbrook were dumped for 67.

In 1934 Purbrook split their home fixtures between Purbrook Common (most games) and Waterlooville Rec (a few games). From Waterlooville CC's perspective, Purbrook were trying to muscle in on their territory, so it's no surprise that at the start of the year the two clubs could not arrange their fixture allocation amicably. The new Urban District Council had to do it for them.

Eventually the Chairman of Havant Council's General Purposes Committee banged the two clubs' heads together, and peace was restored. Ground sharing at Waterlooville Recreation Ground continued until the outbreak of World War Two in 1939. Three clubs were involved: Waterlooville, Purbrook, and Wadhams.

1935 was a slumbering year for Purbrook although one match in May was notable for its high scores. Portchester racked up 148 (Squibb six for 38) and Purbrook replied with a valiant 134. Four home games were played at Waterlooville Rec and it was the same the following season. The team benefited; the track was better and scores were higher. In the first match at the Rec in 1936, Purbrook totalled 171 in a drawn game with Fareham 2nd XI, who were closing fast at 164 for seven.

By contrast, at the RN Barracks in June the Chief Petty Officers were shot out for 60, Fred Brown taking eight wickets in five overs. Purbrook, who batted first, scored 115 for eight. Bad news in August: Rowlands Castle claimed bragging rights again, totalling 92 (Fred Brown five for eleven), whilst Purbrook replied with 71.

Spotted At The Leopard

Harry Friar was a vital cog in Purbrook CC's machinery. Not only was he Secretary and Treasurer, but he was also proprietor of The Leopard Inn, the Club's watering hole. A popular bloke was Harry! But nothing lasts for ever and, after 23 years as licensee, Harry announced last orders in November 1936. A great excuse for a party, and Harry and The Leopard didn't disappoint. Retirement gifts were graciously received.

Cricketers all lived locally in 1931. In the foreground are Hillside Avenue, London Road, The Brow, The Dale, Lily Avenue, Park Avenue and Bushy Mead

Battles On And Off The Field

Throughout 1937 Councillors continued their quest to find land for a new recreation ground, while Purbrook's cricketers simply got on with playing. Ironically scores were improving at the Heath. In June Purbrook notched 159 against Gosport Nondescripts (Reg Brown 43) and the visitors responded with 99. In July Purbrook went even higher, totalling 165 against Fareham 2nd XI, who replied with 152. Good scores, because it rained throughout the match. In the August local derby at Waterlooville, the Ville compiled 140 (Reg Brown five for 30), but Purbrook crumbled to 59 all out. It went a bit quiet at The Leopard after that.

1938 was conspicuous at a political level because of the Purbrook Heath Boundary Inquiry (chapter 14). On the field of play, however, the year was unspectacular. Reg and Fred Brown remained the backbone of the team but progress was patchy. Alexandra Park was a prominent pre-war cricket venue and Purbrook played Southsea Wanderers there in August. The match was something of a bore draw, Southsea making 125, with Purbrook struggling to 84 for seven, Reg Brown making 30.

That's The End Of That

By the time 1939 season broke sweat, cricket was being played against a backdrop of impending war. Purbrook just about squeezed their season in before troop mobilisation knocked sports fixtures on the head from September. The Club had not had a memorable year and a decline had set in. At the beginning of June, for example, Purbrook managed a paltry 28 against Edneys, chasing a total of just 46!

When stumps were drawn for the last time in late summer, Purbrook players knew they could be in for turbulent times, but they had little appreciation of what wartime had in store. With the optimism of youth they hoped to be cutting the wicket on the Common before too long. In reality it would be the best part of a decade before local cricket matches resumed on a regular basis. By then a whole new breed would represent Purbrook. The team of '39 would never reassemble; its old guard would stand down. The team is dead, long live the team.

Chapter 14

Playing The Field

It was back in February 1934 that Alf Murrant rose to his feet in The Leopard and addressed the assembled membership of Purbrook Cricket Club at their AGM.

From Wreck To Rec

As the senior member present, Mr Murrant was pleased to report a healthy bank balance of almost £3. He then moved on to discuss the coming season, and announced that Purbrook's request to use a pitch at Waterlooville Recreation Ground had been met sympathetically by Havant & Waterloo Urban District Council. They had granted Purbrook four Saturday matches, with local club Waterlooville retaining the lion's share. Mr Murrant confirmed that Purbrook's other home fixtures would be played at their traditional Purbrook Heath venue.

The truth was that the old cricket pitch on the topside of Purbrook Heath was being overtaken by the development of other grounds. It had been at its best before the First World War, when the playing surface was heralded throughout the district. During the war years 1914 to 1918, the Purbrook club disbanded and no cricket was played. The untended Heath never really recovered.

Now, a decade and a half on, the players' verdict was that the ground was small, under-prepared, balls were too easily lost in the gorse, and there was a dodgy slope towards the distant brook. When all was said and done, the pitch on the Heath was merely a swatch of common waste on Squire Thistlethwayte's Southwick Park Estate. Not a lot could be done with it.

1934's season of cricket muddled into life, the rivalry between Waterlooville and their older cousins Purbrook bubbling up as usual. In a nail-biter on Purbrook Common Fred Brown (five for 28) and brother Reg (three for 35) skittled Waterlooville out for 50. Batting second, the home side found runs a struggle too, scratching and scraping to a pressure-cooker victory, man of the match Fred Brown contributing 24.

Committee With A General Purpose

The General Purposes Committee on Havant & Waterloo Council were a lively bunch, with a mission to give Purbrook a new recreation ground. During 1934 and 1935 they enquired after half a dozen potential sites, spurred on by entreaties from Purbrook Ratepayers and a petition from Widley residents. Among the Committee's considerations was land in Purbrook Park which they decided not to pursue, and land at Highbank Avenue owned by Squire Thistlethwayte of Southwick Park – he would not sell because of potential building value.

However, the Southwick Park dealings were not altogether negative because, arising from the discussions, a surprise package emerged. Seemingly out of the blue, at their December 1934 meeting the General Purposes Committee recommended that an offer be submitted to Southwick Park Estate.... "for the purchase of Purbrook Heath!"

Manoeuvres

On May 9th 1935, the Committee trekked to the prospective Purbrook Heath site and, after a good sniff around, authorised the Clerk to submit an alternative (new) offer for the entire acreage. This caused a delay and, in June, Walters & Co of Lincoln's Inn communicated that their client, Squire Evelyn Thistlethwayte, could not accept such a low offer. The Committee responded that the Council could not increase their bid.

Nevertheless the Committee were keen on a deal, so a bit of cut and thrust followed and by mid October the two parties were practically warbling from the same willow tree. Matters moved apace and, by the middle of November, a positive Walters & Co returned a draft agreement with suggested amendments.

There was now a gleam in the eye of the General Purposes Committee. They were on a roll, and asked the Engineer to prepare estimates for Purbrook Heath that would include one cricket pitch, two football pitches and two tennis courts. All in all, a comprehensive makeover for this patch of heathland.

Going For Broke

As well as the potential jackpot of Purbrook Heath, the General Purposes Committee continued to plough several other furrows during 1935. Ideally they wanted a playing field and, elsewhere in the village, a children's playground and land simply left as open space.

133

They cast their eyes at almost ten acres south of Park Road belonging to Mr G Cousins; this would cost £1,100 and could be converted into a playing area. And Austin & Wyatt continued to push the sale of five acres in Park Avenue belonging to Mr D Cleeve; this would cost £750 and could become a children's playground. Local residents asked them to buy land in The Dale for a recreation ground, but they dug their heels in and said no.

By April the following year (1936) the Urban District Council resolved to purchase both the Park Road land owned by Mr Cousins and the Park Avenue plot owned by Mr Cleeve. At this point the Minister of Health waded in and ordered a public enquiry into the two potential purchases. His enquiry was immediately deferred, pending a report from the District Valuer.

The End Of An Innings

One important purchase was completed however, and with incredibly little fuss. On April 10th 1936, Council Chairman AC Lane puffed out his chest and announced that the purchase of Purbrook Heath "as an open space" had been agreed for a nominal sum, and that Havant & Waterloo UDC would soon be the proud owners of 18.391 acres known as Purbrook Common.

And so, without much overt wailing or gnashing of teeth the tiny sloping cricket pitch, together with its generous surrounds of gorse and bog, plus the pond and animal pound, wriggled from the ancestral grasp of successive Southwick Squires and passed into the delighted clasp of the local Council. A very astute piece of business when you consider that the price was all of.... £100!

Did the Common jump, or was it pushed? Was it altruism on the part of Squire Evelyn, or practicality? From representations made at a Ministerial Inquiry three years down the line, it's clear that the sale was a reluctant one and that Evelyn Thistlethwayte of Southwick Park did not envisage the land being developed in any way. It's equally clear that the Council nabbed a bargain; the sale of the century despite the acreage in question being wet, wild and woolly.

Guns 'n' Poses

The 18.391 acres of Purbrook Heath changed hands on May 7th 1936. The vendor was described in the conveyance as:

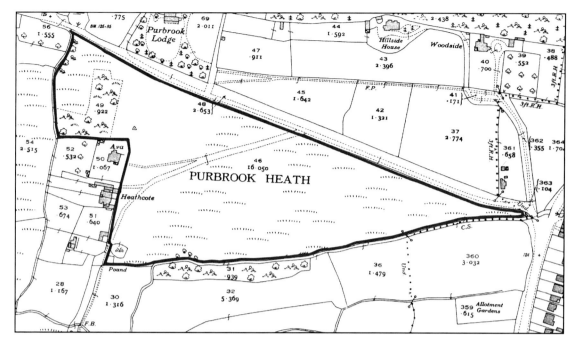

Havant &
Waterloo Urban
District Council
purchased
18.391 acres
of Purbrook
Heath for £100
in May 1936

"Evelyn William Thistlethwayte of Southwick Park Fareham in the County of Southampton a Colonel (retired) in His Majesty's Army."

Less grandly, the purchasers were simply: "the Urban District Council of Havant & Waterloo."

A condition of the sale was that Southwick Park Estate would continue to have use of the pathway that cut across the Heath from Purbrook Heath Road (where the Pavilion car park entrance is today) to the pond in the south west corner. The conveyance contained one quirky clause, a reminder of the lifestyle of the landed gentry and their passion for huntin', shootin' and fishin'.

It read: "The exclusive right for the vendor during his life with friends servants and others of shooting and sporting and taking all manner of animals game and wild fowl thereon with power to enter upon the said land for the purpose aforesaid...."

Safeguarding The Future

Part of the conveyance document, referred to as The Schedule, included the following 59 inspired words intended to protect Purbrook Heath as a recreation ground in perpetuity.

Note 1 of The Schedule said: "The land hereby conveyed shall always hereafter be used for the purpose of a Recreation Ground for the benefit of the neighbourhood and not otherwise and that only such buildings or erections shall be erected thereon as may be reasonably necessary for the equipment of a Recreation Ground or Open Space and not exceeding twenty five feet in height."

Back At The Cricket

Although the 1936 purchase of Purbrook Heath was a seminal event, it caused barely a ripple amongst the bowlers and batters of Purbrook CC. They were more concerned about winning cricket matches, four of which were scheduled for Waterlooville Recreation Ground, with other home games at the Heath. For 1936 season three clubs shared the Rec – Waterlooville were allocated twelve matches, Purbrook four, and Wadhams four.

Across at the smoke-filled committee rooms of the Urban District Council, the red hot topic under discussion early in the year was whether to permit Sunday games on Council-owned grounds. Ultimately a decision was reached at the January 1936 meeting: no games on the Sabbath would be allowed at recreation grounds under Council control. Waterlooville Rec must therefore continue as "strictly Saturdays only."

Dreams Of Schemes

During 1937 the worthy cause of open spaces in Purbrook moved in fits and starts. At the Council-owned Heath they erected railings along the north side. Public access to the pathway below the cricket pitch was maintained and there were spaces at the top to park vehicles when the lower end became too boggy.

Purbrook Common in 1937, looking east. The path where people are seated bisected the Heath, running below the old cricket pitch

Pumped up by the dream of their Purbrook Heath enterprise, in November 1937 the General Purposes Committee proposed a grander layout incorporating cricket and football pitches for seniors and juniors, four tennis courts, a bowling green, a car park, and a fully equipped children's playground with drinking fountain. The full Council endorsed the plan and instructed the Engineer to proceed with all haste, so that the senior cricket pitch could be ready by the upcoming 1938 season. In the bleak midwinter it seemed a tall order.

Two Steps Forward, Two Back

The proposed purchase of land at Park Road (Cousins) and Park Avenue (Cleeve) hit the buffers in 1937. The Minister of Health would not sanction a loan for Mr Cleeve's Park Avenue land because he considered £750 to be too much and, in the case of Mr Cousins' Park Road land, he concluded that the plot was unsuitable for either a playground or an open space.

Undeterred, the Council persevered with the Park Avenue land and made Mr Cleeve a reduced offer of £300. But fate took a hand in September when Mr Cleeve died at his home in The Mound, aged 71. A well-known local character, he had run Chalk Farm and, later on, Flint Farm which at the time of his death was being demolished to make way for the resurrection of The Woodman pub. This mix of events and circumstances caused both the Park Road and Park Avenue projects to slip off the radar. Their time had come and gone.

Hiccups At The Heath

If there were any pouting pessimists on Havant & Waterloo Council, they must have worried that purchasing Purbrook Heath had been far too cosy. They would have been right. The Council were anxious to seal a deal that would see all the approaches to the recreation ground come within their boundary. Currently this wasn't so.

They wanted to replace the old path that traversed the Common with a new roadway running alongside the houses by the Heath. Plans to lay out their sparkling new sports ground were costed at £12,000, a sizeable chunk of cash in the 1930s. Some preparatory work had already been undertaken – a surface water sewer had been laid.

Southwick Park Estate and Southwick & Widley Parish Council resisted the changes and in April 1938 a Boundaries Inquiry took place at Havant. By April 1939 the dispute had blown up into a full Health Ministry Inquiry. This was because Hampshire County Council approved Havant's plan to include Purbrook Heath's adjoining land within the urban district of Havant & Waterloo, and made an Order for the Minister of Health to approve. Southwick & Widley Parish Council promptly appealed against the Order and Droxford Council objected too.

The Inquiry confined itself to the boundary dispute, although the differences between the two camps were far more fundamental. Havant & Waterloo wanted to develop the land as a recreation ground decked out with sports pitches. Southwick Park Estate wanted the land kept rural. They had reluctantly sold the 18.391 acres but had no intention of allowing any development.

They also considered the boundary change incorporating the surrounds to be unnecessary. After the hearing the Inspector popped across to the Heath to see things for himself. Having done that, he made his recommendation to the Health Minister.

A path used to cut diagonally across the Heath towards picturesque Tudor Cottage

Close Of Play

In the big wide world away from Purbrook Heath, boundary disputes were festering on an international scale. Piddling local difficulties like the one on the Common were about as significant as a wandering ant on the outfield. A power crazed fuhrer was on the rampage, intent on Deutschland uberalles. Countries were about to be overrun, and peace in our time was out of time.

Purbrook just about completed cricket commitments before the lid came down in 1939.

Early signs of impending doom included the cancellation of September's British Legion fete at Waterlooville, followed by the ditching of Fareham and Hants Farmers' Club Show. Press announcements called up Army and Air Force reservists, and Royal Navy reservists were told to report to their depots. Young men were sucked away from their sporting activities.

The curtain descended on local cricket's indian summer and the upcoming winter football leagues were curtailed or cancelled. On November 24th 1939, under the headline "Hampshire County Cricket Closes Down," a sombre press announcement read: "County cricket as we know it will not be played during the hostilities."

Purbrook Heath suffered like every other sports project. The National Playing Fields Association had agreed to fund 40% of the estimated £12,000 development costs for the Heath, but in September '39 they wrote to say that in view of the war the grant would lapse. The future lay in deep shadow. Town and country prepared for war.

Chapter 15

Ready To Rumble

Four and a half short years after the last green tram clattered through Purbrook Common siding, Britain was at war with Nazi Germany. Young men of the village laid down their cricket bats, dubbined their football boots one last time, and prepared for battle. At first those between 20 and 23 were called-up but, as war progressed, the conscripted age group broadened and youngsters of eighteen and nineteen woke to find their call-up papers on the mat.

Farming was one of several reserved occupations "essential to the war effort" which meant that farmers around Purbrook were exempt from military service. Many lads volunteered anyway, whether they worked on farms, in offices or in factories. Wadhams Coachbuilders at nearby Waterlooville lost a flood of employees to the Army, Navy and Air Force in September 1939 alone.

Within two years farms and factories were seriously short of manpower, and single women between 20 and 30 were conscripted specifically to work on the land or on production lines for the war effort.

The Phoney War
War was declared on September 3rd 1939, three days after Germany invaded Poland. By this time 12,000 Portsmouth schoolchildren had already been evacuated from the city, to places like Ventnor on the Isle of Wight. But many kids remained in town, because none of the anticipated German attacks materialised and parents were naturally reluctant to wave Jack and Jill goodbye. They called it the phoney war and by the end of 1939 some Portsmouth schools, closed earlier in the year, opened their classes again.

In this uneasy calm food rationing began in January 1940 and coupons became the currency of the time. All the correct procedures were in place; it was a regime of ration books, gas masks, black-outs, air raid drills, and waiting in shelters for the "all clear." All practice and preparation, because the bombers didn't come.

On The Back Foot

War spread from Norway, through Holland and Belgium, into France. At home Winston Churchill bulldogged his way to become Prime Minister on May 10th 1940. By the end of the same month Portsmouth was sending ships to Dunkirk to help rescue 340,000 British and French troops in danger of annihilation. Spirits plummeted further when France fell to German occupation in just six weeks, on June 22nd. Our stubborn island was on its own - resolute, but on its jack jones nevertheless. The waiting was almost over; the south coast braced itself for invasion.

This time the bombers came.

3.7 inch anti-aircraft guns were located on Portsdown Hill's forts from 1940

Devastated Streets, Defiant Spirits

July 11th 1940 was a balmy summer's day. When darkness fell, the first air raid blitzed Portsea Island. Twelve Heinkels escorted by twelve Messerschmitt fighters dropped 20 bombs over and around Kingston Crescent. They missed the mighty dockyard, but this was just a taster. Massive air assaults carried on from August through the rest of the year.

In early 1941 the bombing became even more intense. On January 10th 300 bombers groaned overhead on a bright moonlit night and blasted out the Guildhall, wrecking great swathes of Palmerston Road, Kings Road and Commercial Road. The city was ablaze, whole streets ripped out. Lord Mayor Daley, who lived in our hamlet of Stakes, spat defiance: "We are bruised but we are not daunted."

The battering eventually eased and the precious dockyard lived to fight another day. During the span of World War Two Portsmouth suffered 67 major German air raids which dropped 1,320 bombs and 38,000 incendiaries. Back in July 1940 when the air raids first targeted Portsmouth, any notion of a D-Day invasion force of nearly three million troops from twelve nations heading across the Channel would have seemed pie in the sky. In truth it was still four long and arduous years away.

A Different Life

The city became a dangerous place and many families evacuated, some moving to the safer climes of Purbrook but, though the bombs were meant for Portsmouth's dockyard, stray shells fell on the verdant slopes of Portsdown. Purbrook was safe, but not that safe. Village life carried on but its youthful spark was dimmed. There was no local sport of an organised kind and the cricket pitch at the top of Purbrook Heath lay untended. Gorse bushes moved in from long leg and tall grasses crouched behind the wicket.

Children were much in evidence in the village. Early in the War the Church School closed because it had no air raid shelters but, when these were erected (on the site of the Manor House which had burned down pre-war), it was back to normal classes for the lads and lasses of St John's.

Along at Aldermoor Road Primary, headmaster Leslie E Twigg pulled the strings. First thing in the morning there were hymns to be gargled in Assembly and prayers to be recited, eyes squeezed shut. Later in the day long division lurked in the classroom. Air raid shelters were built on the playing field east of the school block and, when the siren wailed, classes and teachers trooped off to the shelters to carry on their nine times table there. Headmaster Twigg did the rounds in his tin hat.

Many homes had air raid shelters in their back gardens and families spent soggy nights inside, making the best of it until the "all clear" sounded. There were also public shelters, like the one at the corner of Fir Copse and Stakes Road, next to the shop. The war churned on and the prospect of cricketing summers on the Heath was just a pipe dream.

Significantly, in December 1941 the United States joined the war and slowly the Allies turned the corner, enabling those who stalked the corridors of power to make plans for an invasion of Normandy. By 1944 these plans were coming to fruition. From August 1943 the south coast became an exclusion zone with everyone bar locals requiring official sanction to pass through. In anticipation of D-Day, this zone was extended to cover a coastal strip ten miles deep from April 1944.

Spring Is Sprung

The spring that sprang in 1944 was a glorious one in Hampshire. Heavy blossoms of lilac and laburnum; rhododendrons too. It would have been easy to presume that peace was all around. Instead, something stupendous was about to descend upon the quiet anonymity of Purbrook Heath. This great happening would deluge all the naturally camouflaged leafy lanes of neighbouring villages – Bedhampton, Cowplain, Denmead, Hambledon, Havant, Horndean, Rowlands Castle, Southwick, Waterlooville, Widley and others near and far.

Springtime 1944 saw the woods of ancient Bere Forest bloom in a new colour – khaki. Like bees around a hive, the hidden byways and protective woodlands saw thousands of young men in uniform swarm in. Preparations for the Second Front were now in top gear. American General Dwight Eisenhower was D-Day's Supreme Allied Commander, and his administrative HQ had settled in at Bushy Park, near Hampton Court, during December 1943.

Most major players in this huge exercise, codenamed Overlord, arrived in England early in 1944: Montgomery on January 2nd and Eisenhower on January 15th. The first full meeting of staff and commanders took place in London on January 21st. General Sir Frederick Morgan's original plan had already been substantially amended by Montgomery and it was broadly Monty's plan that was adopted at the series of London meetings – the assault on Normandy was increased from three to five divisions, and the area of attack was broadened to five main assault beaches.

A colossal amount of planning, designing, building and testing had been going on for years. After all, massive concrete structures like floating Mulberry Harbours can't be bought off the shelf. Aircraft, ships, vehicles and machinery had to be supplied and gathered together. There was ammunition to be sourced and stockpiled, men to be transported to England and equipped, fed and watered. Camps to plan and set up. Supplies of food, kit and medicines to organise.

Moving an invasion force of three million personnel required super-human skills. This D-Day armada would be the largest shore-to-shore invasion in history. Beach landings were practised on suitable coastlines throughout England, Scotland and Wales, and training on a broad range of equipment and ordnance was being drummed into the troops. Preparations were long and hard.

British General Bernard Montgomery was Commander-in-Chief of 21 Army Group

The Migration South

What Admiral Sir Bertram Ramsey later described at a Southwick House briefing as "the greatest amphibious operation of all time" was on such a vast scale that it was impossible to conceal it from German Intelligence. Instead the Allies successfully concentrated on subterfuge so that, in German eyes, the most likely invasion site was Pas de Calais, hundreds of miles east of the true destination, Normandy.

The Allied masses became an unrelenting force sweeping south into Hampshire and its neighbouring counties. Troops from twelve countries were involved in Overlord, but the bulk of the men and women came from the USA, Britain and Canada. Half of the three million fighting force were American, better equipped and better off than their counterparts. For folks in Cosham and Hilsea there was the novelty of black American faces – United States troops had quarters at the Technical High School.

The masses who assembled for Overlord divided up like this: Air 660,000; Land 1,932,000; and Sea 285,000. Most of the land forces headed for southern England, especially the Solent region, during the glorious spring of '44. The huge army divisions would be supported by 6,500 ships and 12,000 aircraft. The Allies were playing to win.

A House In The Country

In Southwick the last week of April arrived and in a quiet country house on the leafy fringes of the Forest of Bere, something stirred. Lots of gold braid, lots of quiet discipline amid lots of concentration. First, on April 26th, Admiral Sir Bertram Ramsey (Allied Chief Naval Expeditionary Force Commander) took up residence at Southwick House. Not long afterwards, even bigger guns arrived. General Eisenhower decamped from Bushy Park, and then British talisman General Bernard Montgomery breezed in.

But neither Ike nor Monty chose to live in the residences provided for them – Southwick House and Broomfield House respectively. Both were closet caravanners. Eisenhower parked his three and a half ton Circus Wagon in a glade away from Southwick House.

For an American General commanding three million troops, his billet was unpretentious. A tiny bedroom with family photographs, a pile of novels and not much else. His staff lived in tents nearby. As a consequence of his penchant for caravans, the bedrooms of Southwick House were never to have their pillows plumped by the future 34th President of the United States.

Montgomery's camp was set in a shady copse. His personal residence comprised three caravans. One had been captured from the Italians during his desert campaign and now served as his office. The second, another "present" from the Italians, became his bedroom, and the third – new and specially designed for him – was his map room and nerve centre. In here a telephone kept him in direct touch with his commanders. In his Broomfield House compound he was supported by 20 officers and 200 other ranks.

Encampment

Away from the caravanned headquarters of these two big hitters, the southbound avalanche gathered more men and machinery. Schools, church halls and public buildings were collared by the military. Camps, canteens and field kitchens sprouted up; bath houses, showers, latrines too. Places of detention had to be set aside - not every soldier was a good soldier! Hospitals and medical areas were set up too, ready to receive the wounded brought back from France once the campaign was under way.

A gigantic arsenal weighed down upon Hampshire's heaths and hollows. Along the roadsides, in the bridle paths, against the hedgerows and in the glades and coppices, were bumper-to-bumper jeeps, armoured cars, tanks and amphibious vehicles, laced together with entire lanes of anti-aircraft guns and howitzers. Rows of semi-circular metal bays, stacked with tons of artillery shells, stretched up the byways and into the woods. All ready for transportation to France. There were also huge stocks of bulldozers, excavators, pre-fabricated huts, and stores of every kind.

Troops were everywhere; under canvas, in requisitioned buildings, in Nissen huts and outhouses. South Hampshire was transformed into a military waiting room. Purbrook's neck of the woods included two main camps near Denmead at Creech Walk, which together accommodated 3,850 personnel and 550 vehicles.

There was another camp at Stakes, housing 2,500 troops and 250 vehicles, and two camps in the Cowplain area (at Padnell and Queen's Inclosure) each holding 1,500 troops and 215 vehicles. Horndean camp accommodated 1,500 troops and 215 vehicles, and Rowlands Castle camp held 2,000 troops and 200 vehicles.

Close by, Emsworth housed 2,100 troops and 210 vehicles. Bury Lodge between Denmead and Hambledon held 1,000 troops and 140 vehicles, the camp at Greville Hall beyond Hambledon accommodated 1,350 troops and 190 vehicles, and West Walk north of Wickham housed 3,250 troops and 465 vehicles. To the east of Wickham at Rookesbury School, there were 1,250 troops and 278 vehicles.

On Purbrook Common, the drier parts were commandeered by British troops and a bell-tented village blossomed. It was the same on the eastern side of the London Road between Westbrook Grove and Stakes Hill. Sometimes they had to put duckboards on the floor to keep the marshy bits at bay.

"See here soldier boy, cricket is like baseball with brains."

Beyond the Common, Purbrook Heath House was taken over by No. 2 War Office Signals. And there were American troops just up the road; they chose the countryside near Potwell for one of their encampments. All these camps were buttoned into one small region of south Hampshire, roughly the area covered by the ancient, faded, Forest of Bere.

Of course there were countless other similar concentrations - down in Portsmouth and across most of southern England. For these young recruits there were periods of bustle, of anxiety and of contemplation. So many strangers, so far from home.

Sergeant Santa

For a young village lad, such a fusion of men and machines caused great excitement. Brian (Chick) Churcher was one such eleven-year-old. He lived on the main road between Purbrook Church and The Leopard Inn. Purbrook Common was his stamping ground and to have all these British and American troops buzzing round was a big deal. Seeing them camped all over the countryside by the Common was as thrilling as living on a film set.

Chick knew all the long-grassed pathways to the Heath and on to Potwell. Skipping over there with his pals he could see, beneath the ample trees and hedgerows, tanks, lorries and jeeps all the way to the Watersplash. Down the side of the Heath it was the same, as far as the pond and Tudor Cottage. All in all, a crowded house.

To Chick's delight the Americans constructed a bath house on the top side of Purbrook Heath. To a child's eye it was at least 60 feet by 30 feet. Inside the grand structure were two open areas – one down each side – with a changing room at the eastern end. Allied troops queued to use this very popular amenity, with Portsmouth Water Company providing a temporary supply as they did to a number of camps over Purbrook way.

Military vehicles were stacked up all the way to the Watersplash

Sergeant Duke was the amiable American in charge of the bath house facility; one of the older generation of soldiers. He was a kindly soul where children were concerned and a keen distributor of chewing gum and Oh Henry chocolate bars.

Wide-eyed kids viewed him as some kind of khaki-clad Santa Claus. The considerate Sergeant also let the boys use the bath house when it wasn't too crowded. A more innocent age, even in wartime. For Chick and his pals, such adventure put cleanliness right up there with godliness.

On Your Marks

And so to the last days of May. The security belt was tightened another notch. Already Portsmuthians were not permitted to go beyond Cosham without a pass. Troops were sealed in their camps for briefing and issued with maps of France plus what were called invasion francs. Restlessness hung on the breeze that blew from Southwick through Purbrook Heath and onto Stakes.

Into June, and final preparations were in hand. The roadside from Horndean right through to Portsdown was choked with military vehicles. Then these great roadside convoys began to roll, blinking out from their leafy lanes and edging to the coast. Staccatoed policemen on point duty waved them forward. Tens of thousands of troops loaded into lorries and tanks and transported to ships down by the docks. Once aboard, undue delay was not an option.

Back in Purbrook, mums carried their little ones to the front gate to wave the soldiers off. Jean Leaver was almost seven and lived at 58 Stakes Road. Her mum and Mrs Sansom next door made tea and cakes for the troops. Not supposed to, but they did anyway. Jean looked up the road and all she could see were military vehicles and lorryloads of soldiers. Down the road was just the same.

On the trucks, young guns called down to the line of mothers:

"Give us a kiss, love!"

One or two mums responded, one or two blushed and didn't. Another soldier, tall and thin, confided:

"We're off to the Rock; I'll bring you back a stick."

Jean's mum murmured: "Poor devils" and Jean asked what she meant. The bystanders waved them into the distance. Laughter and tears, gratitude and sorrow. The long goodbye.

"OK, Let's Go!"

At Southwick HQ, the decision to go rested with one man – Eisenhower. The big day had already been re-scheduled once, and set for June 5th. Now rough seas and stormy skies scotched that. Meteorologist Group Captain Stagg foresaw a brief window among the squalls. Not perfect, but workable. At 4.15am on Monday June 5th, Eisenhower had a

B. L. Montgomery
General

21 ARMY GROUP

PERSONAL MESSAGE FROM THE C-in-C

To be read out to all Troops

1. The time has come to deal the enemy a terrific blow in Western Europe.

The blow will be struck by the combined sea, land, and air forces of the Allies—together constituting one great Allied team, under the supreme command of General Eisenhower.

2. On the eve of this great adventure I send my best wishes to every soldier in the Allied team.

To us is given the honour of striking a blow for freedom which will live in history; and in the better days that lie ahead men will speak with pride of our doings. We have a great and a righteous cause.

Let us pray that "The Lord Mighty in Battle" will go forth with our armies, and that His special providence will aid us in the struggle.

3. I want every soldier to know that I have complete confidence in the successful outcome of the operations that we are now about to begin.

With stout hearts, and with enthusiasm for the contest, let us go forward to victory.

4. And, as we enter the battle, let us recall the words of a famous soldier spoken many years ago :—

" *He either fears his fate too much,*
Or his deserts are small,
Who dare not put it to the touch,
To win or lose it all."

5. Good luck to each one of you. And good hunting on the main land of Europe.

B. L. Montgomery
General
C.-in-C 21 Army Group.

Monty's message to the troops of 21 Army Group

final, earnest pow-wow with his commanders. After a brief pause, he announced: "OK, let's go!"

D-Day was fixed. Once set in motion, there could be no recall. It would be June 6th, 1944, the 1,453rd day of German occupation in France. The invasion actually started overnight, (late 5th and early 6th) as massive airborne landings centred on Caen.

Portsmouth's Airspeed factory assembled five (of the original seven prototypes) of hundreds of Horsa gliders that now ghosted over Normandy in this overnight assault. Each wooden glider carried up to 25 men and/or equipment. Early on June 6th the mass of Allied shipping with their pent-up human cargoes headed for northern France. 150,000 troops landed in Normandy on the first day, together with a multitude of machinery.

Purbrook folk woke up to comparative silence. The troops had all but disappeared, along with their vehicles and equipment. In the run-up to D-Day the departing hordes had chalked heartfelt thanks on the road surfaces. On the day itself dispatch riders buzzed earnestly to and fro and, high above, allied aircraft flew south, outward bound for the French coast.

By 5.30pm on June 6th staff at Queen Alexandra hospital in Cosham were treating the first casualties brought back from the French beaches. Boundary Oak field hospital in Widley was also pressed into service. Major problems were burns, bullet wounds and exhaustion. Another million and a half troops landed in Normandy in the next few weeks.

Beginning Of The End

Local camps and billets had served their purpose. The troops had gone but evidence of their stay remained. Empty tins and boxes lay strewn over Portsdown Hill and all the way to Denmead, while outside the affluent American and Canadian camps lay wire baskets packed with shoes, raincoats and sweaters.

In the fields around Purbrook Heath (between Sheepwash and the Hill) dozens of stray metal sleepers remained – set down to provide a firm track for the heavy vehicles, now departed. Much of the soldiers' scrap and pap had been deliberately burnt, but much remained, enjoying a mixed afterlife. Some stayed where it was and rotted, some was gathered up and recycled, and some became souvenirs in the prized collections of children or their parents.

Afterglow And Aftermath

Purbrook Heath's shiver of excitement was over, although another year had to be endured before victory in 1945. With the May '45 declaration of VE Day came exhilaration. After years of blacked-out houses and pitch black streets, the sudden night-time brightness seemed extraordinary.

Families skipped to the top of Portsdown to celebrate. Jean from Stakes Road went to the hilltop one evening with her mum. The twinkling city below looked like fairyland. It took a good while longer for Purbrook to get its young soldiers, sailors and airmen back. Such were the demands of managing the peace that many were not demobbed until 1946 or 1947.

Trevor Harfield was one of those. He was eighteen when called up in 1942. Later on he went to Normandy on D-Day plus four, driving amphibious DUKWs. From Arromanches Trevor made it through to Germany and in April 1945 saw the horrors of Belsen at close quarters. He was retained in Germany for two years, finally getting home

Churchill tanks found parking spots along local roadsides in readiness for transportation to Normandy

to Widley Lane in 1947. It wasn't long before the sweet smell of new-mown grass flickered beneath his nostrils, and he made plans to start Widley Cricket Club.

Similarly, Laurie Farmer didn't get back to the UK until 1947. Laurie was a Londoner by birth, his family moving to Widley when he was very young. He joined the Army in 1942 and was part of the D-Day invasion force, fighting through France and Holland into Germany. After that he served in Palestine, finally getting his demob suit in '47. Within a few short winters he would be running Purbrook Football Club.

Doug Doe was a city boy, born in Queen Street Portsea. He joined up in 1943 and was not demobbed until well after the end of the War. A Gunner in the Royal Artillery, Doug served in India and then in the Burma Campaign against the Japanese. His May 1947 release papers described him as "a useful type who can take charge." More than a decade would pass before Doug was enticed to Purbrook Heath by his pals Tony Bonnington and Jim Holder. But once there, he became a key component in the development of Portsdown Cricket Club.

These three combatants – Harfield, Farmer and Doe - and countless others like them came home to a world where sport was down on its uppers. Government helped where it could to provide an infrastructure of facilities and grounds to play on, but the reality at the end of World War Two was that Britain's resources were exhausted.

Among the rank and file there was a mood for change; the wartime coalition was dissolved in July 1945 (even before Japan surrendered in August), and Attlee's Labour Party won the General Election, which took three weeks to complete because UK servicemen worldwide were encouraged to vote.

Purbrook was about to emerge into the daylight of the 1950s. Young people returned from their wartime military service with energy to burn and Local Authorities recognised that facilities were needed to channel this restlessness.

And so it was that a plan hatched before the War by the good burghers of Havant & Waterloo – to convert a ragged heath into a sports ground that would meet the aspirations of a village – was dug out from its bunker and placed on top of the pile. If the plan became reality, it would mean a level playing field at last for Purbrook Heath.

General Sir Miles Dempsey and Christ Church Portsdown

The General was one of Monty's men. He fought with distinction through Sicily and Italy. In January 1944 Sir Miles was called home to take command of the Second Army, ready for D-Day.

He was in good company – the other commanders in 21 Army group were Crerar, Bradley and Patton.

Two days before the D-Day invasion commenced, General Dempsey and

Vicar Gillman organised a "Knight's Vigil" at Christ Church, Portsdown – an eve of battle dedication service, led by Chaplain Reverend Steel. Local records show that so many officers and men attended the service, there was no room for parishioners.

Chaplain Steel called for those present to "dedicate to Almighty God the task which lies before us." Within hours of the Sunday June 4th vigil, Overlord had begun.

Such was General Dempsey's attachment to Christ Church and his Knight's Vigil that, after the war had been won, he returned to Portsdown on June 6th 1948 and unveiled two commemorative stained glass windows, which remain to this day at the front of Squire Deverell's 19th century church.

Remarkably, General Dempsey returned to Christ Church every year from 1948 to 1968 on the Sunday nearest D-Day, usually accompanied by Lady Dempsey, to "resound the call" made in 1944 on the brink of the huge invasion.

General Sir Miles Dempsey, GBE, KCB, DSO, MC was very much the professional soldier, always competent, honourable and loyal.

Significantly, his death in 1969 occurred on the 25th anniversary of the D-Day landings.

Chapter 16

Brave New World

At the end of World War Two, Purbrook's old cricket pitch at the top of the Heath was in a state. But things could have been worse – it might have been a cabbage patch! During the war the Urban District Council notified the County War Agricultural Committee that it would not object to the Heath being used for food production. Nothing came of the offer. On the development front, the National Playing Fields Association stayed loyal to their pre-war pledge. As early as September 1945 they revived their 40% funding offer, suggesting that an application be resuscitated via the County Education Committee.

Let's Play Anywhere But Here

It wasn't until the summer of 1947 that Purbrook restarted their cricket team. The rule was still "Saturdays only" at Council-owned grounds, and the Heath had been Council-owned since 1936. Matches on Purbrook Common cost the club three shillings and ninepence a time and Purbrook played nine games at the Heath in this come-back season. To their credit, Havant Council's General Purposes Committee accepted that Purbrook Heath cricket ground was zonked out and did their best to find better accommodation for the club.

But a po-faced County Council wouldn't allow the old cricket field at the former Industrial School to be used (opposite Gauntlett's Dairy in Stakes Road), because it might be required for school accommodation. There was better news in respect of land in Stakes Hill Road near Waterlooville. Owner CA Knights was agreeable, if suitable terms could be worked out. (This land morphed into the RN and RM Orphanage, and was later called South Africa Lodge).

At down-at-heel Purbrook Heath, "gimme shelter" was the cricketers' cry. They pleaded for a shed to change in and a pot to piss in. The Council coughed up, spending £45 on a sixteen-feet-long portable wooden hut, supplied by AR West the Purbrook builder. An Elsan closet costing

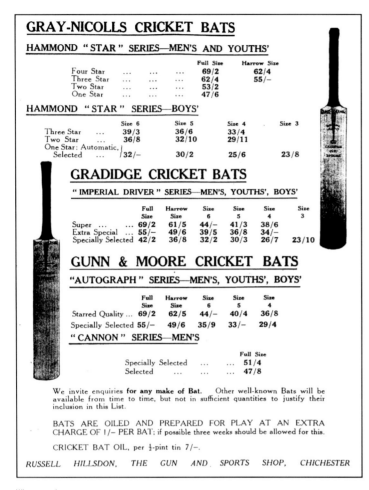

GRAY-NICOLLS CRICKET BATS

HAMMOND "STAR" SERIES—MEN'S AND YOUTHS'

				Full Size	Harrow Size
Four Star	...	...	...	69/2	62/4
Three Star	...	...	...	62/4	55/-
Two Star	...	...	...	53/2	
One Star	...	...	...	47/6	

HAMMOND "STAR" SERIES—BOYS'

	Size 6	Size 5	Size 4	Size 3
Three Star ...	39/3	36/6	33/4	
Two Star ...	36/8	32/10	29/11	
One Star: Automatic, Selected ... /32/-		30/2	25/6	23/8

GRADIDGE CRICKET BATS

"IMPERIAL DRIVER" SERIES—MEN'S, YOUTHS', BOYS'

	Full Size	Harrow Size	Size 6	Size 5	Size 4	Size 3
Super	69/2	61/5	44/-	41/3	38/6	
Extra Special ...	55/-	49/6	39/5	36/8	34/-	
Specially Selected	42/2	36/8	32/2	30/3	26/7	23/10

GUNN & MOORE CRICKET BATS

"AUTOGRAPH" SERIES—MEN'S, YOUTHS', BOYS'

	Full Size	Harrow Size	Size 6	Size 5	Size 4
Starred Quality ...	69/2	62/5	44/-	40/4	36/8
Specially Selected	55/-	49/6	35/9	33/-	29/4

"CANNON" SERIES—MEN'S

			Full Size
Specially Selected	...	...	51/4
Selected	...	...	47/8

We invite enquiries **for any make of Bat.** Other well-known Bats will be available from time to time, but not in sufficient quantities to justify their inclusion in this List.

BATS ARE OILED AND PREPARED FOR PLAY AT AN EXTRA CHARGE OF 1/– PER BAT; if possible three weeks should be allowed for this.

CRICKET BAT OIL, per ½-pint tin 7/–.

RUSSELL HILLSDON, THE GUN AND SPORTS SHOP, CHICHESTER

When good bats cost three pounds ten shillings

another £12 provided the lap of luxury. The portable wooden hut boasted four shuttered windows plus an internal partition, and the whole lot was delivered and assembled for a further sum of £39.

On the pitch the rutted outfield warranted a health warning. Accidents were frequent enough for the Engineer to be consulted as to the wisdom of using Purbrook Common. In addition to Purbrook's match quota, informal games were played there by a group of cricketers calling themselves Old Widley. This didn't help the state of the ground but, in truth, neither did it make things any worse. The put-upon Engineer allowed himself a wry smile when asked by the General Purposes Committee to "level off the outfield." Mission impossible!

Upping The Stakes

Up at Stakes Hill Road in Waterlooville territory, Mr Knights allowed the Council to use his land for cricket during 1947. Purbrook CC applied to use the ground on nine Saturdays...they tried for Sundays too. The General Purposes Committee knocked the Sunday application on the head at first but, when Mr Knights raised no objection, they approved six Sunday games as well.

Looking ahead, CA Knights also agreed to let the Council have free use of his land for the 1947/48 football season. As spring turned to summer in 1947, Purbrook CC were using both Stakes Hill and Purbrook Common but feeling grumpy about their lot.

Before long a letter was winging its way to the Urban District, complaining that Stakes Hill changing accommodation was ropey, and

The cricketers' "local" was The Leopard Inn

urging the Council to provide a better hut. The missive also moaned that balls were frequently being lost in the hedges around the boundary. The Club were promptly put in their place, being told very bluntly that the ground was being loaned free of charge and they would have to lump it.

The use of Stakes Hill Road was reviewed in October 1947. Mr Knights was happy to continue the arrangement through 1948, provided he was paid £20 annual rent and provided the deal could be terminated with three months' notice. There was talk of borrowing a hut from Waterlooville Rec and putting wire netting alongside the hedges, but nothing came of it.

In 1948 the charge per match for using either Stakes Hill Road or Purbrook Heath was three shillings and ninepence. Bedhampton was the same. Up at the posh end, Havant Park and Waterlooville Recreation Ground both cost fifteen shillings, and Emsworth and Hayling ten shillings. Compare this with the Council's estimated annual expenditure (upkeep & maintenance) on each of these grounds for 1948/49: Stakes Hill (which they didn't own) £91; Purbrook Heath £131; Emsworth £407; Hayling £589; Waterlooville £606; Havant £653. No figure at all for Bedhampton!

For 1948 season the plan was for Purbrook to continue using both the Common and Stakes Hill Road. But it seems the long, chill winter of '47 numbed players' spirits because the club wrote to the Council's Engineer saying that they would take the season off and re-form when better playing conditions were available.

Meanwhile Mr Knights decided to terminate his loan arrangement with effect from the end of August '48. What happened in practice was that, by November 1948, there were new owners at Stakes Hill. Mr Knights had gone and the RN & RM Orphanage had taken over.

Don't Forget The Ninepence

But what about the Purbrook Heath redevelopment project? The earnest Purbrook Ratepayers' Association were doing their bit – they urged the Council to get moving and develop the Heath as a "recreation and playing park." There was good news in July 1947, when the General Purposes Committee approved the Engineer's sketch plan, showing how the area could be utilised for cricket and football pitches.

By September 1947 the Engineer had costed the provision of two football pitches and a cricket pitch at £4,937 9s 9d. Such precision. Admittedly this was a knockdown version of the grandiose £12,000 pre-war plan for senior and junior pitches, tennis courts, bowling green, car park and children's playground. Even so, the latest scheme incorporated a great deal of excavation, levelling, draining and developing, and to be able to provide all that for under £5,000 seems remarkable.

Grinding Through Committees

The General Purposes Committee were delighted with an estimate below £5,000 and approved it, passing it to the Finance Committee. They seemed happy with the figure and sought a £5,050 loan from the Minister of Health, also applying to the County Education Committee for a grant in aid.

Between September 1947 and December 1948 the project ground its way through a forest of committees. It was frowned at, enthused over, queried, doubted and disputed, but never discarded. The bureaucracies through which it churned totalled seven – by name: General Purposes, Finance, full Urban District Council, Hampshire & IOW Playing Fields Association, County Education, Further Education, and the Ministry of Education.

The upshot of such longwinded worthiness was that the Minister of Education was amenable to a scaled-down proposal not exceeding £4,000. Havant Council's Engineer duly submitted an amended scheme. In December 1948 the Minister of Education made a provisional grant offer of £1,950 towards the capital cost of £4,000 and the Council accepted this. At last there was a big tick in the box marked "Purbrook Heath Development," but the project's cost had been cut from £5,000 to £4,000. The Engineer would have to wheel and deal.

The plan to purchase and develop Purbrook Heath as a sports ground had been a long time in the making. First mooted in 1934, World War Two parked its tanks all over the plans for a long period but finally, on June 17th 1949, the General Purposes Committee allowed themselves a corporate hug. The Clerk triumphantly reported "receipt of planning approval for the development of Purbrook Heath." The Chairman popped an extra knob of sugar in his cup of tea and cheerfully dunked his rationed chocolate biscuit. Today was a back-slapping bonanza.

Start Digging!

The optimism bouncing around Council corridors encouraged action and, by September, a fired-up Engineer had placed an order with H & VJ Jefferies to start work on September 26th 1949. At the same time the General Purposes Committee set the machinations in train to block up the diagonal pathway across the Heath and replace it with a north-south roadway.

Not straightforward because this latter part of Purbrook Heath remained within Droxford Rural District, and application had to be made to the Minister of Transport for approval to carry out the diversions.

The autumnal bog at Purbrook Heath made progress grindingly slow. The place was waterlogged and the dumper trucks couldn't get on site. And if they did slither on, they couldn't get off. Contractor Jefferies seemed unwilling to provide enough manpower, so almost nobody was around to get on with any work. Through November and December the General Purposes Committee pulled faces and sulked, but they felt powerless.

In their anxiety to keep the contract moving, the Committee made one bad decision. The contract made provision for limited subsoil drainage and the plan was to spread a thick layer of clinker on a third of the total

Purbrook circa 1950. Reg Brown is kneeling in jacket and cap. Behind him are guest Trevor Harfield (centre) and Rube Stallard (two places left)

area, enabling water to run away efficiently. This operation would cost £1,050 but no provision had been made in the contract.

An extra £1,050 would swell the project way over its £4,000 ceiling so they pressed ahead without the vital clinker drainage. As a result of this cock-up in the costings, two generations of cricketers and footballers spent forlorn weekends staring at sodden, unusable pitches.

Dead Slow And Stop

Weeks went by and nothing much happened at the Heath, except that the site was cleared and a sixteen-feet-wide access road took shape. The task of excavating and removing tons of soil was only 10% complete, and stripping off the topsoil was just 25% complete.

The mammoth levelling operation was stuck in a rut. This process involved cutting into the hillside to a depth of up to ten feet and, tapering out towards the brook, excavating an area approximately 150 yards wide. Then, to cap it all, because of heavy rain through October and November, contractor Jefferies wanted to halt excavation work until March 1950. This extended the contract's timescale from five to eight months.

Putting The Boot In

By the time March 1950 edged into view, not a lot had altered heath-side. When the Engineer met contractor Jefferies on site in April, the ground was still very wet. This prompted a letter from Jefferies, saying they hoped to restart soon after Easter. Duly recorded in the General Purposes Committee minutes and reviewed by the full Urban District Council at their April 25th meeting, it caused a tremor in the chamber. There was a lot of froth and bile about, and not much goodwill.

Councillor AJ Kille proposed an amendment and Councillor John Flanders seconded it. Both men knew Purbrook Heath well and the full Council duly amended the General Purposes Committee minutes thus:

"that the Engineer be instructed to arrange for the work to be carried out, to be proceeded with without delay."

Not sparkling English, but the message was clear: "no more delays, no more excuses – get on with it!"

Despite all this high level huffing and puffing, excavation work did not recommence until June 21st 1950, a standstill of six months. On July 14th 1950 the Engineer reported yet more delays with only one man working the machinery on site. The contract completion date had come and gone.

Before the Heath's redevelopment in 1950, this vibrant willow tree (pictured in 2009) had a pond for company

On July 25th 1950 the full Council reviewed the lack of progress. At this distance we can only guess their mood. A volley of teacups launched at the good lady by the tea urn? Possibly. As before, it was forthright Councillors Kille and Flanders who proposed an addition to Minute 260 relating to Purbrook Heath:

"that, if the Engineer reports no progress, the Chairman of the General Purposes Committee be authorised to instruct the Clerk to give notice of the termination of the contract." Carried!

That's what happened. The General Purposes Committee met two months later on September 15th 1950 and reported that the contract had been terminated on August 17th. Following this, the Engineer invited three firms to tender for completion of the work and the Committee proposed that the contract be awarded to SM Tidy of Brighton.

But the Council chamber atmosphere had grown tetchy in respect of Purbrook Heath business and the full Council flexed their muscles, deciding not to follow the recommendation. On December 28th they awarded the Purbrook Heath completion project to En Tout Cas Co. Ltd.

Still Bogged Down

Despite new contractors, the Heath's development crawled along in first gear. Although regular checks were carried out on the waterlogged site, work couldn't start again until the middle of 1951. Through July '51 work went well, but even this optimism couldn't be sustained. Heavy summer rain dampened progress. Then work stopped again during the early part of September. At last, by mid October, levelling was complete, under-drains had been laid apart from the north east corner, and 75% of the area had been covered with soil, harrowed and treated with lime.

The sizeable task of excavating and levelling signalled the end of the line for some of the Common's historic landmarks. The pathway that cut diagonally across the Heath was no more – replaced by a north-south road at the western edge. The pond in the south west corner disappeared, along with one of its willow tree sentries. The solitary willow that survives today used to reside on the far bank. Also gone is the adjacent animal pound.

There was still time for a dispute between the Council and En Tout Cas over completion of the cricket square. With winter '51 whistling and wheezing in the wings, the contractor wanted to delay finishing the square until the better weather of 1952 arrived. The Urban District Councillors had exhausted their capacity to cuddle contractors and pushed hard for completion in '51. Letters flowed and brows furrowed. But weather had the final say, making conditions impractical for En Tout Cas to return any earlier than April of 1952.

En Tout Cas completed the square and seeded the outfield in early May '52. There was work to be done on a boundary fence, on constructing manholes and on clearing the site but, other than that, Purbrook's wow-factor-wonderland was about to come true. Don't dance round the maypole just yet, though. The specification for the cricket table made no provision for a water supply (a bit like a pub with no beer) and the additional cost was £40.

The shoots of this showpiece sports ground were considered too delicate for cricket in '52, and in mid summer it was decided that the grass surface was not ready for the wear and tear of the 1952/53 football season either. Everything seemed set for the summer of 1953.

Lift Off

In December 1952 the Council were overcome by festive good cheer, adding a sum of £800 to their capital expenditure estimates for the provision of a pavilion at the Heath. As for the likelihood of playing cricket on the Common during the summer of '53, the vibes were good: Purbrook's application for ten Saturdays, fourteen Sundays and Whit Monday was approved. Suddenly, the proximity of the new Heath's virginal cricket season brought on a mixture of anxiety and activity.

In March '53 En Tout Cas worried that a second sowing of grass seed was needed and asked the Council to pay for it. The General Purposes Committee refused. Next, the Engineer conceded that concrete steps were needed from the site of the proposed pavilion on top of the bank down to pitch level; an omission that the Committee accepted, recommending expenditure of £70. And lastly, Purbrook CC woke up to the fact that the new ground had nowhere for people to sit. Resulting from the Club's entreaty, the Committee approved some temporary seating.

Reflections

In the seasons leading up to 1953 Purbrook CC continued to use South Africa Lodge in Stakes Hill Road as their home patch. The Leopard's Bill Arnold was a godsend, regularly serving up cricket teas from the back of his woody estate wagon. As an occasional treat players traipsed along to Broadlands restaurant and enjoyed the real deal, tablecloths and all.

South Africa Lodge's new owners, the RN & RM Orphanage, carried on the loan arrangement established by predecessor CA Knights, and Purbrook finished their last season in exile (1952) with two good September victories. Portsmouth Telephones were disconnected for a paltry 29 in response to Purbrook's 120 for six. And finally, Purbrook

Purbrook celebrate the opening of their new ground in 1953. The picture includes Bill Arnold, Len Marchant, Chick Thresher, Cyril Kemp, Lester Hirst, Stan Doe, Frank Marsh, Don New, Sammy Small, Frank Lambert and groundsman Bob Scantlebury

chirruped to a narrow victory over Finchdean, who collapsed to 35 all out chasing a meagre total of 58.

Now it was 1953 and Purbrook's cricketers were geared for change. The boys were back in town and moving to pastures new; a posh playing arena just a six-hit away from pastures old. It had been a long drawn out five years since games had been played regularly at the tiny, rack-and-ruined Heath. By comparison, this fresh-faced facility was a brave new world. This place could be something special, hewn out of the clay, sands and gorse.

"OK, Let's Play"

Sunday May 10th 1953 dawned. The local paper carried a team photo and a brief summary of how the smart new complex had gone from there (heathland) to here (sports ground). Club chairman WE Arnold wielded his bat to the first ceremonial ball bowled and then retired to watch proceedings from the top of the bank – a grandstand view. It was a good day for Bill Arnold; he was custodian of The Leopard Inn and he took a few bob that night!

The inaugural 1953 season bloomed, blossomed and withered as all cricket campaigns do. There were expectations of better things to come.

Better facilities at the ground, better players and better cricket. Purbrook Football Club came to life in these new surroundings too. Within two years versatile publican Bill Arnold managed his local footballers to glory – in a grand finish to 1954/55 season they won the Father Purcell Cup at mighty Fratton Park.

By now two cricket clubs (and a football team) called the Heath their home. The first was long established Purbrook. The second was a new kid on the block: Christ Church CC.

Purbrook FC at the Heath in 1955 with the Father Purcell Cup.
Back row: Angus Munro; Bill Stoat; Trevor Harfield; Sid Allen; Eric Jurd; Ted Sillence; Stan Martin; Bill Arnold
Front row: Ted Rex; Kingsley Daniels; Doug Hall; Billy Daniels; Ted Lamont

Chapter 17

A Notion Of Shopkeepers

Purbrook and Widley were close neighbours by the 1950s. In fact it was impossible to detect a dividing line. Widley was entirely removed from its old westerly location by St Mary Magdalene Church, and was now firmly settled astride the A3 London Road, edging up to the Portsmouth border on the brow of Portsdown. It was spreading out, particularly to the east, with copses and glades being gobbled up by housing.

Shops On Parade

At the crossroads on the top of Portsdown by the old George Inn, 1950s rush-hour traffic grew sufficiently heavy to require a policeman on point duty, oozing symmetry, style and panache. There was no doubt he enjoyed his work; he waved and swept and pointed with a flourish.

Little more than a peak time traffic queue north of him, past Portsdown Filling Station, stood Widley's parade of shops, neatly set back from the main road. There was the Sweet Shop - shelves bedecked with boiled sweets and wine gums in gargantuan glass jars, Greenwood the Chemist, Plumbley's Wool Shop, the Greengrocer, Grinter the Butcher, and at the far end an odd mix called Portsdown Cycles & Radio, run by L Stuart Vigurs.

Tucked away in the hinterland of residential streets was Mr Caizley's grocery, all on its own among the houses in Geoffrey Avenue. In simmering summers Mr Caizley concocted his very own juicy, blackcurrant ice lollies for the kids. Further down the A3 London Road at Bushy Mead, there was a diddy shopping parade that included a Co-op and a post office.

The Co-op laid claim to a miniature cable car – a contraption of wonder that enthralled children shopping with mum. It was called a cash railway and on receipt of mum's ten bob note tendered for her three and ninepence of groceries, the sales assistant would seal invoice and cash into a ceramic cup and send it via overhead wire to the cashier's office at the back of the store. By magic, back would come Co-op divi update, a receipt and six and threepence change. The method of propulsion was catapult.

Further along, past Hants and Dorset Caravans and the beanstalked allotments, Purbrook had its own selection of shopping parades. By the brook there was a proper fish shop – cold, wet and scaly...and that was just the customers! Alongside was newsagent Nuttall and wine merchant Smeeds. Nearby were huge advertising hoardings – a bit garish for prim Purbrook – separating road users from the soggy bog behind.

Next door was another shopping parade that included greengrocer Bravo and Wilkes the immaculately dressed chemist – all bow tie and half glasses. A few shops further along was George's Hairdressing Salon, where the barbers' combs rested reassuringly in jars labelled "Disinfectant." The cynical young streak in me suspected it was simply water. In the same block was the Post Office run by always-affable Mr Mills. In bygone days, the original Post Office was further up the street.

Opposite The Woodman, the 19th century Old Manor House (simply an imposing old house in the manor) had burned down before the War (WWII) leaving only its stables intact, and had given way to Manor Filling Station, whose repair workshops were up at Stakes Hill Road.

Purbrook's main road was well off for grocers – at one time there had been Voysey by the brook, Lever who "delivered to your door" and Roper on the corner of Stakes. An old wrought iron seat offered rest and recuperation at this spot. In the mid years of the decade you might espy two blond lads from Queen's Grove monitoring the London Road traffic from this very seat. They studiously recorded the cars and their registrations, with plenty of time for a yawn and a good scratch between vehicles.

Not so much a barber's shop, more a hairdressing salon!

LADIES' AND GENTLEMEN'S HAIRDRESSER

GEORGES SALON

Satisfaction Guaranteed

16 London Road, Purbrook Hants.

On Your Bike

Further north in London Road, JE Saunders butcher's shop loomed large: "Purveyor of best English and imported meat." At the beginning of the '50s Ted Lamont had a Saturday job making deliveries on Saunders' cumbersome trade bicycle. The sign on the bike frame made him chuckle: "Express Delivery Service." Alongside butcher Saunders was Worleys, selling antiques the old fashioned way.

Opposite JE Saunders was another butcher called Haywards (previously Cottons). At the end of the '50s (just like Ted Lamont at the start), a bespectacled lad named Peter pedalled a chain-ganged butcher's bike around Purbrook streets, delivering for Haywards. A cavernous front basket carried the meat and on several slate-grey slippery Saturdays the bike keeled over, spraying Peter plus his beef and sausages all over the pathway. The grit and gravel added bite to the sausages, but it was no place for vegetarians.

J. E. SAUNDERS

Prop.: J. Taylor

PURVEYOR OF BEST ENGLISH AND IMPORTED MEAT

LONDON ROAD

PURBROOK

Telephone Waterlooville 3127

A butcher's bike provided the "Express Delivery Service"

Shop Till You Drop

Meanwhile, hairdresser Christopher coiffured into the corner shop in Stakes Road. It was in this neat establishment that my barnet had its first brief romance with Brylcreem - if only I needed it now! Sothcott's hardware shop stood by the bus stop and next door was the cobbler's hut where Purbrook's engaging country shoe mender stitched and glued in a haze of leather.

Next to him was Battman's yard, which stretched round into Stakes Road on land that once hosted the Vicarage. Opposite, past 1844 April Cottage, was a four-square building whose ample front wall advertised A H Clear & Sons, Builders and Funeral Directors. This family firm had built St John's Church in the 19th century.

A few steps along the south side of Stakes Road was a trim shopping parade, separated from the street by its own deep frontage. Especially attractive to kids homeward bound from Aldermoor Road Primary were lip-smacking penny buns pertly wedged on shelves in the Black and White Bakery. They baked their bread on the premises, but it was their penny buns that put the gilt on their gingerbread.

Next door was confectioner Dyer, whose matronly owner clearly had a taste for many of the sweets she sold. Her red and yellow gobstoppers worked miracles – they kept schoolkids quiet all the way to the bus stop! Further along, grocer Gregory traded busily at the west end of the row. This precinct survived another 50 years before being converted into housing. Nowadays not even a weathered gobstopper remains as evidence of a tasty past.

Deeper into Purbrook village there were other patches of shops, notably Roseblade's store: "Deliverers of pink paraffin and sharpeners of lawn mowers" on the corner of Stakes and Fir Copse, Nuttall's other newsagent branch in Park Avenue, and Hicks the small general store further up on the corner of Privett Road.

On The Buses

Public transport was the key to getting around, either to the shopping magnets of Waterlooville and Cosham, or further afield to Portsmouth and Southsea. Southdown provided green and cream double-deckers up and over the Hill to Horndean (route 41) or as far as Petersfield (route 42 direct or 40 via Clanfield). There were also services to Waterlooville that went round the houses via Park Avenue and Stakes Hill (routes 37 and 137). For a short time these two routes were taken over by the wine-red buses of Portsmouth Corporation, but then reverted to Southdown.

Purbrook folk also had their bikes, motor bikes, Morris Minors and Vespas, but double-decker buses stacked with passengers ruled the roost. Smoking was permitted upstairs and Corporation buses displayed signs on the lower deck saying: "Spitting Prohibited," such exhortation apparently unnecessary for Southdown's discerning customers.

The decade of the '50s was still a time for working horses. Milk carts from Gauntlett's dairy delivered around village streets, pulled by strong impassive greys. On the corner of The Brow, milkman Mr Lambert normally allowed his horse to dive into the nosebag for a good munch.

Purbrook Football Club regularly met in the car park before setting off to "away" games

Hidden away at the end of The Dale were Rita's stables where children took riding lessons, parading Black Beauty and Champion along the avenues in regulation single file.

Education, Education, Education

For their primary education, the kids of Purbrook and Widley went either to posh Boundary Oak Prep (which moved to Roche Court in 1961), or to the tiny Church school attached to St John's on the main road or, most likely, to Aldermoor Road where pigeon-toed Mr Twigg held sway. He and Mrs Twigg lived in Stakes Road not far from Clear the Builder, their privacy assured by a fulsome front hedge.

Miss Bambury (later Mrs York) was his deputy, and other worthy teachers included Miss Blades and Miss Dent for the five-year-olds over by the dinner huts (later, Mrs Ballinger assumed their mantle). In the adjacent hut was formidable Mrs Brown (wife of cricketing stalwart Reg Brown), and back in the neatly quadrangled main school were Mrs Thomas, Mrs Wallis, Mr Packwood (who gave lads their first exciting taste of organised football and cricket), and Mr Bence who had a kindly disposition and a wooden leg. A good school, despite the nauseous crates of free milk a-curdling outside each classroom on hot summer mornings.

The only senior school in the immediate locality was Purbrook Park County High School, domiciled in Squire Deverell's old Park Avenue mansion plus their new annexe 200 yards south. It was at Purbrook High, between 1948 and 1955, that my sister Jean quenched her thirst for knowledge. At least that's what she tells me she did. Mr Le Min was her headmaster and Fred Coley was her favourite (music) teacher.

The other senior schools were Cowplain Secondary Modern, which was a Southdown bus ride north of Purbrook, and the Convent of the Cross round in Stakes Hill, housed in Charles Napier's former home, Oaklands.

Cubs And Clubs And Rock 'n' Roll

Lord Baden would have Powelled with delight at Christ Church Portsdown's achievements in the mid '50s. They had a full set of Guides, Brownies, Scouts and Cubs. In the hall next to the church, Mrs Naish looked after the Cubs with spirit and gusto. The Pack reached their peak winning the citywide Rounders competition and Akela Naish was proud of her boisterous charges.

The older lads who formed the 72nd Portsmouth/1st Portsdown Scout Troop were a step up in class from their green-capped juniors. They unquestionably showed more discipline, but undoubtedly had less

Purbrook Scout troop, late 1950s. In the back row are leaders Don Pitman (right of centre), and Joyce Singleton and Alex Ferrier on the extreme right.
Picture courtesy of Mervyn Liversidge

fun. Sunday morning church parades, once a month at Christ Church, displayed the Guides and Scouts at their ceremonial best.

A mile away in deepest Purbrook, the Methodist Church built a new hall round the back in 1953. Within a couple of years its Saturday evening Youth Club was the place to be. John Goddard's Navy pal Stephen rigged up his electronic wizardry, soldered a bit of this to a bit of that and eased a tremulous turntable into action. Their limited collection of delicate 78s crackled into tinny life and a polite mob of village teenagers jived and smooched at the very dawn of rock 'n' roll.

By 1957 this Stakes Road church felt confident enough to set up its own Scout Troop, run by good eggs Don Pitman and Alex Ferrier. Then, in the early years of the 1960s the church hall became a proving ground for tuneful 16-year-old Pete Connor who cobbled together a rock group with brother Mick on rhythm and pal Merv Liversidge on bass. Pete's first electric guitars were built in his garden shed – with homespun Stratocaster threaded through mega-pumped-up amplifier, Pete practised till the valves began to smoke!

The next step saw Rube Tyler and his drum kit snared from Leigh Park and "FORCE 5" were up and running. Admittedly their rustic stagecraft was more Reg Presley than Elvis Presley, but the band were in business. Within a year they had ditched their dodgy singer and kitchen sink guitars, turning semi-pro at the height of Mersey beat mania. "FORCE 4" adapted well....they were easily the best band in Purbrook. Come to think of it, they were the only band in Purbrook.

Ministering To Others

The three churches in the locality were St John's in the heart of Purbrook, Christ Church up on Portsdown, and the Methodists in Stakes Road. Providing pastoral stability were dedicated men of the cloth: Vicar Harry Maber at St John's and Vicar Frank Worwood at Christ Church. Purbrook Methodists had two ministers at the helm through the '50s; Eric Gulliford served until 1955 and Tom Welch for the next five years. Both Worwood and Welch had cricket in their soul. Canon Worwood formed Christ Church CC in 1953 and played regularly. Reverend Welch turned out for Purbrook when duties permitted.

At Stakes Road Methodists, meeter and greeter on the front porch for Sunday services was retired Purbrook cricketer Reg Brown. Jovial and avuncular, he had a dodgy joke for allcomers. Brother Fred under-

FORCE 5 practising in 1962. Pete Connor, Dodgy Singer, Mick Connor and Merv Liversidge are hard at it, but drummer Rube Tyler is missing. *Picture courtesy of Mervyn Liversidge*

took duties inside the church. Their cricketing days now harrowed and harvested, both men were frequent spectators at the "new" Purbrook Heath ground. Regular spot was on the bench outside pavilion number 2 at the top of the steps, from where they watched their successors battle on in Purbrook's name. Mind you, it was always better in their day!

Watering Holes

Pubs in the stretched-out village were in most cases long established. At the northern end was The White Hart, and a few doors down lurked The Leopard where Mrs Arnold's labrador would ring "time" each evening by nuzzling through the bar with a bell neatly trapped between its teeth.

Next was the re-sited Woodman, then a long haul up to Widley's grand Hampshire Rose whose ample car park was the meeting place for Laurie Farmer's Purbrook footballers whenever they set off to "away" games. Nestling within Purbrook's residential tapestry was The Mount William Club, running since 1928 as a social club. Its first address had been The Dell, evolving into Frances Road. Mount William finally hung out the white flag in 2009.

At the top of Portsdown overlooking the city was The George Inn, its chalk-bored well still in evidence. And we mustn't forget the hamlet of

Stakes a mile or so to the north east, where The Fox and Hounds had traded for many a year. One hundred years ago the Fox's landlord was fined £3 for allowing gambling on his premises – high Stakes perhaps?

Developing Appetites

In Widley, developers were salivating over the wooded area between Fir Copse and The Dale; at the commencement of the 1950s both roads were dead ends and didn't connect. On the western side of London Road, when Boundary Oak School moved on in 1961, the site on the brow of the Hill (within the Portsmouth boundary) was sold for residential development, street names Oak Tree Close and Boundary Crescent bearing reference to the old school.

In 1950s Purbrook, developers with similar appetites were eyeing up the mix of heath and scrub that lay adjacent to Queens Grove and Shaftesbury Avenue. Close by, Westbrook Grove already had plenty of houses fronting up to the roadside and was an oft-used thoroughfare. Despite this it stayed unadopted, its road surface a nightmare of stones and potholes as had been the norm a century before. Its saving grace was a double line of proud poplars that guarded the street.

In their heyday, Mount William Club ran their own football team

A decade on, in February 1965, Portsmouth City Council approved the purchase of Crookhorn Farm for £485,000. The plan for these 127 acres included 700 homes for Portsmouth's overspill population, plus educational and recreational provision, with half an acre reserved for a church.

This building programme followed hard on the heels of the development of much of Gauntlett's farmland on the other (western) side of Crookhorn Lane, known as Purbrook Chase or the Money Estate, stretching westwards to St John's Avenue which until then was a gravelly cul-de-sac off Stakes Road. And further on, in Purbrook's old heart by the A3 London Road, land behind Purbrook House came within the developers' gaze. A small estate called Purbrook Gardens was built there.

Such examples of Purbrook and Widley's building boom don't tell the whole story; this tide was not for turning. The designs were on the table and the bricks were in the kiln. Open spaces were beginning to fill with housing: detached, semi-detached, terrace and bungalow.

Most of the building was taking place on the eastern side of the A3 London Road. To the west, Purbrook Heath's surrounds escaped a battering from the house builders. Our precious Common had already been shredded by excavators between 1950 and 1953, but this wasn't mutilation, it was improvement! The Heath's new order stemmed from the Council resurrecting their pre-war plan for a makeover. And it was all in a good cause – a Common cause, as already described in chapter 16.

"It happens every time he plays Great Balls Of Fire!"

How Purbrook Grew Between 1920 and 1965

The years show when mains water was first supplied, synonymous with the start of house building

Central Area

Stakes Road: 1920s – see end note

Park Farm Road: late 1920s

Westbrook Grove: late 1920s; north section 1931

Queens Grove and Woodlands Grove west: not recorded, but as for Westbrook Grove

Chace Gardens: 1924

Aldermoor Road: 1928, 1933, 1934

Aldermoor Road East (by the school): 1936

Alsford Road: 1928, 1933, 1934

Penjar Avenue: 1929, 1931

Shaftesbury Avenue west section: 1933, 1936, 1939

Eastern Area and Purbrook Chase

St John's Avenue: to Craigwell Rd 1927, 1938; east section 1961, 1962

Craigwell Road: 1929

Morelands Road: east section 1936; rest 1957

Capel Ley: 1957

Shillinglee: 1957

Timberlane (Fishers Lane): 1958

Crowns Close: 1960

The Florins: 1960, 1961

The Guelders: 1961

Penny Place: 1961

Sovereign Lane: 1961, 1962

Minters Lepe: 1962

Tanners Ridge: 1962

Halfpenny Dell: 1963

Purbrook Park Area and Widley

Park Road: 1921

The Crescent: 1921

Bushy Mead: 1925

Fir Copse: north to south 1925, 1927, 1937, 1938

Privett Road (The Mound): 1925, 1933, 1937

Privett Road (Privett Copse Road): 1927; east section 1957

Park Avenue: 1925, 1926, 1927, 1928

Hillside Avenue: 1926

The Brow: west to east 1926, 1927, 1928, 1931, 1933

The Dale: west to east 1927, 1934, 1936, 1937, 1958

Frances Road (The Dell): 1927

Sandy Brow: 1927

Geoffrey Avenue: 1927

Lily Avenue: 1927

The Crest: 1928

Lansdowne Avenue: 1931

Victoria Avenue: 1931

Highbank Avenue: 1933

Alameda Road: between 1939 and 1949

Lone Valley: east section 1939, rest 1947

Serpentine Road: 1946, 1948, 1949

The Thicket: 1949, 1952, 1954, 1955

Alameda Way: 1952

The Rise: 1954

Underdown Avenue: 1954

Deverell Place: 1955

Greenacre Gardens: 1960

Northern Area

Kentidge Road: 1937

Bursledon Road: 1938, 1946

Dayslondon Road: 1946

Campbell Crescent: 1955

Purbrook Gardens: 1961 (and 1967)

Newlands Road: 1963

Corbett Road: 1963, 1964

Alexander Close: 1965

Marlborough Close: 1965

Montgomery Walk: 1965

Also London Road between Purbrook and Waterlooville: 1933, 1934

NB: Stakes Road (and some other isolated dwellings) existed before the year shown, but had no mains water supply. Wells were dug instead.

Chapter 18

Short And Sweet

When Trevor Harfield finally arrived home from his long war in 1947, it seemed the best day of his life. Purbrook Common was just a canter from 3 Widley Lane and he was keen to play some cricket. What confronted him at the old cricket pitch was not good for the soul. No organised cricket had been played there since 1939 and nature had taken it back.

Making The Best Of Things

The lads did what they could to restore the playing area above the path that crossed to Heathcote and Tudor Cottage. They ended up with a small clearing surrounded by gorse and scrub. Games were organised mostly for the evenings, but availability was a problem and matches often went ahead with no more than seven per side. Post-war cricket at the Heath was a sorry spectacle – made worse because few players possessed "whites." But never mind the quality; Trevor's team (informally known as Old Widley) were up and running. It wasn't Lords, but it was cricket.

Widley cricketers preened when they first made the sports page of the local journal although, to be blunt, it wasn't headline copy. The weekly paper accorded them one solitary line on August 22nd 1947, stating: "Widley 118 for 8; Hayling 75." On September 5th the same paper recorded a match between Widley and Purbrook with equal brevity: "Widley 56; Purbrook 77 (Stan Doe 20)." Nothing more, nothing less.

Church Field, Heaven Sent

The number of homes in Widley Lane was small but, proportionately, the number of cricketers living there was huge. These sporty neighbours decided the game was up for Purbrook's blasted heath. For Widley to survive and prosper, a new home was needed. A place they could nurture and call their own. Down the lane and round a couple of bends was a broad field that belonged to Widley Farm. The field had two things in its favour: it was currently under-utilised and it was flat.

Vic Grant and Trevor Harfield asked farmer Wilfred Cleeve if he would let them use Church Field as Widley's home ground. It would take a deal of preparatory work, but the field had potential. Farmer Cleeve was sympathetic to the cause of local cricket, but he was a tenant on the land and referred Vic and Trevor to the owners, Southwick Estate.

Trevor Harfield wasted no time, knocking on landowner Hugh Borthwick-Norton's front door to seek permission. Mr Borthwick-Norton was currently battling in vain to wrest the family seat (Southwick House and its surrounding parkland) from the military who had requisitioned it during the War in Squire Evelyn Thistlethwayte's time. Nevertheless, Hugh B-N offered no objection, provided that Farmer Cleeve was suitably recompensed by the Club.

Reaping What You Sow

The biggest hurdle had been cleared and it was all systems go for Church Field. Wilfred Cleeve cut the field in readiness, and the Cricket Club agreed to pay the farmer £7 per year for the hire of the ground (in later years this rose to £10). Optimism abounded, and volunteers set about getting the place into shape. Harry Bailey, who worked over by Newlands Farm, made an instant impact by putting a barbed wire fence

A cricket ground was fashioned from this farmer's field in 1950. Quite an achievement.

around the boundary, to keep the cows at bay. Other volunteers made good use of a hand mower, and the pitch and surrounds were steadily transformed.

The Club soon inherited a motor mower – not entirely a blessing because the machine had seen better days. Urgently, a bomb crater had to be filled in because, though not strictly in the line of cricket-ball fire, it had the capacity to lure unsuspecting outfielders into an early grave!

The graft paid dividends. Beyond the stile by the oak tree, the boundary wire was in place, the grass was trimmed, the field was flat, and the wicket was cut north to south to avoid the track of the setting sun. Admittedly, the cricket square was of the same composition as the stony outfield, but the boys did the best with what they had.

Every cricket club needs four walls and a roof. Somewhere to prepare, somewhere to lay out the tea and sandwiches. Widley cricketers made do with benches on the boundary for a while, but Trevor Harfield had a grander plan. At Wadham's of Waterlooville he was a carpenter with indentures, and by his hand a corrugated iron and timber structure was built, positioned not far from the oak tree at the northern side of the ground.

Now Widley CC had a pavilion, twenty feet by ten, that opened up like a stable door supported by two poles. The left hand side was a changing area, the middle part had two tables and benches for teas, and the right hand side acted as a small kitchen with a gas bottle for heating water. The loo was round the back in the bushes! A changing area was less vital than today, because almost nobody owned a kit bag and most players arrived already changed and ready to play.

The pavilion was so grand it required planning permission from Droxford Rural District Council in May 1951, granted for five years. In his supporting documentation, Droxford's Building Surveyor demeaned the artful structure by referring to it as "a shed." The remarkable "shed" gave generous service to Widley CC before embarking on a second career as a detached residence for chickens on the farm.

Widley Cricket Club played at Church Field from 1950. The venue established itself sufficiently to feature on Ordnance Survey maps as "Cricket Ground" and, although the Club faded completely by 1962, maps continued to designate it as a cricket ground into the 1990s. By then it was a farmer's field once more. Today, the sentinel oak tree and rustic stile remain, but there's nothing else left from cricketing times.

Green For Go

Widley CC held their first Annual General Meeting on May 10th 1950. The Club had been playing informally for a season or two, but now they had their own ground. No mean achievement starting from scratch. Trevor Harfield's neighbours in Widley Lane provided the backbone of the Club. Vic Grant lived at number 1; Uncle Bill Harfield at number 2; Trevor at 3; Charlie Perkins at 4; Uncle John Harfield at 5; Alf Norgate at 7; and Doug Hall at number 8. Roly Hall was another player who lived in the block, and although Mr Gregory at number 6 had no connection with Widley, he reinforced the Lane's cricketing pedigree by umpiring for Wadhams CC.

Widley's fixture list ebbed and flowed as such lists always do, but regular opponents included Purbrook (now playing at South Africa Lodge in Waterlooville), Bird In Hand Fareham, Brickwoods Brewery, Cowplain, Denmead, Rowlands Castle, Swanmore, Tadley, Warnford, and Wickham.

The mood in St John's church hall for Widley's AGM on May 10th was awash with enthusiasm. Alf Norgate was elected Chairman and Captain, and the members voted to buy Trevor Harfield a cricket bat in appreciation of his hard work. There was enough in the kitty to be

"Ethel, I've thought of a name for this cow....Pat."

generous; expenditure over the year had totalled £79, leaving a credit balance of £24 7s 0d.

Mr Norgate said that the Club was making its mark locally and urged all players to wear regulation whites from now on. In respect of their Church Field ground, the meeting expressed a vote of thanks to Squire Hugh Borthwick-Norton and Mr Wilfred Cleeve of Widley Farm. The meeting closed at 9.30pm; perfect timing for a pint up the road.

The Squire Bows Out

A sad footnote to this upbeat tale is that Hugh Borthwick-Norton, stressed by his fruitless endeavours to reclaim Southwick House, died before the year was out, on October 5th 1950. His latter years had been spent at Purbook Heath House which he had purchased privately soon after the end of the War. He married his Secretary Eva Sardinia Burrows in January 1944, and it was widow Eva who now took the reins of the Southwick Estate.

Meetings, Bloody Meetings

Church Field was available for matches on both Saturdays and Sundays, but Widley enjoyed their quota of away games too. If their opponents were far distant, Widley CC travelled in style, hiring a small coach from Provincial of Fareham for a fiver a day.

For Widley's first season at Church Field (1950) Trevor Harfield's pavilion was still on the drawing board. Mr D Hollis volunteered for umpiring duties and Miss M Cleeve was appointed scorer. Two wicketkeepers had to be kept happy, so Bill Harfield kept wicket one week and Arthur Bartlett the next. With Chairman Norgate's uniform plea in mind, the Club purchased eleven cricket caps for regular players.

The next AGM was held early, on September 21st, before members' minds drifted to wintry matters such as football. With surplus funds of £21 14s 9d, the meeting resolved that the Club's monies should be placed in a bank account rather than under the Treasurer's mattress!

Kingsley Daniels was voted the season's best all-rounder and was awarded a bat in recognition. There were important matters to be dealt with in respect of Church Field. Firstly, Charlie Perkins was unanimously elected groundsman and given complete control. Secondly, sightscreens were proposed for 1951 season. Skipper Alf Norgate ended an upbeat AGM, saying that it had been "a pleasure to captain such a fine set of fellows." All matters were wrapped up by 9.30pm, allowing the assembled heroes to hasten to the hostelry.

Over the winter, a multitude of Matters Arising necessitated a pre-season General Meeting on April 12th 1951 at St John's church hall. Secretary and Treasurer Trevor Harfield reported that the Club's credit balance of £29 11s 4d was now, genuinely, a balance at bank. He had opened an account for Widley CC at the National Provincial. The Club's umpire for 1951 would be Mr W Bartlett, with Miss R Hall as scorer. Alf Norgate was re-elected Captain with a landslide of votes.

Annual subscriptions were agreed at sixpence (a tanner) a week, and there would be no match fees. Fixture Cards were already available, priced sixpence, and coaches had been booked for the long-haul away matches. A stack of procedural business was transacted in staccato manner, enabling the meeting to finish on the dot of 9.30pm.

Church Field from above, circa 1950. The area shaped like a balloon is the pitch, and the road alongside is Widley Walk. *Picture courtesy of Peter Rogers*

Widley Cricket Club

Work In Progress

After two encouraging seasons, maintenance of Church Field remains hard graft. The wicket needs constant repair and grass on the outfield is too long. Cutting the entire playing area is a mammoth task. And, whilst the barbed wire fence helps considerably, cows still manage to infiltrate the playing area, dumping cowpats anywhere from fine leg to long on. Also, the location of the square is such that the northern boundary is vulnerable to a big hit, with agricultural sloggers able to loft the ball into the woods, causing breaks in play.

At the November 1951 AGM, the Club decided not

to continue with the election of a groundsman. A proposal to buy 100 turfs was turfed out, but erection of a larger wire fence was approved. Harry Bailey would purchase 100 pickets and four rolls of barbed wire and invoice the Club. Farmer Cleeve had already agreed to let the cricketers fence off a larger portion of the field.

As far as last season's cricket was concerned (1951), Widley had played 25 matches, winning twelve, losing twelve and drawing one. Trevor Harfield took 51 wickets and scored 289 runs, and Kingsley Daniels bowled consistently well, taking 83 wickets at an average of 5.19. Even though expenditure on the new "shed" made a hole in Club finances, there was still a healthy balance of £26.

1952 And All That

For the upcoming 1952 summer, Trevor Harfield was in overload mode. The Club elected him Secretary, Treasurer, and Captain. He was also a one-man selection committee. This heavy workload proved unsettling and would eventually bite Widley on the backside. Other problems in 1952 were a) the drain of young players called up for National Service, and b) Church Field's long grass. New members would satisfy the first issue, whilst the second was eased by Vic Grant and Bill Harfield volunteering to mow the field each week.

Despite the niggles of running a cricket club, Widley CC members were pleased with themselves. After all, they were proudly playing on their own patch at Church Field, whereas homeless Purbrook were making the best of things exiled up at South Africa Lodge in Waterlooville. Despite this, Purbrook Cricket Club were undoubtedly regarded as the senior team in and around the village. They proved their point in the fixture between the two clubs at the start of 1952 season. Purbrook reached 50 for five declared, and bowled Widley out for nineteen. Over far too soon, with little credit to either club.

Come July, the Church Field crew had their revenge. They shot Purbrook out for a paltry 33 (Kingsley Daniels five for nine) and won the battle by a handsome 43 runs. Even the cows celebrated! Low scores continued to be the theme of Widley's summer: Mayles crept to 104, with Vic Grant taking seven for 43, but Widley's reply was dismal: 28 all out.

By the season's end Widley had played 29 matches, winning eleven, losing seventeen, and drawing one. Vic Grant excelled, taking 100 wickets including a prized hat trick against Purbrook, and Arthur Bartlett topped the batting averages. Reviewing 1952 and looking forwards to '53 at their General Meeting, members agreed that maintenance of Church Field was the sticking point. Preparing the square, cutting the outfield, maintaining the fence round the boundary - all were a heavy drain on volunteers.

And what about the cowpats? They were proving impossible to prevent, and difficult to ignore when fielding. More in hope than expectation, 25 more pickets and another roll of barbed wire were ordered. Where there's muck there's flies, and there were plenty of them on Church Field. Fortunately, the good ladies who provided teas – Mrs Cleeve, Mrs Grant, and Mrs Biddle – fought valiantly to keep these buzzing hordes off the food, their efforts much appreciated. As a token of esteem, the Club presented each lady with a pair of gloves.

Two Grounds And Three Clubs

By 1953 season Chairman Norgate had stepped down and John Harfield had replaced him. Trevor Harfield remained as Secretary, Treasurer and lone Selector. He continued as Saturday Captain but abdicated from the Sunday job. Vic Grant stepped up for the Sabbath. Practice nights were formalised for Wednesdays; cattle not invited.

In the summer of '53, up the road and round the corner great expectations were coming to fruition at Purbrook Heath. A brand new ground, cut into the clay banks of the Common, emerged in full glory and was available for use. And the cherry on the trifle was the Council's decision to provide a full time groundsman to tend this new sports field. Purbrook CC came scuttling back from South Africa Lodge to find that a brand new rival Club, Christ Church, were pitching in for a share of Saturday matches.

Proud Widley carried on at Church Field, cutting their own grass and preparing their own wickets. Low scores were still the norm, typified by Widley's total of 74 in May 1953 - they defeated Leigh Park by twenty runs! Away from Church Field, scores were no better. Cowplain scored 49 in August, Kingsley Daniels and Trevor Harfield sharing all ten wickets, but Widley could muster only 30 in reply. The beaten team that Saturday comprised Trevor Harfield, Billy Daniels, Kingsley Daniels, K Hudson, J Mahoney, Charlie Perkins, Dave Cleeve, Vernon Hunt, R Bailey, Denny Daniels, and Roly Hall.

Good use was made of official stationery. His Majesty would have approved!

Matters Of The Moment

On November 25th 1953 John Harfield chaired Widley's AGM and congratulated Doug Hall on heading the batting averages and Kingsley Daniels on topping the bowling. Weighty discussion centred on the playing area at Church Field. The square required much attention and the batting strips produced uneven bounce. Some deliveries didn't bounce at all!

A matting wicket was proposed but opinion was divided; and there was only £12 8s 6d in the kitty. They decided to carry on with grass. Bullying the motor mower to work better was essential; £7 9s 9d had already been spent and the iron clodhopper was still farting and failing. To cheers all round, Peter Batley said he would sort it out.

Ch...Ch...Ch...Changes

1954 season hove into view. There was a full quota of Saturday and Sunday matches, mostly against neighbouring villages. League cricket was on no-one's agenda, although it was tiptoeing onto the summer stage over the Hill, where a Portsmouth & District Cricket Association established three divisions.

The Harfields still had a significant presence in Widley CC's hierarchy, but founder member Trevor was edging away from the limelight. He had become overburdened with commitments and ultimately opted for a quieter playing life, joining his pal Rube Stallard in the ranks of Cormorants CC downtown. He still turned out for Widley now and then (and Purbrook too) but relinquished all administrative duties.

1954 bobbined along. Kingsley Daniels took seven for thirteen as Cottons were dismissed for 44. Such a pity that Widley amassed just 25. In July Widley turned the tables, scoring 74 (Cleeve 27), before Cottons lost the thread and were all out for 30 (Kingsley Daniels four for seventeen and guest Trevor Harfield four for eight).

In August Vic Grant weighed in with seven for 30 against Cowplain who totalled 53. Widley replied with 30. The following weekend Widley amassed 63 against Good Intent's 44, and then 30 in reply to Bedhampton's 91 (Hall five for 40). Sometimes matches were over so quickly that tea was taken after the game had finished.

The cracks in Widley's edifice were widening. Players come and go at every cricket club, but good administrators are vital to a club's success and Trevor Harfield was a hard act to follow. Now, to a large degree the fate and future of Widley CC passed into the willing hands of Cyril Sparrow from Cowplain. Throughout 1955 season batting continued to be Widley's downfall. At Church Field in July, rivals Bedhampton whittled the home side out for 37, winning by 90 runs. Low scores were happening all too frequently.

Fading Away

Through the remaining five years of the 1950s Widley CC battled on, although their star was on the wane. They found it tough when key bowler Kingsley Daniels joined neighbouring Purbrook – his teammate Doug Hall was already there. The magnet of a well appointed Heath only five minutes up the road made it hard for Widley to bring in new recruits. And there were three clubs vying for players: Purbrook, Christ Church, and Widley, whereas in the years of Purbrook's exile at South Africa Lodge, Widley had been the only team playing locally.

In 1957, 1958 and 1959, scoring runs continued to be Widley's Achilles heel, especially at Church Field. The home games against regular opponents Cowplain are typical examples. In May '57, Cowplain reached 96 (Vic Grant five for 28) but Widley folded for just 38. In August the following year Cowplain scored 104, and Widley were bowled out for 31. In May '59 Cowplain had another field day, amassing 186 (Ray Cleeve five for 56). Widley tottered to 53.

Perhaps the lowest point was reached in a twelve-a-side match with Mariners at the end of May '59. Selby took five for 32 as Mariners reached 105, but Widley folded for only 23. No Widley batsman reached double

The make-up of soil around Widley Farm is complex. Conditions are ripe for this pond to thrive nearby

figures and the last six batsmen failed to score a run between them.

It was hard to take. The team that reached 125 against Horndean's 173 (Ray Cleeve six for 52) in August '59 included but two survivors from the August team of six years before. The 1959 line-up was: Roger Flake, Fields, Ray Cleeve, Denny Daniels, Alan Day, M Oldman, R Oldman, Hayday, Bottom, Charlie Perkins and Tullett.

Roger Flake was one promising new recruit. He played for Denmead as a youngster, but joined brother-in-law Roger Rasell at Church Field. Opening batsman Flake lived in Fir Copse Road for a couple of years, and was a butcher at Cottons, down the road from The Leopard Inn.

Several players came up and over the Hill to play for Widley. Notable among these were Alan Day, and father and son Oldman. Their route to Church Field was up Portsdown Hill, and then a country stroll down Widley Lane among hedgerows, fields and birdsong. Church Field's rustic setting had a charm and aroma all its own. Upkeep was still in the dutiful hands of the Widley Lane clan. By the end of the 1950s a few players had graduated to car ownership, and there was just room to park a car or two by the oak tree. Arrive in style, hop over the stile, play with style (hopefully).

The first season of the Swinging 60s was now in session. But if Widley's bats were swinging, they weren't connecting. In June 1960 they were crushed by 178 runs by Mariners, who sailed to 227. Widley limped to 49. At Horndean in August, a desperately low-scoring affair was stretched to two innings in an attempt to make the game last beyond 4 o'clock. Horndean limped to seventeen and 55, then Widley wimped to 26 and eight. Roger Rasell took ten wickets for 26 in the match and ended up on the losing side!

Rasell and Day took plenty of wickets in '61, although more games were lost than won. When Shipfitters laudably reached 154 for four in August, Widley responded bravely with 130. Incredibly good totals for Church Field, especially as the local press described the wicket as "boisterous."

Widley's administration was all of a crumble now. The centre of the club's universe was shifting, a pub in Cosham serving as their HQ more often than the homely hostelries of Purbrook. Widley CC was functioning much more informally, with matters frequently decided on the hoof. Twenty three-year-old Roger Flake topped the batting averages and was asked whether he would prefer a memento or a few pints. He opted for the pints.

The End Of The Affair

The Club clawed their way through 1962 season, but the assembled throng decided to call it a day at the pub, when no-one was willing or able to run Widley CC's affairs. Age and effort had wearied the members and there was nobody to grab hold of the reins. The last record of Widley Cricket Club appeared in the local press on July 13th 1962.

It read: "At Widley on Sunday high scores were not forthcoming and only three batsmen on each side reached double figures. Shedfield 95; Widley 88. Widley: Hunt, Flake, Day, Rasell, Cleeve, Holland, Harry, Button, Atkinson, Petley, Sprake."

Back in August 1947 one line in the local journal announced Widley's debut. Fifteen years later, four lines signalled their finale. A quiet end for this friends-and-neighbours club from Widley Lane. Their star had burned out.

Chapter 19

A Vicarious Pursuit

Frank Worwood was a cricket nut. He was also Vicar of Christ Church, Portsdown from 1948 until 1961. During the first summers of the 1950s, after giving due attention to pastoral duties the effervescent Canon turned his thoughts to a rump of clerical-collared cricket keenies who worked in the Portsmouth diocese. He set about inspiring this hallelujah chorus to blanco up their boots, dust down their cream flannels and transform themselves into a sporting collective known as The Bishop of Portsmouth's XI.

Expanding The Boundaries

The Bishop of Portsmouth's XI played sporadic midweek matches, often against other men of the cloth such as Chichester Cathedral XI. Organiser Worwood had to think on his feet. Last minute withdrawals came with the territory.

"Sorry Frank, can't make it, I've got a funeral to do," was typical. The Canon became adept at eleventh hour bolstering of the Bishop's team with a sprinkling of laymen, like Stan the Guild Secretary or Norman the builder.

With the Bishop's XI ticking over, the Christ Church Canon shifted closer to home. He began organising matches under the Christ Church cloak, gathering players from the parish who either didn't play for a club or could be persuaded to turn out for one grand epilogue. Midweek matches were arranged against Price's School at Fareham or the Navy team from Whale Island. Now and then a Saturday game was undertaken, one of the first being against Widley at their new Church Field venue.

From his manse on top of Portsdown, Vicar Worwood enjoyed a peerless view over chalk downs to the battleship-grey city below, and way beyond that to the Isle of Wight. Despite this favoured canvas it was often the sound of lads playing football on the flat hilltop in front of the Vicarage that fired his enthusiasm. On occasion, he would break off preparation of Sunday's sermon and dash over to join in. Sleeves rolled up, dog collar hanging loose, the Vicar played to win.

So it was with his cricket team, his infectious spirit carrying the day. But despite all this gung-ho endeavour, the ambitions of Christ Church Cricket XI might have been blunted then and there had it not been for a verdant little miracle one mile down the road. A new cricket ground was being hewn out of the soil on Purbrook Common, and the Christ Church visionary saw this as manna from heaven.

Let's Go Clubbing

Canon Worwood was used to facilitating meetings, but the one he presided over on Wednesday January 21st 1953 afforded him special pleasure. At this gathering, parishioners made the decision to form Christ Church Cricket Club. Frank Worwood's plan was to play regular Saturday matches with the team selected primarily from the congregation.

The Vicar was voted in as President, Stan Baynham as Chairman, Roy Searle as Secretary, T Mighell as Treasurer, and Messrs Burlay, Batty and Asley as Committee members. Application was made to the Urban

Christ Church
Portsdown,
where it all
began

District Council for an allocation of matches at Purbrook Heath, the Vicar using his influence to good effect. Secretary Roy Searle was the catalyst in arranging fixtures; he was the best cricketer and knew the local scene. In their initial press release, Christ Church felt confident that they "could prove a successful rival to the older (Purbrook) Club."

Purbrook CC were not sure what to make of these gatecrashers. Some welcomed them and some dismissed them as bible thumpers. But at least they would never book the ground on the Sabbath! The first Christ Church Captain was Norman Davies, with John Batty as Vice Captain.

The Council gave the new club a wad of Saturday matches at the Heath, and on June 20th 1953 Christ Church registered their first success with a convincing victory over Havant NALGO. The July parish magazine was suitably impressed – not surprising as Chairman Baynham wrote the adoration.

Stan Baynham and Roy Searle were crucial to the Club's wellbeing. Chairman Stan and his wife Kath had moved to Widley from north London in 1948, having already lived in Cosham between 1938 and 1941. Stan, Kath and family (John, Jan and Mary) were residents of Hillside Avenue, five minutes from the church. Kath was destined to supervise Christ Church's catering for many glorious summers, while son John, a sharp bowler and even sharper fielder, would soon become a regular in the team.

Roy Searle lived less than a mile from Stan in Serpentine Road, Purbrook. Schoolmaster Roy was a fine bowler in local cricket: windmill action, away-swing, plenty of wickets. He had a love affair with Senior Service ciggies; during bowling spells he would finish his over, retire to third man, light up, have a few puffs, place the fag packet neatly back in his pocket and be ready for the first ball from the other end.

The ritual seemed to work - he continued playing deep into his twilight zone. Fair minded, his mantra was discipline and respect. Young players called him "Mr Searle" and only if they played regularly did this graduate to "Roy." That's simply how it was.

Catering For Cricket Tastes

From 1953 the life and times of Christ Church CC clicked into gear, their new showpiece ground at Purbrook Heath shared with Purbrook CC. The two clubs tolerated each other but were never easy bedfellows. Their first pavilion was a basic wooden model, painted green with metal bits. It offered very little room in which to change, and the elemental cinder floor prohibited mincing about in bare feet.

Tea ladies valiantly used the same space as the players, so if Fred came in to strap his box on, tea ladies promptly exited stage front. Kath Baynham was practical and prepared her teas at home in Hillside Avenue. She then wheeled the food on the 20-minute walk to the Heath, with twins Jan and Mary in tow. Upon arrival teas were laid out, with gas bottle primed for heating water at Typhoo-time. The hut held few home comforts but there was a minuscule loo at the back – urinal only! Before too long the Council removed the hut to the far corner of the sports field, where the ribby ruin enjoyed a second innings as the groundsman's store. 'Twas better suited.

Seasons Of Mellow Fruitfulness

Christ Church's first seasons were blessed with hope. Players were settling in and Purbrook Heath was a great venue for a new club. Tea arrangements worked well with wives and girlfriends chipping in. The Saturday fixture list was full and both Whit Monday and August Bank Holiday Monday hosted matches. All this achievement was worthy of celebration and prior to their third season, 1955, Christ Church splashed out with a Dinner Dance. Seventeen days later came the Club's AGM – a reasonable attendance, but there were more people at the Dinner!

At the March 22nd AGM, President Worwood spoke of how far the Club had come in two years. Eighteen matches had been played in 1954, with seven wins, six losses, and five draws. For the approaching season, a shift behind the scenes saw SWP Martin elected Treasurer, with Lyn Ratsey stepping up to skipper the side.

Practice sessions expanded to two nights per week and catering touched a new peak - Whit Monday's fixture against Portsmouth NALGO commenced at 11.30am with "luncheon served at half past one." The parish magazine summed up succinctly: "Our cricket in 1955 was memorable."

Wet, Wet, Wet

The parish magazine maintained a honeyed theme towards cricket, its April 1956 edition describing Purbrook Heath as delightful. The Urban District Council thought so too. They dug out funds for a block and brick pavilion (pavilion number 2) to replace the shoddy shed. It wouldn't be ready for cricket in 1956 but construction was under way.

Season '56 turned out bad for weather, good for Christ Church. Roy Searle scalped 89 victims in the damp conditions and Skipper Ratsey topped the batting with 320 runs, averaging 23. In contrast, Canon Worwood was firing blanks. He played in a creditable sixteen games but had a top score of just eighteen against Denmead in May. He also took three for seventeen in the same match but managed a summer haul of only five wickets from 35 overs. The Christ Church statistics were fourteen wins, five losses and four draws.

Part Of The Furniture

Years 1957 to 1960 hosted unremarkable consolidation for Vicar Worwood's dream team. The Club's '57 record was similar to the previous

A stylish Bob Scantlebury with his wife in 1954, at daughter June's wedding. Bob was groundsman at Purbrook Heath for over 20 years

Picture courtesy of June Blythe

year, although batsmen struggled, even at well-tended Purbrook Heath. The June game at Buriton summed things up. Buriton totalled 53, Roy Searle swinging in with five for 25, with Paul Christopher claiming four for ten. The match was there for the taking but Christ Church crumpled for 33.

Revamped Purbrook Heath was now five seasons old, with a sturdy new pavilion and a solid full-time groundsman – Welshman Bob Scantlebury, who knew his onions. The table was settling and the outfield too, although down at grass roots the Common remained soft and squelchy.

Membership strengthened in 1958, '59 and '60, although results didn't keep pace and money was tight. Increased membership led to better attendances at Monday and Wednesday practice nights, and spirits were high. Frank Worwood reflected this in July's newsletter: "mixed success but much enjoyment." By the time the season's last ball had dug into the Heath's green top, a wet summer had produced a wonderless season.

The annual Dinner Dance was a close season highlight by now – more successful than the cricket some would say. Chairman Stan announced a posh new venue: The Bear Hotel at Havant. Tickets costing fourteen shillings for the November 19th bash could be purchased from Stan or from Secretary Roy Searle. "Both of us are on the telephone" added Stan....quite a bonus in 1960.

New Names, New Faces

Jim Holder completed his Army National Service in 1958. He'd been caught up in both Suez and Cyprus (EOKA) crises and was glad to get home. Football was his game and cricket had never been on Jim's radar. He began working at McMurdo with Christ Church wicketkeeper Arthur Moppett and during car journeys to and fro, Arthur enthused about the subtleties of the summer game.

The old stumper's yarns found a willing ear and, when Christ Church were short one Saturday, young Holder was dragged to the party. JR Holder was about to enter the promised land. He played his first match for Christ Church in 1961 at Hayling Park against Havant NALGO. If this was step one of Jim's three steps to heaven, step two followed immediately: an invitation to net practice.

Jim had been impressed by the poise of one of Christ Church's main players. The luminary in question was Paul Christopher, who never played for England but looked as though he might have done. His peppery bowling delivery came at the end of a long and winding run, oozing style over substance.

But this was outdone by one spectacular stroke in his batting armoury. He shouldered arms to balls outside off stump better than any man on planet Earth. Arms and bat would be extended high above his head, front pad thrust forward, with his entire body arched like a Sherwood Forester's longbow. This was by some measure the best shot in P J Christopher's repertoire and by its very nature it never earned him a single run! Nevertheless, when style guru Paul suggested nets to rookie Jim, he was on parade at 7pm sharp.

Step three for Jim was luring pal Tony Bonnington to Purbrook Heath's leather and willow wonderland. Tony knew no more about cricket than Jim, but he was good at ball games and fancied a dabble at something new. Wicketkeeping appealed to his extrovert nature, and very soon he had replaced ageing Arthur Moppett with the latter's blessing. Tony performed his keeping duties with a liberal dash of vaudeville, and there were no dull games at Christ Church when he was around.

Newcomers drifted in: some good, some not, but all willing. Colin Bench-Capon, Trevor Cole, Mike Emmerson, Roger Evans, Dick Farrell, Brian Gould, Phil Kille and Ken Fullalove were all new names on the scorecard. Ken also played for Portsmouth Chemists, and from their ranks he brought along Tony Dindar, Avi Muley and Moni Nijkar.

So many new faces, but Captain Roy Searle prodded this team of odds and sods into a reasonable outfit. Jim Holder cajoled workmate Douglas Doe into playing at the Heath, thereby bringing together three men (Stan Baynham, Jim and Doug) who would become the bedrock of a team as yet unborn: Portsdown CC.

The Good Old Bad Old Days

Team selection in the 1960s centred around 1) selection cards; 2) the telephone; and 3) car ownership. Roy Searle selected the team with a modicum of consultation. He posted a selection card to each player, although one or two exalted beings got the nod at the end of the previous game. Roy's fall-back option was the telephone, but not all players were on the dog & bone way back then.

The half-dozen car owners had a leg-up in the selection stakes, especially for matches away from Purbrook Heath. The point of embarkation was the slipway in front of Christ Church hall. Car owners waited for their charges to arrive, then whisked them off to village greens hither and thither. These magnificent men in their motoring machines were excused a match fee in return for chauffeuring duties.

The car with the biggest boot carried the Club bag. Hidden within the bag's cavernous crevices were an assortment of battered bats, canvas pads whose cream had crackered, pimpled batting gloves with rotted palms, distressed wicketkeeping gloves with withered webbing, heinous strap-on boxes, a dribbling bottle of horse liniment, muddy rolls of crepe bandage, mottled cricket balls, and stray buckles long since torn from their vestments.

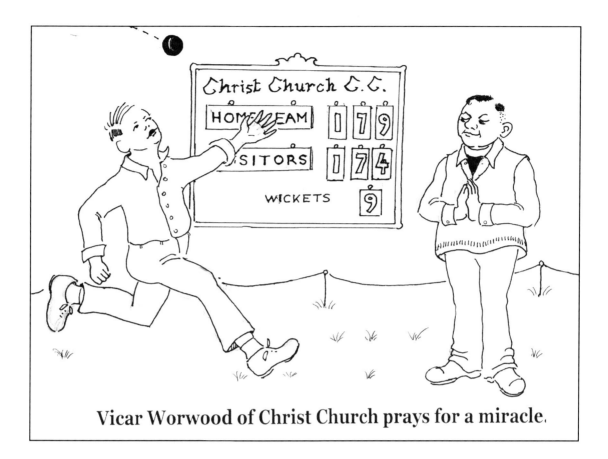

Vicar Worwood of Christ Church prays for a miracle.

As for the players, one or two owned a bat but most players raided the Club bag. A fair number of batsmen had boxes and jockstraps, but there were others who simply didn't bother. The only helmets on show were those paraded by the Lambretta luvvers as they scooted to matches. New balls were a precious item, their scarcity fostering a cottage industry polishing up old ones.

Players made do with a duffel bag for their vestiges of gear. Their possessions comprised cream flannels, white shirt (though rarely a pukka cricket shirt), sweater of doubtful provenance, much-darned socks, maybe a dusty cap with fraying peak, and leather or canvas boots that stretched right up to the ankles.

Matches started at 2.30pm with tea at five, and drinks breaks were unheard of. Bad pitches outnumbered good ones and scores were low; once batsmen six and seven were accounted for, the rest crumbled. Most clubs had pavilions - often without showers - but few teams had a bar. Post-match socialising took place in the pub down the road, with visitors expected to stay for several rounds of drinks in this pre "don't drink and drive" era. If the "away" team sloped off early, they risked a hole in their fixture list next season.

The Canon Goes Off

July 21st 1961 was a sad day for cricketers representing the homely church on the hill. Vicar Frank Worwood, the founder and heartbeat of the Club, had played his final game and was moving to Nottingham. He wrote a final epistle to his faithful parishioners:

"My dear Friends, this is the last letter I shall write to you as Vicar of Christ Church, Portsdown. Over thirteen years, each month has come round with its familiar pattern....as my days in Portsdown draw to a close....(I offer) thankfulness to God the Father that He brought us here from Battersea to be with you...."

And so the guiding light was dimmed. Christ Church CC would survive, but they would be a different club with different aspirations.

......And The Secretary Too

After Vicar Frank's departure, Roy Searle put in three more seasons of commitment before his pivotal association with Christ Church Cricket Club ended too, after a couple of seasons as Skipper. There had been grumbles over selection and one thing led to another. The AGM voted Doug Doe as Captain, which sparked Roy into a move to Purbrook for the 1965 season. Of the original three wise men (Worwood, Searle and Baynham), only Chairman Stan was left to follow the star.

A First Class Addition

The prevailing westerly blew in a star turn for the season of '65. His name was Andy Dindar and he was a class apart. The South African had caught the eye of Gloucestershire County Cricket Club, making his 1st XI debut for them in 1962. Serious misdemeanours caused his professional career to be brief, but in 1962 and 1963 he played seven first class matches with a top score of 55, taking three wickets for 25 in his one bowling spell.

His county appetiser was followed by a main course of porridge, but by 1965 he was back in the big wide world, looking for a new start down south. Dindar split his cricketing allegiance, turning out for Christ Church on Saturdays and South Hants on Sundays.

In June 1965 he made a tidy start for Christ Church, taking four wickets in a nine-wicket drubbing of Rowlands Castle. After that he nudged Christ Church to victories throughout the summer. In a succession of low team totals, his batting scores were sufficient to ensure that games were won. At the Heath in August, he pumped the throttle, taking nine Purbrook wickets for 45. Christ Church had totalled 143 and went on to win the local derby by 26 runs.

1966 – Don't Think It's All Over

Christ Church played some stirring stuff during the World Cup-winning summer of '66. Ken Fullalove took plenty of wickets, as did fellow seam bowler Avi Muley, whilst Moni Nijkar weighed in with useful runs. Others played their part too, but Andy Dindar was on top of the heap. From May through to August Christ Church claimed the scalps of Compton, Lavant, King Alfred's College, Bishops Waltham, and a host of others. Ordnance Survey and Old Portsmuthians were not so compliant and Christ Church scrambled draws in both matches.

One of the season's tougher games came at the Heath against Yorkshire Nomads on June 2nd. The home team comprised: Dindar, Muley, M Nijkar, Connolly, A Nijkar, Graham, Emmerson, Richards, Bonnington, Fullalove and John Baynham. In village cricket terms Yorkshire Nomads were a strong outfit, but Dindar dominated with 92 out of 180, following this up with three for 36 as Nomads forced a draw, scoring 138 for six. The

Christ Church on their travels in 1962.
Back row:
Phil Kille,
Roy Searle,
Dave Martin,
Moni Nijkar,
Mike Emmerson,
Brian Scarth,
Stan Baynham.
Middle row:
Jim Holder, Colin Bench-Capon,
Tony Bonnington,
Dave Nicholson.
Front row:
Avi Muley,
Paul Christopher,
Ken Fullalove

bubble finally burst in August, after 39 games stretching back two seasons. A Portsmouth & District XI did the damage, scoring 180 at the Heath and then humbling Christ Church for 145. Even in defeat Dindar scored 74.

Success brought more recruits and a 2nd XI was launched, captained by Douglas H Doe. It was a role that suited him admirably, especially with Jim Holder as his aide de camp. Doug's marauders didn't win too often, but they had a great time coming second.

One significant ripple on the surface of Christ Church's pond happened at Bishops Waltham on July 14th 1966. The significance wasn't that Dindar took six for 22 and Muley four for sixteen, nor that Christ Church won by a comfortable 69 runs. This ripple had a far greater impact: the Club played their match on a Sunday....the writing was on the wall.

Cricket All Day Every Day

For the time being, the Christ Church garden continued to be rosy. In August 1967 Club elders organised Purbrook Heath's first Cricket Week. It ran from Monday the 7th to Friday the 11th and enabled the Club to invite guest players. In the years that followed, many promising young cricketers fell for the seduction of Cricket Week.

The potion was irresistible: first enjoy a good bat or bowl, then enjoy being wined and dined, and finally enjoy being Dugg'd and Jimm'd by those recruitment master blasters Doe and Holder. Game over; just sign on the dotted line!

Cricket Week matches began at 11.30am, with an expansive lunch served at half past one. Opponents in that first week were: HMS Collingwood; Bobbington Court; SMP Richards' XI; Old Tenisonians; and an England Women's XI who scrapped hard, losing by 184 to 117. This "international" match was a coup for organiser Steve Richards, attracting 200 spectators and much publicity.

Cricket Week continued for 35 years at Purbrook Heath, easily outlasting the Club that spawned it. 1967 opponents Old Tenisonians (Surrey Unicorns) included Purbrook Heath in their tour itinerary for 30 years, and Old Hertfordians lasted nearly as long.

New Tricks, New Treats

The cricketing stock was improving. Accomplished opening bat Don Rock joined up, and Doug Doe trapped a cracking recruit in his spider's web when a young pro footballer strolled to Purbrook Heath one lazy Sunday. Bob Smith had been part of manager Freddie Cox's football coterie that took him from Bournemouth to Pompey to Gillingham.

At the end of it all he and Trissie came to live in Widley. Sherlock Doe's investigations very quickly uncovered a five-star wicketkeeper, and by the following weekend Bob was in harness behind the stumps.

By this time veteran Chick Thresher was twirling his generous moustache plus his slow left-armers for Christ Church rather than Purbrook, and the team sheet versus King Alfred's Winchester was: Steve Richards, Bob Smith, David Younghusband, Day, Phil Aston, Chick Thresher, David Nicholson, Steve Pierce, Nick Snelling, John Mackney and Ken Fullalove. The new breed didn't cash in straight-away; King Alfred's modestly totalled 111, but Christ Church succumbed for a meagre 37.

From Triumph To Disaster

In 1968 Captain and Secretary Steve Richards presided over a comfortable summer. The August Cricket Week roster included 38 Club members and 23 guests – recruiters Doe and Holder rubbed their hands. 55-year-

Christ Church at Purbrook Heath around 1968.
Back Row:
Ray Tiller, Steve Pierce, Doug Doe, Jim Holder, Don Rock, Ken Fullalove, Alan Exall
Front Row:
Only John Mackney second from the right, and captain Steve Richards in the centre have been identified!

old Chick Thresher was selected for all eight matches and by the end of the week was praying for rain! The season's low point was losing to Purbrook on August 17th. Christ Church were all out for 62 and Purbrook replied with 65 for two.

In the close season dark clouds gathered. Maybe the root of the problem harked back to 1961, when cricketing-Vicar Worwood left for Nottingham and Vicar CV Herbert replaced him at Portsdown Vicarage. Although the incumbent Vicar was President of the Club, the post had become notional. The Club's base was The Leopard Inn, the link with the pub now closer than their link with the church. The straw that broke the camel's back was Sunday cricket.

Christ Church CC had an initial Sunday dabble in 1966, following up with six Sunday games the next season and fifteen in 1968. Sunday cricket proved popular with players but didn't go down well with the Parochial Church Council, who voted heavily against it. They told the Club either to stop Sunday play or to alter their name. Vicar Herbert considered the link tenuous anyway, as the sole Cricket Club member attending Christ Church was Stan Baynham. A parting of the ways was inevitable. On December 5th 1968 the Hampshire Telegraph ran a front page feature:

"Bowled out by the Parochial Church Council."

And from the dawn of 1969 the Club started afresh as Portsdown Cricket Club. Vicar Herbert wished them well and Chairman Baynham commendably maintained loyalty to both Church and Cricket Club.

Even as the lid slammed shut on Christ Church CC's coffin, another problem sprang to life. Hanky panky involving players and girlfriends caused an abrupt haemorrhaging of cricketers. A manpower crisis resulted and the guardians of newborn Portsdown were left holding the baby.

In the lull before this Portsdown storm, spare a thought for Christ Church Cricket Club as it fades into the mist between hilltop and heath. Thanks for the memory.

Chapter 20

In A Different League

Stan Baynham started 1969 with that sinking feeling. He was up the creek without a paddle and when he called for all hands on deck, there were precious few survivors from Christ Church days. In the cold light of January, he was Chairman of a newly-constituted cricket club abruptly shorn of many tried-and-tested players. Rumpy pumpy had been the major cause of this hasty haemorrhage and the players involved, both innocent and guilty, were gone for good.

Apart from this athletic exodus, Stan's concern was the loss of administrators, so he took the bull by the horns and doubled up as Chairman and Secretary, with Ray Tilford supporting him as Treasurer.

The Survival Instinct

Income was vital for the nascent Club, and Treasurer Tilford set about hauling in as many annual subscriptions as possible. This didn't harvest a fortune, but it kept the cricketing bailiffs away. Annual subscriptions were £1 10s, and match fees were 3s 6d. All things considered, the outlook for Portsdown's first foray was pretty bleak. Money was tight, playing resources were threadbare and team spirit was muted as the early matches whispered into life.

Dire straits brought out the best in Chairman Stan. Survival meant fulfilling fixtures by getting eleven players onto the pitch each Saturday, and doing it all over again on Sunday. As for the preparatory stuff: confirming fixtures, booking pitches, arranging catering, sorting out travel and balls and stumps and umpire and scorer, plus collecting match fees – this was all concentrated in the hands of a thin band of stalwarts.

Unsurprisingly, Portsdown's first Sunday match saw them mauled by Crofton over at Stubbington. The home side soared to 161 for five but Portsdown plummeted to 28 all out. Stan's trim moustache teetered on a stiff upper lip as his Club struggled through the next month, although

John Mackney bowled well in a losing side against Knowle Hospital, taking six for 46. Portsdown were losing games, but at least they were managing to put two sides out every weekend and maybe, just maybe, they were through the worst.

The Only Way Is Up

On June 7th 1969 they hung out the flags and banged a gong. Portsdown won a game, beating Bedhampton's 143 for the loss of four wickets. Paul Christopher swashbuckled 39 and a young spark called John Austin ground out a priceless 67. It was a couple of years earlier that this same John Austin first dangled a stodgy bat between his lefthanded legs at Purbrook Heath, as a guest of Christ Church CC in a Cricket Week fixture.

From the start he displayed a unique style which he developed to exasperating effect over the next 25 seasons. His great assets were concentration and stickability. Opening the batting, he'd nudge and nurdle till the cows came home. If he didn't want to play a ball in that corridor of uncertainty, the demon dangler would simply withdraw his bat and dangle it limply between his pads. Effective, though not a thing of beauty, and you definitely won't find the stroke in any coaching manual. Doc Austin has the patent still pending.

Portsdown won their first silverware in 1971 – the Lord Mayor's Knockout competition. *Back row:* Jim Holder, Terry Carter, Russell Kyte, Derek Dyer, John Hawley, David Young-husband, Bob Smith, Nick Snelling *Front row:* Jon Floyd, Andy Cragg, John Bradley, Dick Farrell, Mike Hunter, Pete Elloway

This Austin & Christopher-inspired victory against Bedhampton signalled a glorious second half of June. Wins followed against Purbrook (newcomer John Jeffries took six for 42), Rowlands Castle (Paul Christopher five for 22), and Bognor (John Mackney six for six).

After that results cooled somewhat, before coming back to the boil against Portsmouth NALGO when Purbrook footballer Paul Walder (who played cricket at the Heath as a youngster and was now returning for a second bite) scored 70 in a total of 146 for seven. Bowlers Jeffries and Mackney polished off NALGO for 48.

Thus Portsdown took their first faltering steps on the cricketing stage. Treasurer Tilford kept finances on a tight rein and a refreshing number of new faces were reeled in. But there was still much to do.

Bailed Out

Like the River Pur, 1969 season flowed gently on, unspectacular apart from July's game against Bishops Waltham. This otherwise mundane village cricket match made the newspapers because it was Mr Askew's lucky day. The Bishops Waltham batsman was beaten by a ball that hit his wicket and lifted one bail. This awkward 10.95 centimetres of wood refused the call of gravity and instead fell back onto leg stump.

Despite indelicate coughing and wheezing by the Portsdown keeper, the bail refused to shift from its perch and the man in the white coat, after much scratching of lacquered quiff, ruled the batsman "Not Out." See Law 28 for confirmation. Crestfallen, Portsdown slid to defeat by 32 runs.

At the end of a back-to-basics season, Portsdown's slim hierarchy reviewed their first year which had begun in such disarray: "fixtures fulfilled; finances in the black; membership increasing; management committee dazed but undaunted." It could have been better, but it could have been an awful lot worse.

All Change Please

During the winter of '69/'70 Portsdown's committee room saw a whole lotta shakin' going on. Paul Christopher stepped up to become a stylish President and Doug Doe took guard as Secretary. Playing reinforcements were lining up thanks to the evangelism of Doug Doe, Jim Holder and Stan Baynham. They had already roped and branded one belligerent young batsman, Terry Carter, as Portsdown's next skipper.

Belligerence in batting is a positive trait and it became a recurring theme as batsman John Hawley signed on, followed by Derek Dyer. They both liked winning and were distinctly unimpressed with any other type of result. Young Hawley's batting had a sprinkling of stardust and he was a treat to watch. Des Dyer had several strings to his bow. He scored quickly, he was an up-your-nose opening bowler and a crafty close fielder. Whether batting, bowling or fielding, there wasn't much he couldn't do.

Another refreshing newcomer was John Bradley. At first glance he was a toff, a gentleman among players by virtue of the Persil-white cravat that topped off his cricket attire. But such pigeonholing was wide of the mark. From his jet black hair to his jet white boots he was a grinding, grunting seam bowler, his neckerchief simply an attempt to soak up the rash of sweat from his toil and torture. Much later, in his Saga years, John confessed that this sparkling cravat was nothing grander than a baby's muslin nappy.

"Unused!" he added, defensively.

Nappy days.

As counterweights to the creaking bones of senior statesmen Rock and Thresher, a clutch of bright youngsters enrolled, among them batsmen Mike Hunter and Jon Floyd, keeper Adey Voss and bowler Nick Snelling (engagingly monikered Nick Swelling and then Nick Smelling by

Portsdown's first season of Hampshire League cricket was in 1973. *Back row:* Stan Baynham, Bob Smith, Andy Cragg, Jon Floyd, Peter Bennett, John Hawley, Mike Hunter, Steve Sims (scorer); *Front row:* Mick Huntley, Derek Dyer, Russell Kyte, Dave Martin, Glen Ivett

successive editions of the local paper). Doug and Jim's recruitment wagon rolled on throughout 1970 – I was one who benefited from being corralled by Butch Cassidy & the Sundance Kid one sultry weekend. It's nice to be wanted.

The upshot of this trawl for new members was a change in fortunes. The Club attracted better players and enjoyed a highly successful season. Don Rock scored heavily, Carter and Hawley scattered fielders with heart-warming regularity, Derek Dyer marauded around gobbling up wickets and runs, and keeper Bob Smith had an heroic season with the gloves in his no nonsense manner. In a year, Portsdown moved from no-hopers to some-hopers.

1971 saw more of the same. It was still village cricket, although Portsdown's fixture list was gradually toughening up. Against their traditional opponents they were winning most games by a street. Portsmouth Rovers were dumped for 25; Rowlands Castle managed just 57; Bentalls at Kingston crept to 62, IBM reached 93, both Moneyfields and Compton tottered to 95; and so on. Sometimes the wheels came off – at Stansted Park in May, the pride of Portsdown collapsed to 51 all out and were trounced by six wickets. Every dog has its day.

A significant newcomer to Portsdown in 1971 was Midlands lad Russell Kyte. After watching him bat for barely a minute in the nets, Jim Holder nodded: "He'll do for us." Fine all-rounder though Kytey was, what Portsdown didn't know in this era of friendly cricket was that his biggest contribution would stem from his experience of senior league cricket back home in Warwickshire.

The Beer Tent

In most respects Portsdown was the love child of Christ Church Cricket Club, and one much-valued heirloom was Cricket Week. The Beer Tent was the centre of Portsdown's August universe. All-day matches required all-day lubrication, so a marquee was hired and a temporary alcohol licence secured in cahoots with a Lovedean pub. With up to 30 lunches and 30 teas sold each day, the booze 'n' food facility kept Stan's cash register ringing merrily.

The marquee was large and stocks of booze were piled high. But you can't lock a beer tent at the end of the day, so Portsdown players doubled as nightwatchmen, a rota of sentries kipping in the marquee each night. Chick Thresher bagged the trestle table, scorer Steve Sims snoozed in his

Big but not
beautiful.
Pavilion number
3 began life
in 1975

van by the tent flap, and an unlucky few were blanketed on the floor.
John Mackney organised the card school, and midnight cigars and wine
became an occasional treat.

Another occasional treat for one married Club member was the opportunity for him to bonk his secretary on the bench seat of his company car,
parked a polite distance from the tent flap. Playing a second innings, he
was caught in the act by Chairman Baynham who was not amused. The
shamed Executive got a wigging, not because of his nocturnal nuzzling
but because he should have been guarding the beer!

Sleep was in short supply, not helped by August rainstorms coursing
through the sodden marquee. But such hardships added to the fun and
beer tent tales grew more fanciful with each passing year. Then suddenly,
in 1975, the frolics ended. A new pavilion of unexpected grandeur
appeared on the bank (pavilion number 3), complete with clubroom
and bar. No longer would a marquee be required for Cricket Week, no
longer would bouncers have to guard the booze. The Portsdown beer
tent sank into the mudheap of history.

Half A League Onward

In January 1972 there were stirrings in the valleys of Hampshire village
cricket. Proposals were in hand for a Hampshire Cricket League, incorporating county and regional divisions. For whatever reason, the new
league didn't begin in 1972 as planned and in the hiatus Portsdown

woke up to what was being organised. Their committee considered the options: they could remain in non-league cricket or they could join the bandwagon. Initially Chairman Baynham was in favour of retaining the status quo, but most players in the Club were young and ambitious and wanted the buzz that a league format would provide.

Democracy ruled and the Club applied to join the Hampshire League for its inaugural 1973 season. County Division 1 was already sealed down, however, and Portsdown – to their immense frustration ('cos they were not a patient bunch) – were deposited in County Division 2 along with Purbrook.

Go Forth And Come 4th

Russell Kyte was a shoo-in as Captain for the first league season of 1973, and Portsdown fared well, winning eight and losing five. At the end of the season the top four teams were Lymington, Petersfield, Tichborne Park and Portsdown. John Hawley came fourth in the League batting averages (43.33) and Des Dyer also featured. Skipper Kyte came third in the bowling with Andy Cragg a fistful of places below him.

The top four teams were promoted to Division 1 for 1974 season. Chairman Baynham realised that league cricket was the shape of things to come and manoeuvred himself onto the League Committee for 1974. If you can't beat 'em, join 'em.

John Austin and Bob Smith watch Petersfield's Bob Pullin nudge another run (Hampshire League mid 70s). *Picture courtesy of The News, Portsmouth*

Seasons 1974 to 1977 were good for Portsdown. The Club had by now attracted a rich seam of bowlers including Peter Bennett, Alan Brown, Mike Turner, and Dave Martin who returned from the wilderness. New to the area was Keith Storey (younger sibling of Surrey's Stuart Storey), whose talent for leg spin seemed worthy of the County circuit. Only a diffident temperament sold him short. Capable batsmen had joined too – Mick Huntley, Glen Ivett, Terry Stallard, and Terry Heywood among them.

An added bonus was the development of a young off-spinner named Kelvan Finch. He picked up good habits at Portsdown and learned a few bad ones too. There was an abrasive air about the team which umpires didn't take to. Although Skipper Kyte always kept the lid on things, sometimes opposing Clubs took umbrage.

One encounter with Follands was a case in point. A legitimate short ball felled their opening batsman and, as he lay crumpled on the deck, the non-striker (Follands' best bat) strode urgently up the pitch to check on his mate's health. Ever alert, Des Dyer nipped in and ran him out. All's fair in love and war.

The Best Of Times

Portsdown's dressing room had a spirited, humorous edge, league cricket acting like a drug. County Division 1 placings were commendable: in consecutive seasons from 1974 Portsdown came third, fourth, ninth and sixth. Captain Kyte was indisputably the boss and troops rallied to his call. Des Dyer took 46 league wickets in the summer of 1974 and Andy Cragg claimed 100 wickets in the two seasons that followed (56 in '75 and 44 in '76). They owed much to the catching talents of keeper Bob Smith and first slip John Austin.

Mike Turner switched from Follands in 1975 and would become Portsdown's most dependable bowler, but it was with his paddle of a bat that he put a dent in the Surrey League Representative XI in 1976. Paddling at number ten for the Hampshire Cricket League, he scythed and hoicked ten fours in a riotous 63, having previously taken four Surrey wickets for 76.

A week later another Portsdown recruit, irrepressible Terry Heywood, smote 105 for the Hampshire League against Hampshire 2nd XI at the County Ground Southampton. Mike Turner took five for 68 in the same (drawn) match. Also featuring in Hampshire League Rep matches that year were John Austin, Des Dyer, Bob Smith and slip-of-a-lad Kelvan Finch. The villagers of Portsdown CC were starting to perform on a bigger stage.

Over The Top

Around this time Chairman Baynham staked a claim for "legend in his own leaguetime." Arriving for a match at Purbrook Heath with no time to spare, Stan parked his sturdy Hillman on top of the grass bank overlooking the pitch.

Mindful of pre-match umpiring duties, he loped off towards the pavilion leaving wife Kath in the passenger seat. But in lurching from the motor Stan unknowingly disengaged the handbrake and, with gearbox in neutral and Stan attending to matters elsewhere, the car began to inch towards the precipice.

The imperious saloon crunched through a concrete post, split three metal rails and plunged over the 60 degree bank. The nosediving vehicle stayed upright and kept rolling. In the manner of third man moving in to cut off a second run, the Minx headed towards the Square with Kath clinging on inside.

"Give me a brake, Stan!"

Eventually the motor rock 'n' rolled to a halt. The onrushing Portsdown posse, including contrite Chairman Stan, found a roughed-up Mrs Baynham none the worse for her skydive. In the line of duty she walked off to help diligent Mary Holder with cricket teas as usual. The Hillman, bruised but unbowed, was driven away for more adventures with Stan.

Quick, Quick, Slow

It was in this same epoch that Portsdown Cricket Week reached its zenith. All-day games were much coveted - obdurate opener John Austin felt free to jettison all dastardly thoughts of attack while, at the heavy metal end of the batting spectrum, Terry Heywood could welly the ball around the park as opposition bowlers toiled through a long day.

One Wednesday versus Old Tenisonians, Terry crashed and banged his way into the 90s, at which point he "went delicate," intent on nudging gently towards his ton. For several overs Terry paddled and poked to no effect whatsoever. Runs dried up so completely that the acerbic Tenisonians' skipper – now wholly unemployed down at deep long-on - could bear this painful exhibition of dab and tickle no longer.

"Oh for Christ's sake," he hollered in exasperation, "switch him back to SLOG!"

The entreaty worked. Terence smacked the next ball high over the stream and everyone lived happily ever after.

That Sinking Feeling

On the face of it, 1977 was another progressive year for Portsdown. They finished sixth out of eighteen in County Division 1, introduced a 2nd XI to the Hampshire League South East Division (captained by ex-Waterlooville veteran Ricky Travis), undertook a Midlands tour against some serious opposition, and joined a Colts League that included Gosport and Havant.

On the home front, the Heath's spacious new Pavilion was two years old and had bedded in. With extensive changing rooms, tearoom, clubroom and bar, it seemed light years away from its predecessors. On the debit side, the roof leaked and there was mould on the ceiling!

And then the roof fell in. Not literally, but in terms of Portsdown's ambitions. The moribund Southern Cricket League decided to get their

Portsdown take the field, circa 1976. Derek Dyer, Bob Smith, Russell Kyte, John Austin, Adey Voss, Andy Cragg, Terry Stallard, Mike Turner, Jake Cable

act together and modernise. Still undeniably the home of Hampshire's leading dozen clubs, word seeped out that they might invite leading Hampshire League clubs to join them.

Portsdown considered themselves well placed to benefit and were shell-shocked when Hythe & Dibden, Lymington, New Milton and Petersfield received the call to join the Southern League for 1978. After all, Portsdown had finished 1977 season above both Hythe & Dibden and Lymington. But entry was by invitation and there could be no appeal. Unlike the anointed four, Portsdown was neither town nor village – it was a hazy, undefined district that just happened to have a cricket team.

For the dejected Portsdown troops, normal service resumed for 1978. Kyte remained Captain, Turner became Secretary, and veteran Holder skippered the 2nd XI. But below decks Portsdown's hull was grinding against icebergs. A dribble of players walked the plank to join Southern League clubs and others were about to abandon ship. Portsdown did well to finish ninth.

In 1979 Captain Kyte upped sticks to pursue Southern League cricket with Deanery (after a short, ill-fated spell at Waterlooville). Des Dyer was there too; playing at the County Ground Northlands Road was an obvious attraction for both of them. Mike Turner took on the Portsdown captaincy but Portsdown players knew that County Division 1 (shorn of four major clubs) was now a diminished league.

The Grand Tour

It was not all gloom at Portsdown though. Summer tours were a bright feature through the mid '70s and early '80s. Wherever the tour was based, Chairman Baynham knew a devilish short-cut and many gullible drivers followed his dodgy directions. Stan was an enthusiastic organiser and loved every moment. He knew the best routes and booked the best accommodation. One stroke of genius saw him book Portsdown's pint-swillers into the Carfax at Bath in 1979. It was a temperance hotel!

Tours went far and wide: South Wales, the Midlands, Somerset, and Devon. The Somerset itinerary included Wells, Keynsham, Midsomer Norton and Yeovil, and cavalier John Hawley hit form in the Keynsham game, repeatedly belting the ball into Mr Grumpy's garden until the enraged householder refused to give it back. Portsdown's affronted batsman brusquely advised Mr Grumpy where he could stick the next ball that sailed over his privet hedge!

A penchant for touring spread through the Club. Doug Doe welcomed Southsea solicitor Nick Lang to his Colts' management team and together they took Portsdown Colts to a higher plane, running Under-

Portsdown missed Derek Dyer's close fielding when he joined Deanery. This smart catch nicks a wicket for Peter Bennett, bowling from the stream end

15 and Under-17 teams. Nick, ever enthusiastic for his protegés, broadened their cricket horizons with a '79 tour to Lancashire. He repeated the expedition the following summer, and trumped this with tours to the Midlands in 1981, Yorkshire in '82, Kent in '83 (following the merger with Purbrook), Lancashire again in '84, and finally Yorkshire in 1985. Lawyer Lang loved his tours; so did his Colts.

The End Is Nigh

At the end of the '70s, Portsdown's prognosis didn't appear terminal. League positions from '79 to '81 were healthy: third, sixth and fifth. Opener John Austin ground out 400 league runs consistently, Mike Turner captured around 40 league wickets most summers, and Terry Heywood (46 wickets in 1981) was dangerous with bat and ball.

Behind the stumps keeper Bob Smith cleaned up and, when he wasn't around, Adey Voss was neat and tidy. Also handy was Vossy's temperamental batting. With heavy blade in hand he could make mincemeat of thoughtful field settings – lofted off drives had a habit of soaring far and wide over mid wicket, causing captains to sob uncontrollably whilst ditching coaching manuals in the bin.

County Division 1 took another dip in strength when Alton clambered up to the Southern League after the 1979 season. Portsdown wanted the same escape route for themselves....so their committee formed a subcommittee! They were charged with recommending ways to move the Club onwards and upwards and into the Southern League.

The four just men included businessman and greyhound-racer Vic Brooks who knew a thing or two, and Roger Clarke who had the best job in the Royal Navy. He boffined away in the heart of the South Downs at HMS Mercury, and on midweek summer afternoons he played cricket for United Services – just part of the job! Nice work if you can get it.

The sub-committee recommended amalgamation with Purbrook CC, an idea first mooted back in 1975. The plan was to preserve Portsdown's County Division 1 status and make Purbrook Heath the home of one club. It would also boost Purbrook who were languishing in regional South East Division 1. On April 9th 1979 Portsdown CC wrote to neighbours Purbrook:

"If your club were interested in a possible merger, we would suggest a meeting is arranged between our sub-committee and representatives of your club."

Mergers are never simple matters. There are positions to protect and clubs fear a loss of identity. At the Heath progress was slow, but in the cold light of day both committees recognised the advantages of having one club with several teams.

"Amalgamate Mate"

Following league placings of third, sixth and fifth, Portsdown's star descended alarmingly in 1982 when they finished thirteenth out of eighteen. Their 2nd XI also finished thirteenth in South East Division 2. Neighbours Purbrook were suffering too; they finished bottom of South East Division 1.

In November 1982 three years of intermittent negotiation paid off and Portsdown threw in their lot with neighbours Purbrook. To protect sensitivities and maintain Division 1 league status, the merged Club was called Purbrook & Portsdown, with every intention that this would be simplified to Purbrook Cricket Club in time. Everyone knew it made sense.

Portsdown held a happy but soggy reunion in 2007. It was 30 years since this group last played together
Standing:
Paul Walder,
Dave Martin,
John Bradley,
John Austin,
Mike Turner,
Bob Smith,
Derek Dyer,
Terry Heywood,
Russell Kyte,
Kelvan Finch,
Roger Clarke
Kneeling:
Andy Cragg,
Mark Smith

Chapter 21

From Here To Fraternity

By the 1950s cricket is much changed from the sport that sponsored the birth of Lord's Cricket Ground in 1814 and humble Purbrook Heath around 1815. In those 19th century days the gentry organised both game and players but now, in mid 20th century, village cricketers run their own sporting affairs. And with a posh new ground from 1953 and a prissy new single storey brick pavilion a few years later, "Purbrook have never had it so good," as Prime Minister Harold Macmillan so very nearly said.

Yet despite their splendid surroundings, the cricket club are suffering an identity crisis. Sometimes they are called Purbrook and Widley, sometimes they are Widley and Purbrook, and sometimes they are plain and simple Purbrook. Adding to the confusion another club, Widley CC, exist too and play nearby at Church Field. So if Widley and Purbrook play Widley at Purbrook, and Purbrook and Widley beat Widley, readers of the local sports pages have no idea who the hell has beaten whom!

Bring 'em On!

Purbrook's fixture list was mostly bread and dripping with little in the way of scones and jam. Opponents included the respectable villages of Bedhampton, Cowplain, Denmead, Finchdean and Hawkley, plus the diverse attractions of Civil Service, Co-op, Mayles, Palmer Sports, Portsmouth Banks, Red Company and Twilfits. Homage was paid to the cuddly new NHS by including fixtures against St Mary's Hospital and St James' Casuals.

Locally the balance of power had shifted – Waterlooville CC were a mere 50 years old, but already Purbrook's seasonal battles had been relegated to the Ville's 2nd XI fixture list. In 1955 Purbrook played them on consecutive weekends and narrowly won both encounters. In the first match Purbrook batsmen V and R Timms, Furlong, Small, Brown, Finch and Hall inched the visitors to 94 before bowlers Freddie

Furlong, Forsythe and Kingsley Daniels nipped Ville out for 90. Next weekend was similar – Lambert hit 26 in Purbrook's 93 and Ville were squeezed out for 82.

In May 1958 Portchester's total of 116 was described as "formidable" in the Hampshire Telegraph – how times change. Purbrook tiptoed to victory by one wicket. The team was Stan Doe, Chris Bazalgette, Chapman, Tony Wagg, Trevor Boulton, Kingsley Daniels, Doug Hall, Marsh, New, Favell and young Roger Boulton. Doug Hall scored 39 in his drover's pads, so called because with an extra bolster down the outside they resembled a cowboy's leathers.

Over at Havant the Urban District Council were measuring up sporting improvements for the Heath. £250 was included in capital estimates so that preparatory work could begin....tennis courts were in session and there would soon be a racket on the Common.

Lie Back And Think Of Cricket

The 1960s were unspectacular in Purbrook's camp, although these days they had to put up with interlopers Christ Church CC and there were inevitable player transfers between the clubs.

Typical of the cricket fare was a July 1960 game versus Portsmouth Rovers, played in bad light on a damp wicket. Chick Thresher (later of Portsdown) spun out seven batsmen for 50 as Rovers plodded to 123. Purbrook peered into the gloom after tea and squirted to 121 for seven at the close. The team was Freddie Furlong, Jack Wright, Mick Harfield, Tony Wagg, Beadle, Chick Thresher, Stevenson, Crocker and Cyril Kemp, plus two more who didn't make the score card.

The cricket club meandered on. They viewed the demise of Widley CC with tepid detachment, and they learned that Vicar Worwood of Christ Church CC was leaving in July '61 but it didn't break their hearts. More disturbing was the sudden death of teammate Trevor Boulton who collapsed at the Heath after batting against Portchester in May 1963. Son Roger was playing in the same game. A couple of weeks later, after the funeral, Roger returned to the Heath and spread his dad's ashes on the cricket square. It just seemed right.

Playing conditions on the new Common improved as the sports field settled down. Groundsman Bob Scantlebury bestrode his empire of green in paternal manner. Uniformed in blue denim dungarees, face beetrooted red by the midsummer sun, Bob cared about his square, protectively leaving the grass a shade long as he fashioned neat and tidy wickets. He cut and rolled the pitch on the morning of the match, and marked out boundaries last of all. For Sunday's game on a new track he would ensure Saturday's battered strip still looked in good order by sprinkling freshly-mown grass cuttings on the rough patches.

The Common's banked contours demanded a bespoke sightscreen with a top flap, lifted into place using a long pole. The scoreboard was austerity personified - a three foot square blackboard secured by a metal pole in the ground. Numbers for "Total" and "Wickets" slid into place on runners.

Pavilion number 2 at the top of the steps was an Aladdin's cave. Peering through the central door you espied two changing areas. The home room to the right was dominated by a wooden kit box in the middle that doubled up as the tea table. Venerated tea ladies served goodies through a hatch from their cramped Cell Block H kitchen round the back. Beyond the changing area was a loo and groundsman Bob's desk with pin board above. Showers were tucked in near the hatch from Cell Block H which had its own murky entrance at the rear of the building.

Purbrook at the end of the 1960s decade.
Back Row: Tom Jones, Peter Jones, Phil Sanders, Greg Carson, Brian Andreae, Guest;
Front Row: Roy Searle, Guest, John Burrell, Andy Ferrier, Steve Richards (ex Christ Church)

Tea And Cakes

Despite these underarm facilities, tea was much treasured. A large brown pot dispensed the brew. Displayed alongside on the kit box were cucumber sandwiches, scones and battenburg slices. There was a separate charge for tea – some players brought their own, so the overworked skipper had to tot up numbers and inform the tea ladies pronto. In respect of next weekend's matches, players ticked an Availability Book hanging by the door.

A subsequent line through your tick means you've been selected and notified. If you're not present, a card through your letterbox during the week will confirm. During matches, a chore in these hard-up times is rattling a collection box under the noses of spectators sunning themselves on the bank. Roy Searle (ex Christ Church) is especially good at this. He pauses for a chat at pressure points along the way and the dosh comes rolling in!

The snoozing summers slumber on. In June 1966 England noisily win the World Cup at Wembley and Purbrook (73) quietly beat Fareham United (67) at the Heath. Representing Purbrook are Jack Wright, Chapman, Ricketts, Chick Thresher, Dave Martin, John Beamish, Phil Sanders, Symonds, Nigel Lloyd, Fred White and Chris Millett. 1969 brings re-packaged cricketing neighbours – a butterfly called Portsdown emerges from the chrysalis of Christ Church....or is it a moth? Anyway, the first encounter follows in June: Steve Edge scores 36 in Purbrook's total of 107 but Portsdown edge in front with 108 for six.

The March Of Events

The approach of a new decade brought new faces. One was fresh-faced accountant John Burrell who bowled up, marked out his short run and started clipping off stump regularly, a gift that rarely left him in the next 25 years. Among JB's contemporaries were Derek White, Tim Durston and Steve Edge.

Along came batsman Greg Carson, who previously played for Christ Church when Ken Fullalove was skipper. Living at Copnor (and taking a season off), Greg watched Purbrook play an away fixture at Rugby Camp one Saturday. Roy Searle spotted him and slotted him. Greg played in Purbrook's next game, albeit batting at number nine! He learned a simple truth very early: "value your wicket." Throughout a long career, the maxim served him well.

Back at the Heath, it wasn't long before veteran Jack Wright (1958 to 1973) began relishing his batting partnerships with young Carson. Their 1971 encounter with Emsworth was typical. Pursuing a target of 157 Purbrook reached it for the loss of six wickets, Carson scoring 56 and Wright 34.

Pattering alongside events on the field were matters off it. The superb new setting of Purbrook Common was now two decades old and facilities were in need of a massage. In April 1972 a joint meeting of Purbrook CC and Portsdown CC resolved to seek help from the Council. Their wish list included practice nets, a heavy roller and a larger pavilion incorporating a clubroom.

Greg Carson and Jack Wright open the batting for Purbrook, circa 1970

But the Council's concerns were centred more on football than cricket, because the pavilion's two crunched-up changing rooms couldn't cope with four soccer teams muscling in to use them on Saturday afternoons. A further worry on the horizon was the impending retirement of long-time groundsman Bob Scantlebury (on duty since 1953). Replacement Pat Vincent had never maintained a cricket square and would have to learn as he trudged along.

Ups And Downs

The fresh-faced Hampshire Cricket League bounded onstage in 1973, putting a spring in Purbrook's step even though participation was costly. Happily, Purbrook's finances were shaping up....thanks to strip-tease nights. Organised by club members who knew about these things, vestal virgins were hired from a Leigh Park agency and zipped off to Purbrook's party venues by willing Club regulars. Duly ensconced (and following cricket tradition), the girls tossed up before opening their innings, bringing joy to the watching punters and to Purbrook's treasurer.

Like neighbours Portsdown, Purbrook were plonked into County Division 2 for their first taste of Hampshire League cricket in 1973. They finished a creditable seventh, with Bob Gillmore and Greg Carson featuring in the Division 2 batting averages. League cricket was different from the previous diet of friendly matches and Purbrook needed an astute captain to pull them through. For the onset of their League campaign Greg Carson was Purbrook's canny skipper, approaching every fixture with a game plan, and making sure he understood the Rules of Play from cover to cover. It was evident that captains of many other clubs didn't.

The club that shared the Heath, Portsdown, won promotion to Division 1 at the end of this inaugural season, which damaged Purbrook's ability to attract and retain players. By 1975 league cricket was proving tough and Purbrook finished sixteenth in a relegation slot. Phil Sanders was the one bright spark, finishing seventh in the bowling averages.

Portsdown Chairman Stan Baynham and Purbrook Chairman Brian Andreae celebrate the opening of Pavilion number 3 in 1975, in the company of the Mayor and Mayoress of Havant, Mr and Mrs Ken Berry

Big But Not Beautiful

1975 was a strange year: gloom on the pitch, grand designs off it. Pavilion number 2 at the top of the steps was relegated to a groundsman's hut and loo, and pavilion number 3 rose in red-brick angular vastness next door. On the positive side the two clubs (Purbrook and Portsdown) had a clubroom at last, for which they had to dig deep and contribute £1,500 each to Council coffers – it was touch and go, and revenue from striptease nights proved timely for Purbrook.

There were four changing rooms and a capacious shower room in the new building, plus a generous tearoom on the first floor. But on the negative side the front of the building was offset at an odd angle to the pitch, the huge veranda above the clubroom was isolated and rarely used, and two ill-sited public loos faced directly onto the cricket field.

Pavilioned in splendour possibly, but this Tricornesque edifice was an unsympathetic lump and no mistake. A shame, because it was an expensive statement of intent by the Council. Worst of all, the clubroom's flat roof began to leak almost as soon as the first pint was pulled, and never relented. Despite repairs, refurbs and even a false ceiling, nothing stopped the rot. Through 25 subsequent summers Purbrook's clubroom mouldered into manky decay. Finally, in 2002 the entire awkward pile was knocked down and carted away.

Bowling Along

In September 1975 a brief but seminal letter winged its way to Purbrook's committee from Portsdown chairman Stan Baynham. The topic was amalgamation, but the idea didn't get far. Newly elected Purbrook Secretary Brian Woolley was tasked with responding. (Brian, wife Maureen and sons Grant, Darren and Avan lived at Copse Close Widley, an appropriate address as BW was a policeman). His polite reply to Chairman Baynham on October 28th was along the lines: "thanks but no thanks!"

But by 1977 the outlook for Purbrook CC was cloudy, with their 1st XI competing in the same regional South East Division as Portsdown's 2nd XI. On the credit side, Secretary Woolley set up a Colts section and in 1978 the Under 13s played nineteen games, Under 15s played five, Under 16s played six and Under 17s played ten. Not bad for starters.

What about the adults, though? They held their own with league placings of ninth, seventh and eighth in 1978-80. Their bowlers tucked in

Purbrook visit Goodwood CC in 1978.
Back Row:
Vernon Delaney, Bob Jenkins, Bill Stenning, Richard Manning, Rube Stallard, Will Kimber, Les Rose;
Front Row:
Bob Gillmore, David Ullah, Brian Woolley, John Burrell, Mick Webb

and feasted: John Burrell (fourth in the 1979 averages) knocked over plenty of wickets thanks to a classic side-on action, and new broom Bob Jenkins proceeded to bowl a prodigious number of overs from the stream end for the next several seasons.

Bob was a man of many parts; the Job Experience section of his CV (if he had one) would include House Removals and Mobile Disc Jockey. His bowling partner John Burrell whispered recently that Bob was a good deal more mobile as a DJ than he ever was as a fielder!

In 1980 Purbrook's batting was boosted by the charismatic arrival of youthful veteran Peter de Cambra from Havant CC. He breezed in with 325 runs at an average of 36, displaying the deftest late cut this side of Georgetown Guyana. 1981 results went up a notch and Purbrook finished seventh in South East Division 1.

Bob Jenkins' in-duckers brought him 62 wickets including all ten for nineteen at Burridge, the first time this feat had been achieved in the Hampshire League. The same Zapata desperado churned out 222 league overs that summer....come September Bob was a foot shorter and his black moustache had drooped to ghosty white.

Biting The Bullet

Such steady improvement made 1982's stuttering performance hard to take; Purbrook dropped to eighteenth and last in South East Division 1. There were still decent cricketers in the ranks, but simply not enough of them. At the end of this depressing campaign, with relegation to the bottom tier about to become reality, the hitherto dormant amalgamation with Portsdown promised salvation. By November 1982 it had come to pass and Purbrook became "Purbrook & Portsdown." Fraternising with the enemy, and ultimately relieved to do so.

1970s & '80s opening bowler John Burrell ponders a 2010 comeback after buying this cheap bat on the internet. Ground attendant Malcolm Alford gives his verdict!

Chapter 22

The Good, The Bad & The Googly

Newly combined Purbrook & Portsdown overdosed on cricket in the summer of 1983. They had two Hampshire League teams and a 3rd XI playing friendlies, plus midweek and Sunday teams, and a full hand of Colts cricket.

Green Shoots Of Success

Results supported the wisdom of amalgamation: 1st XI sixth in County Division 1 and 2nd XI promoted from South East Division 2. Dave Martin had his best ever season with 40 Division 1 wickets, and claimed his best ever scalp playing for the Hampshire Cricket League against Hampshire County 2nd XI in August when he clean-bowled putative England superstar Robin Smith for 39. One ossified observer opined that young prodigy Smith was never the same again. The same Sanatogen'd spectator said that old campaigner Martin never fully recovered either!

In the South East Division 2 promotion side, Greg Carson scored heavily and youngster Mark Howe seared his way to the Division's highest individual score of 155. The Club's upbeat mood was enhanced by prodigal sons returning for a second helping of Purbrook Heath: Kelvan Finch rejoined after a successful Southern League sabbatical and Jon Floyd sniffed the country air once more. Jon was a spirited lefthander whose expansive cover drives were a joy. On his dodgy leg stump his swash might buckle, but overall he gave the 1st XI's batting plenty of zest.

The 1984 fare tasted even better. 1st XI fifth, 2nd XI promoted again and 3rd XI mid table in their first League foray. Before the lid shuts on the season, let's hear it for evergreen demon dangler John Austin who featured in five century partnerships in Division 1, involving Peter de Cambra, Jon Floyd and Kelvan Finch. Crowning a regal year, Roger Clarke skippered his 1st XI to victory in the Noel Fisher Memorial Trophy, beating Andover in the final. It felt good to be a Brookie.

Purbrook &
Portsdown 1st XI
1984.
Back Row:
Stan Baynham,
Paul Matthews,
Roger Clarke,
Ian Bath, Mike
Turner, Bob
Smith, Jon Floyd,
Mike Salmon
(scorer).
Front Row:
Kelvan Finch,
Mark Howe,
John Austin,
Peter de Cambra,
Derek Dyer

A Fall And A Record Haul

1985 was ordinary by comparison, all three League teams finishing in lower mid table. The 2nd XI's highlight in Division 3 was a first league ton (119) for whippersnapper Pete Yearworth (Jobsworth to his elders). In 1986 progress seized up: 1st XI relegated; 2nd XI relegated; 3rd XI fifteenth in South East Division 2. Playing strength had crumbled through old age and prodigals leaving because of jobs and families.

For the next two seasons the 1st XI wallowed in Division 2, despite the emergence of opening bowlers Graham McCoy (see later pages) and Paul Musselwhite – though Paul's stay was short. A product of manager Les Rose's Under-15 Colts, he graduated to the 1st XI in 1987 and promised a bright future. His bright future turned out to be 600 games between the sticks at Scunthorpe United, Port Vale and Hull City, but in a couple of good seasons for Purbrook he bowled with genuine zip despite his dibble-dobble run up.

Paul's parting gift was all ten for 32 in a friendly versus Civil Service... not civil at all! The Musselwhite moniker lived on, because nephew Wayne (only two years younger) took on the mantle when goalkeeper Paul headed north.

Purbrook waited until the summer of 1989 for the good times to roll. With a very young captain (Ian Limb), the new brooms swept clean. Paul Ancell, Mark Howe, Mike Seal, Graham McCoy and Wayne Musselwhite (plus veteran Austin) all made the League averages as they amassed a record haul of 303 points, bouncing back to Division 1.

Anticipation Of Precipitation

As counterpoint to League pressures Purbrook hosted Hampshire CCC in June 1991, supporting Mark Nicholas's benefit season. On a soggy day Nicholas foreshadowed his TV credentials with vignettes on the veranda, while Robin Smith hot-footed down from a victorious Test match, his car boot laden with alcoholic booty.

The crowd gathered, the bar brimmed and Hampshire's stars were ready to shine. Purbrook's Chunky McCoy had other ideas and took five meaty wickets, but downpours made a codpiece of the showpiece. They started but they didn't finish.

Magic Moments

Brian Robbins in his Hampshire days....and 50 years later flanked by batsman Sean Figgins and Secretary Brian Woolley at the Heath (2009)

Slicing off their Portsdown appendage for 1991, Purbrook's investment in Colts' cricket paid off as the youth of the '80s provided the backbone of the '90s. But the glister didn't turn to gold because players drained away to other clubs. Purbrook's lowest league slot in the decade (sixteenth) came early, in 1990, and their highest position

(fifth) followed in 1995 when Greg Carson took charge for a season.

There were four high spots en route: 1) in 1990 captain Ian Limb held eight outfield catches at home to Hartley Wintney and bowled out the remaining two batsmen for good measure; 2) three seasons later he penguin'd back to his mark and tweaked out nine Romsey batsmen for just 27 runs; 3) in 1995 openers Steve Parker and Colin Pay celebrated five century partnerships, their best a steepling 215; and 4) in 1996 Colin Pay scored bucketloads when he topped the Division 1 honours board with 592 runs, averaging 84.57.

At the start of the 1990s Chairman Ken Johnson used his recruiting skills, plus several pints of brown and mild, to lure ex Hampshire County spinner Brian Robbins (1958-1962) out of retirement for one last hurrah. Ditching pipe and slippers, "Colonel" Robbins enjoyed his revival so much that he carried on twirling into the new millennium, playing for the 1st, 2nd and 3rd teams. By the end his joints were tweaking more than his off breaks!

Overseas Aid

Throughout the '90s "nearly but not quite" summarised Purbrook's Hampshire League labours and the Management Committee sensed salvation in recruiting a quality overseas player. Initially the South Africans who answered this maiden's prayer were not good enough to make a difference, but in 1994 Purbrook cracked it with Barry de Waal who hit 484 lively runs.

The Club persevered with Overseas Aid but the solution sometimes worked and sometimes wobbled. Some imports were good, notably Martin Lazenby who scored 634 runs in 1998 and 580 the following summer, but one or two of the '90s foreign legion flattered to deceive and the costly exercise saw successive Treasurers diving for the Prozac.

As the club moved into the new millennium there's no doubt that South African players helped Purbrook's Southern League excursion, but there were pros and cons. If we asked Purbrook's committee for an umpire's decision on Overseas Aid, they might stick two fingers up rather than one!

Of The Female Persuasion

For three summers from 1996 the conservative tone of Purbrook's committee went a bit dulally. They fell for the charms of a group of ambitious female cricketers and Purbrook Women's XI were born. They were good too; competing in a league that included Andover, Brighton and Romsey, they won at the first attempt. Pat Ready and Kathy Adams provided their administrative backbone and batsman Marina Steele was their star player.

Though it's tempting to describe the interlude as perpetual wine, women and song, this wasn't the case. The females sensed zero interest in their matches from the rest of the club. They also had problems securing games at overused Purbrook Heath and most matches were played at Barton's Green or Emsworth. From the male perspective the women didn't support the clubroom, the bar or even the pavilion, preferring to use the Heath's grassy bank as their playing HQ.

Both male and female sections tried to forge closer links but in outlook and aspiration they remained worlds apart. For three seasons a courtship endured but there were irreconcilable differences. At the end of 1998 the Women's team decamped to Hambledon with a legitimate claim that they needed better facilities to progress. Nobody cried.

Draining Experiences

On a crystal June morning in 1998, long-serving Purbrook batsman Pete Martin motored to the Heath for a net practice with his pal. What they saw heathside stopped them in their tracks. A clunking great machine was gouging 100-yard-long drainage trenches across the entire eastern side of the outfield. The two cricketers stropped over to the lone contractor, only to be told matter-of-factly that Havant Borough had hired him...in the middle of the cricket season! He said that all 28 slits would be filled with sand and gravel by the end of the day and he'd be on his way.

For the rest of the summer wary outfielders felt like coconuts in a shy, and it was touch and go whether cricket could continue to be played on such a ploughed field. Common sense on the Common? Not that summer.

More issues crunched Purbrook firmly in the box in 1998. Mick Wainwright's good work running Colts' cricket ended, and replacement Angela Mansfield's brief spell in charge concluded too. The resulting vacuum meant that there was no Colts' cricket. Within a year Treasurer Duncan Garland valiantly resurrected the comatose Colts' section and the youngsters were on track once again. Along in the musty clubroom, Mel and Jane Snook quit running the bar and the Club were bailed out by ex skipper Mike Turner and wife Anita.

An unexpected testing of the amalgamation waters occurred in July 1999. It began as a fact-finding meeting between representatives of Waterlooville and Purbrook at The Woodpecker pub. A major sticking point was Purbrook's insistence that the Heath should be ground number one with Rowland's Avenue (Waterlooville Rec) being ground number two. Understandably this upset Ville's dyed-in-the-wool patrons and the initiative stuck in the crease. Little to gain and much to lose.

Someone Up There Likes Us

Purbrook CC had reasons to be cheerful in year 2000. The format of league cricket changed-up a gear with the birth of an ECB accredited Southern Premier League. Division 1 had ten teams as did Division 2, while Division 3 comprised eighteen teams including Purbrook. There was promotion and relegation, but progression depended not solely on results but also on having "the non-playing set-up suitable....." At last, 22 years after the Heath's other club, Portsdown, had been thwarted in their desire to join the original Southern League, the Heath's oldest club, Purbrook, made it to the new plateau.

The other reason to be cheerful was stunning. In early 2000 the Councillors and Officers at Havant Borough (clearly a wise bunch!) budgeted

Pavilion number 4 was completed in 2001 and officially opened in July 2002

for a swanky new sports pavilion to be built at the Heath, asking the Club for significant input into architect Parnell's final design. Birthday and Christmas rolled into one. The modern steel and brick structure (pavilion number 4) rose to maturity on the site of single storey pavilion number 2 at the top of the boundary steps, and was completed in August 2001.

All Hands To The Pump

Pavilion number 4 enjoyed spacious changing facilities plus clubroom, function room, balcony and electronic scoreboard, admitting to a final cost approaching £600,000. Purbrook finished 2001 season in their leaking 25-year-old pavilion next door, which was then demolished in the blink of an eye.

Roger Clarke, Keith Todd and Bob Smith took on the task of fitting out the new clubroom. When they first peered into this hulk of emptiness, there was an exposed metal girder holding up the roof, a shuttered balcony and not much else. Plans were drawn and favours sought. HMS Mercury and Cosham Police were raided for materials from their redundant social clubs and Club regulars came up trumps too; Andy Holder magicked up a forest of wood for bar fronts, shelves, work tops, battens and panels, and Alan Hellyer conjured up sparkling customised mirrors.

Old sea dogs Clarke and Todd and old firefighter Smith worked long hours sorting out the infrastructure, although whenever they paused for breath as mature men must, hind legs and donkeys became their sociable tea-break companions! The function room downstairs was furnished at a stroke thanks to the Coffee Pot in Rowlands Castle, whose owner was retiring after a long stint. Purbrook's Chairman salivated over a final lingering breakfast there before snaffling their tables and chairs for £100.

Purbrook swooned in the fresh surrounds of pavilion number 4 from the start of 2002 season. On July 12th in front of a sea of supporters, the notional red carpet was rolled out for a ceremonial opening by local Councillor Gwen Blackett. Havant MP David Willetts was guest of honour and made a generous speech....politically correct, naturally.

Electric Cricket

Graham McCoy had been captain for five of the ten summers in the 1990s, so it was fitting that he was in charge for Purbrook's first season (2000) in Division 3 of the new Southern Premier League. His team stepped up to finish fifth. South African Piet Botha totted up 442 runs and Mark Stanley's left arm swung profitably. He bowled even better the next year, topping the Divisional averages with 25 victims at 11.32. Once again Purbrook finished a creditable fifth in what was now a sponsored Southern Electric Premier League.

Replacing Jimmy Repsold for 2002 was a fellow South African who disarmingly promised the Chairman that he would win the division for Purbrook. Will Prozesky was as good as his word. Responding to wicketkeeper Alan Mengham's front foot captaincy, Prozesky thumped 988 runs in sixteen knocks, launching 113 fours and 40 sixes. He also broke four bats along the way! Purbrook won the Division 3 title, with major contributions from Billy Hunter (482 runs), Mark Stanley (30 wickets) and Graham McCoy (23 wickets). High jinks at the Heath!

Yo-Yo-Yo

Full of optimism for 2003, Purbrook's Division 2 bubble burst and they came tenth and last. Apart from Prozesky's 410 runs (and 25 wickets) no other batsman reached 200. Experienced Billy Hunter took the helm in 2004 and Purbrook finished comfortably in mid table back in Division 3, although the season was blighted by Will Prozesky's transfer to Havant after six games.

In 2006 Purbrook came 7th in Southern Electric Premier League Division 2.
Back Row:
James Iles,
Sam Pearce,
Alan Mengham,
Billy Hunter,
Bashir;
Front Row:
Sean Figgins,
Wayne Musselwhite,
Will Prozesky,
Ian Limb,
Colin Pay,
Christie Viljoen.

Picture courtesy of The News, Portsmouth

In 2005 Purbrook yo-yo'd upwards again, winning Division 3. South African Herman Wessels settled quickly with 539 runs, supported by Steve Mitchell (347) and Sean Figgins (311), and Ian Limb limelighted with 29 wickets. Will Prozesky yo-yo'd back from Havant in June and filled his boots. He clouted 961 runs in just ten innings, averaging 120.12.

Up in Division 2 again, Will Prozesky (2006) and Alan Mengham (2007) held the reins while Purbrook finished seventh two seasons in a row. 2007 was a particular triumph because a week before the first league match, elected skipper Prozesky yo-yo'd to Havant for a second time, leaving Alan Mengham to fill the breach. He commendably kept spirits high and everyone chipped in. South African youngster Ernest Kemm and Jamie Mitchell batted consistently, and both Billy Hunter and Steve Mitchell bagged 25 wickets.

For 2008, another mid table position seemed within Purbrook's scope but it wasn't to be. Individual performances faltered and they were dumped out of the division in last place. Someone was fiddling with that damned yo-yo again.

Promotion Devotion

Away from this yo-yo-ing in the Southern Premier, the club's three other Saturday teams scrapped away in the Hampshire League. The 2nd XI basked in two successive promotion seasons, skippered in 2006 by loyal

"We've got to put up with another 45 overs of this, lads!" Purbrook keeper Andy Holder and fielders Dave Cleeve and Graham McCoy face up to a weary afternoon.

Picture courtesy of The News, Portsmouth

one-club-man Dave Cleeve and in 2007 by Andy Holder, who proved a class act with the bat.

The team benefited from the good form of Gordy Charles (25 wickets in 2006), Trevor Biffen and Dirk Iles (both scored tons in 2007), and Chunky McCoy who snatched 29 wickets in 2007...he was happy but his knees grumbled from May till September.

(2007 2nd XI captain Andy Holder's best years were played away from his Purbrook Heath roots. Long ago in 1981 young Holder, son of Jim, was a top prospect with the Heath's other club, Portsdown. Having represented England Schools Under 15s, he was a target for Southern League clubs and Havant stepped in. Wicketkeeper/batsman Andy returned to homely Purbrook Heath in 1994, by which time he had picked up three Southern League winners' medals during a decade with South Hants Touring Club. Jim was glad to see him back).

Wherever I Lay My Hat

Purbrook 3rd XI's major problem was finding a pitch that they could call home. The Heath was buttoned up by the 1sts and 2nds so the 3rd team were used to house hunting. Since the 1990s Purbrook 3rds had been tenants at Bartons Green, Emsworth, Hollybank and Hayling.

In 2005, 3rd XI captain David Pugsley pulled a rabbit out of his club cap, sweet-talking St John's College into allowing Purbrook's 3rd team youngsters (and a few old'uns) to utilise their manicured ground at Farlington. The 4th XI (carefully nurtured by Roy Marsh from a bunch of youngsters playing occasional friendlies into a fully competitive league team) benefited too.

St John's provided house and home for three seasons, but in 2008 Purbrook Stiffs migrated over Portsdown to the artificial track at Southwick Park. Veteran Pugsley dug out his Jim'll Fix It badge, however, and in 2009 the 3rds and 4ths reverted to St John's. In 2010 it was all change once more – this time over the hills and faraway to East Meon's countryside venue.

In The Old Fashioned Way

In the sheltered climes of Sunday cricket, captain Brian Woolley (now in his fourth decade as Hon Sec) continued his love-in with Purbrook Heath. Relaxed Sunday matches offered that link with friendly cricket from way back when.

Brian's emphasis was on playing genial opposition, giving everyone a bat or a bowl where possible, insuring against defeat by batting second (a draw is as good as a win!), enjoying a handsome tea with scones and jam, and chilling with a gentle half-pint at the conclusion of the game. Not everyone's idea of fun and frolics but, for loyal participants, it's what village greens were made for.

Happy Daze

While cricket fortunes waxed and waned, Purbrook's new clubroom jollied up a feel good factor. When hosts Mike and Anita Turner called time, Carol Coley and Alan Figgins rallied to the flag. Their summer programme of barbecues, chilli nights and curry evenings proved to be... the icing on the cake.

In 2004 Jim Holder, who had surveyed his club's faltering social activities since their days at The Leopard Inn back in the 1960s, confided that the social scene was "better than it's ever been." Admittedly he was polishing off a lip-smacking, tongue-tingling plate of chicken korma at the time. But Jim was absolutely right.

Carol Coley is monarch of all she surveys in Purbrook's clubroom. Mark Hamson lends a hand while bar manager Alan Figgins nips outside for a smoke!

Mark's Mark

Mark Hamson was a fresh face in the director's box for 2007. The new Chairman was a latecomer to Purbrook's paradise isle. Colts manager Dave May encouraged Mark to get involved back in 2000 and he took charge of the Under 9s a few years later when youngest son George was in the team.

Upon election to the hot seat in 2007, Chairman Hamson's priority was the ECB Clubmark – an externally assessed quality control incorporating risk assessments, coaching ratios, first aider ratios, membership criteria and all the other paraphernalia that weighs heavy on sports clubs in this age of health and safety obsession. The Club knuckled down and satisfied the 80-page requirement in eighteen months, and Purbrook were awarded their notional gong (the ECB Clubmark) at Hampshire's celebrated Rose Bowl in September 2008.

May Finishes In June

For Hamson-recruiter Dave May, the date June 23rd 2003 bears comparison with more famous historical occasions like the first Moon landing. On Dave's special date, 23.6.03, he scored his first and only century (134) against Newport Gents. After luxuriating through a back-slapping tea interval, Dave came out to field at 5.30, tore his hamstring at 5.45 and was carried grimly up the boundary steps at 5.46. He never played again!

"One small step for Dave, one giant leap for his hamstring."

Dave May's other legacy was his reinstatement of the annual cricket tour. In days of old, Portsdown CC's Corsairs and Cortinas travelled in convoy behind Stan Baynham's Hillman Minx. In modern times, satnav'd Alan Figgins chauffeured his rump of stars in a seventeen-seater minibus, with coffin-carrier Roy Marsh straining through the gears in the fun bus just behind.

Other than that, the banter and bullshit was remarkably similar to times past, although "old Portsdown's" dick-of-the-day silly tie was hugely improved by "new Purbrook's" frock, hat and handbag – the wearer's daily reward for being voted an idiot by the Fines Committee.

"Frock, hat and handbag" buyer for Purbrook is James (call me Dirk) Iles. If you're of rugged disposition you may feel sturdy enough to witness a disturbing ceremony that takes place in Southsea each summer. Dirk makes a pre-tour parade of the charity shops requesting "something for the larger lady" from bewildered store volunteers. The drama continues as next he catwalks in a succession of outsized frocks, pouting and posing before ultimately making his purchase. It's not pretty.

"Gotta try 'em on, mate. Gotta fit some very chunky people."

The Fines Committee habitually take a dim view of proceedings and for 2010 ordered Dirk to try an Asbo on for size rather than the frocks.

200 Up, 200 More Ahead

Chairman Hamson's laudable objective – to provide cricket for everyone at the highest possible level – was dealt a severe kicking in 2009 when the 1st XI plummeted out of the Southern Electric Premier League. Relegation two years in a row was painful – back in the Hampshire League from whence they came a decade before. Considering that Purbrook fielded more teams than any other club for miles around - four on Saturdays, two on Sundays, and four Colts XIs – the heathside Club were punching below their weight.

James Iles has a pint in his hand and a glint in his eye....charity shops look out!

On the positive side Roy Marsh's 4th XI won promotion from

Regional Division 4, and first team batsman Sean Figgins hauled himself up the greasy pole towards becoming an ECB accredited "Club Coach" – not many of them to the pound. And in 2010 brand new non-turf practice facilities arrived at the Heath, thanks to a generous ECB grant. These new "nets" cost £27,000.

Looking ahead, Purbrook's future seemed in good hands with a lively Colts' set-up producing youngsters who promised much, in good time for the Club's 200th anniversary in 2015.

With this in mind, Chairman

Hamson took time out to ruminate on a suitable 200th birthday toast. As he Winston Churchill'd his speech in front of the bathroom mirror, he visualised generations of players and supporters gathered in Purbrook's cosy clubroom. Pray silence for the Chairman. In sonorous baritone, his closing words would ring out thus:

"Friends, please raise your glasses to Purbrook Cricket Club and this glorious summer of 2015, our best season in living memory. And here's to the next 200 years."

Alan Mengham hands the reins of captaincy to Steve Mitchell (left) for 2010

Purbrook Heath House

Five minutes' walk west of Purbrook Heath lies Purbrook Heath House (PHH). The history of this country seat is as long as its front drive. Originally called Shallots, the house was built in the last years of the 1790s. In 1800 Andrew Lindegren (Junior) was living there. He was a merchant and Portsmouth agent for the East India Company. A few years later Captain Hayes was the owner, prior to his move to Plymouth in 1819.

William Harvey (1805-93) had a long tenure at PHH. He owned the seven-bedroom residence when he wed Mary in 1849 and their children Elizabeth and Thomas grew up there. Intriguingly, in the 1881 census their home was referred to as The Shallows, not Shallots.

William Harvey had personalty worth £60,000 when he died in April 1893. Daughter Elizabeth was left £23,000 while son Thomas inherited Purbrook Heath House. Brother and sister continued living at PHH until Thomas

died in 1905. Elizabeth, "a generous and charitable lady," lived on in the grand house until her death in 1941.

PHH then passed to cousin Edward Murray who planned to live there once World War Two ended, but he was killed in an air raid on Bath in 1942 and the property was left to his eldest son James Murray.

The history of PHH then took a dramatic twist. At the height of World War Two in 1942, it was requisitioned by the Army and the Royal Corps Of Signals took it over. They installed electricity and a mains water supply. In the run-up to D-Day on June 6th 1944, PHH was home to No. 2 War Office Signals. PHH had an Officers' Mess with waiting staff, and the hay loft in the adjacent stables was converted into a dormitory for the military's rank and file.

When the Squire of Southwick, Evelyn Thistlethwayte, died in November 1943 his nephew Hugh Frank Pakenham Borthwick succeeded him as Squire, immediately adding the surname Norton. He battled in vain to wrest Southwick House back from the Royal Navy who had firstly requisitioned it in 1941, and secondly compulsorily purchased it in 1948.

Hugh Borthwick Norton needed some-where suitable to live and bought PHH. With bitter irony Hugh and wife Eva renamed their new home "Southwick House." Hugh B-N died in 1950 and Eva – "petite, firm but fair" – ran the extensive Southwick Estate from then until her death in 1988.

Eva Borthwick Norton was for many years President of Purbrook Cricket Club, prior to their amalgamation with Portsdown Cricket Club in 1982. She was a loyal, albeit "arms-length," President, local folklore suggesting that she had never actually seen a ball bowled in her life!

When Mrs Borthwick Norton died in 1988, the house (which was not part of the Southwick Estate), was sold privately under its former name "Purbrook Heath House" along with the treasure trove of contents....there were taxes to pay! These contents included fifteen paintings by Old Masters including Rubens and Gainsborough. They were bequeathed by Eva in lieu of tax and were expected to be displayed in Scotland's National Gallery. However, her will stipulated that the collection be exhibited at the Royal Scottish Academy, and the resultant dispute took seventeen years to resolve – in favour of the National Gallery.

Chapter 23

Home Is Where The Heath Is

In the several hundred years of its life, Purbrook village has graduated from a clutch of houses above a babbling brook to a regulation urban sprawl. Today's residential spread is not unpleasant, but not distinctive either. As the traffic grumbles through, as the shops dwindle and the pubs call their very last orders, the village heart beats ever quieter, ever shallower. With heavy irony, the brook that spawned Purbrook's genesis now creeps wholly underground through the village. The brook has lost its babble.

Streetwise

Back in the mists, Purbrook's very first roads and carriageways bestowed a dash of grandeur on the village that recent urban-creep has not destroyed, and happily the contours of London Road, Stakes Road and Park Avenue retain their sweeping generosity today. Some of the subsequent crests and crescents have pleasing features too, so it's not all bad... just a tad dull in places.

Piecemeal development is to blame for the mundane bits, pressing in from all sides until the once-dominant farmland ebbs away in the tide of concrete. Like ten thousand other rural idylls across the land, the English countryside is first chewed up and then dumbed down.

But it would be uncharitable to end negatively. Although the picturesque old village has undoubtedly disappeared, its modern replacement remains wonderfully situated, close to town and country and seashore. As Westbrook Grove's Ted and Annie confirmed: "Purbrook is still a good place to live."

And Quiet Flows The Pur

If modern Purbrook suggests a reel of monochrome, then joyous technicolour is very close at hand. The soft green shades of Portsdown Hill and Purbrook Heath are moments away, Hampshire landscapes to their core. And on the Heath in sumptuous summer, leather and willow war games add colour to this pageant, embroidered by the wit and occasional wisdom of the combatants.

But even this wonderful heathside has a downside. Now and then a burned out car is miserably dumped on the outfield by some space invader with brain detached, and very occasionally cricket intensities are disturbed by overboozed birdbrains hell-bent on interrupting play.

One Saturday back in Portsdown's prime, Terry Heywood's crisp left hook was needed to sort out two numpties who refused to stop clambering on the sightscreens, all the while gobbing obscenities at the cricketers. One clump from Terry and it was "goodnight nurse" - Haystacks was a big lad.

Two decades later, the Heath's quiet Sunday game with Pagham was invaded by a druggy band of blockheads from the nearby halfway house. Before most of us had gathered our senses, Ricky McIntosh waded into the lot of them...and waded out victorious. Amazing bravura, worthy of a mention in despatches, so I'm mentioning it here in recognition.

Over And Out

Fortunately our patch of green is the essence of tranquillity most of the time and we treasure its quality. Russell Kyte, Portsdown's much revered skipper of the 1970s, said that playing at Purbrook Heath was, for him, "the best of times." More recently Purbrook Chairman Hamson summed up unfussily: "Where else would you want to play cricket?"

As for me, when I gaze across the cricket square and its skimming swallows to the oaks beyond, and past them to the rolling hills of Portsdown, I'm gratified to have played a recent part in 200 years of battles on the Common. And we had some laughs along the way; the edgy sarcasm of a winning dressing room can be chokingly funny. I miss it already!

Let's leave it at that and hope that the dog walkers, farmers, groundsmen, nature lovers and ramblers, as well as the bowling-greeners, cricketers, footballers, tennis players and spectators continue to enjoy Purbrook Heath down all their days. I wish them well.

Portsdown began life in 1969. This picture shows their team in 1970.
Back Row: David Marks (scorer), Bob Smith, Nick Snelling, Mike Hunter, Adey Voss, John Bradley, Jon Floyd, Bill Hunter.
Front Row: Jim Holder, Dick Farrell, Don Rock, Chick Thresher, Brian Durdey

In 1971 Portsdown existed on a diet of friendly matches.
Back Row: Andy Cragg, Nick Snelling, Jim Holder, Dave Fancey, Brian Durdey, Derek Dyer.
Front Row: Mike Hunter, Adey Voss, Terry Carter, Chick Thresher, Don Rock

Portsdown's 1972 photo includes some new recruits.
Back Row: Steve Sims (scorer), Andy Cragg, Pete Elloway, Geoff Maidment, Nick Snelling, Derek Dyer, Stan Baynham.
Front Row: Dave Martin, Mike Hunter, Russell Kyte, Adey Voss, Bob Smith, John Jeffries

Portsdown in front of their new clubroom, June 1975.
Back Row: Ricky Travis, Alan Brown, Mike Turner, Andy Cragg, Adey Voss, Jake Cable, Julian Travis, Keith Williams (scorer).
Front Row: Dave Martin, Jim Holder, Russell Kyte, Derek Dyer, Bob Smith, Terry Stallard

Portsdown's Hampshire League XI, August 1975.
Back Row: Mike Turner, Andy Cragg, Jake Cable, Glen Ivett, Adey Voss, Terry Stallard, Stan Baynham.
Front Row: Kelvan Finch, Derek Dyer, Russell Kyte, John Austin, Bob Smith

Portsdown's clubroom reunion 2007, after a 30-year gap.
John Austin, John Bradley, Mike Turner, Kelvan Finch, Derek Dyer, Bob Smith

Purbrook
in 1968.
Back Row:
Ernie Gregory,
Derek White,
Nigel Lloyd,
Phil Sanders,
Tim Durston,
Martin Rich-
ardson,
Brian Andreae.
Front Row:
Adey Voss,
John Burrell,
Jack Wright,
Ron Davies,
Fred White

Purbrook in
1972, a year
before the
start of league
cricket.
Back Row:
K. Justice
(scorer),
Terry Stallard,
John Dover,
Terry Stockwell,
Greg Carson,
Tim Durston,
Brian Burrows,
T. George.
Front Row:
Jack Wright,
Steve Richards,
Brian Andreae,
Steve Edge,
Phil Sanders

Purbrook 1st XI in 1995 with sponsors Haines Watts. *Back Row:* Angela Mansfield (scorer), Andy Holder, Graham McCoy, Doug Doe (Vice Chairman), Rob Hamber, Steve Parker, Mark Howe, Colin Pay, Brian Woolley (Secretary). *Front Row:* Tim Wakeley, Chris Potter, Sponsor, Greg Carson, Sponsor, Simon Barnard, Wayne Musselwhite

In 2005, Purbrook 1st XI won Division 3 of the Southern Electric Premier League. *Back Row:* Craig Williams, Billy Hunter, James Iles, Nigel Kenny, Steve Mitchell, Nick Parker (manager). *Front Row:* Jamie Mitchell, Wayne Musselwhite, Sean Figgins, Alan Mengham, Herman Wessels, Ian Limb. *Picture courtesy of The News, Portsmouth*

Purbrook scorer Carol Cooper celebrates 20 years in the hot seat (2009).... she's a campanologist too!

Purbrook optimist Trevor Biffen's glass is always half full. Alongside him is "the Colonel," Brian Robbins

249

Portsdown's Leading Hampshire League Averages, 1973-1982

1973   1st XI 4th in County Division 2 (first season of League)

			Inns	N.O	Runs	H.S	Average
Batting	4th	John Hawley	9	3	260	79	43.33
	18th	Derek Dyer	11	-	282	90	25.44

			Overs	Maid	Runs	Wicks	Average
Bowling	3rd	Russell Kyte	56	14	177	18	9.83
	16th	Andy Cragg	83	17	259	20	12.95

1974   1st XI 3rd in County Division 1

Batting		No qualifiers – only top 15 published					
Bowling	4th	Derek Dyer	164	39	399	46	8.67

1975   1st XI 4th in County Division 1

Batting		No qualifiers – only top 12 published					
Bowling	3rd	Andy Cragg	188	26	509	56	9.09

1976   1st XI 9th in County Division 1

Batting		No qualifiers					
Bowling	11th	Andy Cragg	196	32	544	44	12.36

1977   1st XI 6th in County Division 1

Batting	8th	Terry Heywood	15	-	435	71	32.33
	17th	Russell Kyte	15	1	376	74	26.85
Bowling	3rd	Mike Turner	140	26	376	34	11.02

2nd XI 12th in South East Division

Batting	7th	Jim Holder	11	1	229	53	22.90
Bowling	13th	Dave Martin	124	22	360	28	12.85

1978   1st XI 9th in County Division 1

Batting	10th	John Austin	14	1	400	95	30.76
	20th	Terry Heywood	14	-	361	61	25.78
Bowling	5th	Terry Heywood	95	22	238	22	10.81
	10th	Mike Turner	214	48	581	44	13.20

2nd XI 16th in South East Division

Batting		No qualifiers					
Bowling	5th	**Dave Martin**	107	29	278	32	8.68

1979   1st XI 3rd in County Division 1

Batting	9th	**John Hawley**	13	2	350	69	31.82
	10th	**John Austin**	13	1	364	63	30.33
Bowling	11th	**Dave Martin**	126	24	449	34	13.20

2nd XI 16th in South East Division

Batting		No qualifiers					
Bowling	3rd	**Micky Broad**	167	48	387	43	9.00

1980   1st XI 6th in County Division 1

Batting	9th	**John Austin**	15	2	402	83*	30.92
	12th	**Jon Floyd**	13	1	328	59	27.33
	18th	**Terry Heywood**	12	0	297	79	24.75
Bowling	9th	**Mike Turner**	213	60	515	43	11.98
	15th	**Dave Martin**	118	17	351	24	14.63

2nd XI 18th in South East Division

Batting & Bowling		No qualifiers					

1981   1st XI 5th in County Division 1

Batting	11th	**Jon Floyd**	10	1	263	99	29.22
Bowling	5th	**Terry Heywood**	202	53	534	46	11.61
	19th	**Mike Turner**	248	67	633	46	13.76

2nd XI 11th in South East Division 2

Batting	2nd	**John Hawley**	12	1	389	97	35.36
	12th	**Peter Bennett**	13	1	280	80	23.33
Bowling	11th	**Dave Martin**	224	51	555	59	9.40

1982   1st XI 13th in County Division 1

Batting & Bowling   No qualifiers

2nd XI 13th in South East Division 2

Batting & Bowling   No qualifiers

Purbrook's Leading Hampshire League Averages, 1973-1982

1973 **7th in County Division 2** (first season of League)

			Inns	N.O	Runs	H.S	Average
Batting	8th	**Bob Gillmore**	7	1	198	63	33
	20th	**Greg Carson**	13	2	278	88	25.27
Bowling		No qualifiers	Overs	Maid	Runs	Wicks	Average

1974 **12th in County Division 2**

Batting	9th	**Vernon Delaney**	10	7	94	26*	31.33
	15th	**Greg Carson**	14	3	311	102*	28.27
Bowling	6th	**Steve Edge**	85	10	292	25	11.68
	11th	**John Burrell**	169	48	410	33	12.42

1975 **16th in County Division 2**

Batting		No qualifiers – only top 12 published					
Bowling	7th	**Phil Sanders**	129	28	384	34	11.29

1976 **13th in South East Division**

Batting	8th	**Greg Carson**	17	2	389	79	25.93
Bowling	9th	**Kenny Noy**	151	48	354	38	9.31
	17th	**John Burrell**	148	40	383	37	10.35

1977 **15th in South East Division**

Batting	3rd	**Dave Farley**	11	1	345	58	34.50
Bowling	2nd	**John Burrell**	95	28	197	29	6.79

1978 **9th in South East Division**

Batting	17th	**Bill Stenning**	10	1	205	66	22.77
Bowling	12th	**Bob Jenkins**	183	42	537	49	10.95
	17th	**John Burrell**	190	47	408	35	11.65

1979 **7th in South East Division**

Batting	14th	**Tim Durston**	14	2	276	63*	23
Bowling	4th	**John Burrell**	139	41	298	33	9
	8th	**Bob Jenkins**	159	44	362	37	9.78

1980   8th in South East Division 1

Batting	7th	**Pete de Cambra**	10	1	325	80	36.11
Bowling	11th	**John Burrell**	134	35	277	25	11.08

1981   7th in South East Division 1

Batting		No qualifiers					
Bowling	5th	**Bob Jenkins**	222	66	533	62	8.60

1982   18th in South East Division 1

Batting & Bowling   No qualifiers

Purbrook & Portsdown's Leading Hampshire League Averages, 1983-1990
(after amalgamation of the two clubs)

1983   **1st XI 6th in County Division 1**

			Inns	N.O	Runs	H.S	Average
Batting		No qualifiers					
			Overs	Maid	Runs	Wicks	Average
Bowling	14th	Dave Martin	162	22	561	40	14.05

2nd XI 2nd in South East Division 2

			Inns	N.O	Runs	H.S	Average
Batting	2nd	Greg Carson	11	3	382	108*	47.75
	4th	Mark Howe	12	2	437	155	43.70
Bowling	8th	Darrell Barnes	98	28	255	24	10.62

1984   **1st XI 5th in County Division 1**

			Inns	N.O	Runs	H.S	Average
Batting	9th	Jon Floyd	12	1	429	109*	39
	20th	Kelvan Finch	10	1	255	81	28.33
Bowling	8th	Kelvan Finch	101	17	347	29	11.96

2nd XI 1st in South East Division 1

			Inns	N.O	Runs	H.S	Average
Batting	6th	Gary Hounsome	9	2	239	63*	34.14
	11th	Andy Cragg	11	5	176	64*	30.67
	12th	M Anderson	16	0	480	68	30
	14th	Greg Carson	15	1	395	73*	28.21
Bowling	5th	John Burrell	122	28	382	30	12.73
	8th	Peter Bennett	161	36	422	31	13.61

3rd XI 8th in South East Division 2

			Inns	N.O	Runs	H.S	Average
Batting	11th	Ian Limb	12	1	307	97*	27.91
Bowling	3rd	Dave Evans	91	22	234	27	8.66
	20th	Darrell Barnes	103	16	323	22	14.68

1985   **1st XI 11th in County Division 1**

			Inns	N.O	Runs	H.S	Average
Batting	6th	John Austin	9	4	184	56*	36.80
	8th	Jon Floyd	10	0	356	109	35.60
	17th	Mark Howe	11	5	182	85*	30.33

Bowling	19th	Mike Turner	103	20	389	26	14.96

2nd XI 12th in County Division 3

Batting	10th	Gary Rogers	7	1	177	72	29.50
Bowling		No qualifiers					

3rd XI 14th in South East Division 2

Batting		No qualifiers					
Bowling	13th	C Lyons	114	36	268	22	12.18

1986   1st XI 18th in County Division 1

Batting & Bowling   No qualifiers

2nd XI 17th in County Division 3

Batting		No qualifiers					
Bowling	13th	John Burrell	126	28	345	27	12.78

3rd XI 15th in South East Division 2

Batting		No qualifiers					
Bowling	6th	Paul Musselwhite	102	29	217	21	10.33

1987   1st XI 10th in County Division 2

Batting	10th	Ian Limb	15	1	465	82*	33.21
	17th	John Austin	16	3	343	62*	26.38
Bowling	5th	Graham McCoy	104	16	334	26	12.85
	8th	Paul Musselwhite	107	28	282	21	13.43

2nd XI 4th in County Division 4

Batting	13th	Keith Noyce	11	1	304	67*	30.40
	18th	Mike Lowe	10	2	235	55*	29.37
Bowling	9th	Wayne Musselwhite	95	18	250	20	12.50
	12th	Dave Evans	139	27	441	33	13.36

3rd XI 15th in South East Division 2

Batting		No qualifiers					
Bowling	13th	Ken Burton	90	13	263	20	13.15
	17th	Rube Stallard	200	53	514	35	14.67

1988 1st XI 10th in County Division 2

Batting	13th	Mike Foster	9	2	225	78*	32.14
Bowling	6th	Paul Musselwhite	100	22	259	27	9.59
	16th	Mike Turner	135	18	377	28	13.46

2nd XI 13th in County Division 4

Batting & Bowling No qualifiers

3rd XI 15th in South East Division 2

Batting		No qualifiers					
Bowling	13th	Brian Woolley	85	9	355	28	12.68

1989 1st XI 1st in County Division 2

Batting	6th	Mike Seal	16	2	524	113*	37.42
	9th	John Austin	15	5	358	64	35.80
	12th	Paul Ancell	15	1	480	94	34.28
	19th	Graham McCoy	11	6	141	46	28.20
	20th	Mark Howe	10	4	166	66	27.66
Bowling	5th	Paul Ancell	132	20	420	34	12.35
	16th	Wayne Musselwhite	116	32	314	22	14.27

2nd XI 12th in County Division 4

Batting & Bowling No qualifiers

3rd XI 14th in South East Division 2

Batting & Bowling No qualifiers

1990 1st XI 16th in County Division 1

Batting	16th	Paul Ancell	17	2	522	110*	34.80
Bowling	18th	Ian Limb	100	9	373	22	16.95

2nd XI 13th in County Division 4

Batting & Bowling No qualifiers

3rd XI 13th in South East Division 2

Batting	12th	**Darrell Barnes**	13	2	325	73	29.54
Bowling	10th	**Phil Andrews**	72	14	215	20	10.75

Purbrook's Leading Hampshire League Averages, 1991-1999

(NB No Longer Purbrook & Portsdown)

1991   1st XI 10th in County Division 1

			Inns	N.O	Runs	H.S	Average
Batting	16th	Paul Ancell	13	1	422	124	35.16

			Overs	Maid	Runs	Wicks	Average
Bowling		No qualifiers					

2nd XI 2nd In County Division 4

Batting	1st	John Austin	13	5	533	90	66.63
Bowling	18th	Brian Robbins	135	30	407	30	13.57

3rd XI 13th in East Division 3

Batting & Bowling   No qualifiers

1992   1st XI 7th in County Division 1

Batting	20th	Jon Floyd	13	2	375	92*	34.09
Bowling	18th	Dave Oliver	83	8	356	21	16.95

2nd XI 2nd in County Division 4

Batting	2nd	John Austin	11	2	421	90*	46.78
	19th	Paul McLaughlin	10	0	271	88	27.10
Bowling	16th	Derek Dyer	100	20	306	19	16.10

3rd XI 4th in East Division 3

Batting	3rd	Grant Woolley	13	3	358	49	35.80
	14th	Andy Cragg	9	4	127	38	25.40
Bowling	4th	Andy Cragg	140	35	309	37	8.35

1993   1st XI 9th in County Division 1

Batting	16th	Jon Floyd	12	2	366	108*	36.60
Bowling	16th	Ian Limb	135	18	515	30	17.17

2nd XI 15th in County Division 3

Batting	10th	John Austin	10	2	297	70	37.12
Bowling	4th	Dave Davies	70	11	252	21	12

3rd XI 9th in East Division 3

Batting	4th	Chris Evans	10	4	269	70	44.83
	6th	Grant Woolley	13	4	356	66	39.56
	16th	Pete Martin	12	4	208	46	26
	18th	Pete de Cambra	11	0	274	54	24.91
Bowling		No qualifiers					

1994   1st XI 11th in County Division 1

Batting	10th	Barry de Waal (SA)	12	1	484	106	44
Bowling	16th	Mark Stanley	123	22	472	26	18.15

2nd XI 15th in County Division 3

Batting & Bowling   No qualifiers

3rd XI 8th in East Division 2

Batting		No qualifiers					
Bowling	5th	Stuart Merritt	82	17	242	20	12.10

1995   1st XI 5th in County Division 1

Batting	12th	Simon Barnard	9	3	309	76	51.50
	15th	Steve Parker	13	1	561	118*	46.75
	17th	Colin Pay	15	2	577	98	44.38
Bowling	9th	Colin Pay	114	19	447	25	17.88

2nd XI 7th in County Division 3

Batting	20th	Simon Kyte	14	5	288	55*	32
Bowling	12th	Mike Turner	112	30	343	22	15.59

3rd XI 6th in East Division 2

Batting	19th	Andy Shewring	11	0	336	75	30.54
Bowling	3rd	Dave Pugsley	66	9	225	21	10.71
	5th	Andy Cragg	109	15	375	33	11.36
	10th	Stuart Merritt	163	39	451	32	14.09

1996   1st XI 14th in County Division 1

Batting							
	1st	Colin Pay	11	4	592	161*	84.57
	19th	Andy Holder	15	2	494	73	38
	20th	George du Toit (SA)	15	1	485	99	34.64

Bowling   No qualifiers

2nd XI 16th in County Division 3

Batting & Bowling No qualifiers

3rd XI 17th in East Division 2

Batting   No qualifiers

Bowling							
	1st	Dave Davies	78	32	133	15	8.87

1997   1st XI 9th in County Division 1

No statistics available for 1st XI because no averages were sent to the League by Purbrook!

2nd XI 10th in County Division 3

Batting							
	2nd	Mike Burrows	9	4	246	66*	49.20
	15th	John Austin	11	0	369	61	33.54
Bowling	20th	Phil Andrews	94	13	359	18	19.94

3rd XI 7th in East Division 3

Batting							
	8th	Grant Woolley	10	4	224	49*	37.33
	15th	Dave Davies	12	3	292	52*	32.44
Bowling	1st	Dave Davies	143	56	335	36	9.30
	13th	Andy Cragg	104	22	317	20	15.85

1998   1st XI 7th in County Division 1

Batting	5th	Martin Lazenby (SA)	14	2	634	99	52.83
Bowling	10th	Graham McCoy	138	33	433	26	16.65

2nd XI 17th in County Division 3

Batting & Bowling No qualifiers

3rd XI 16th in East Division 3

Batting & Bowling   No averages sent to League; probably no qualifiers

1999   1st XI 14th in County Division 1

Batting	14th	**Martin Lazenby** (SA)	16	0	580	89	36.25
Bowling	10th	**Graham McCoy**	161	39	462	27	17.11

2nd XI 8th in County Division 4

Batting & Bowling   No qualifiers

3rd XI 16th in East Division 3

Batting	14th	**Duncan Garland**	14	3	353	72	32.09
Bowling		No qualifiers					

Key: (SA) means registered "Overseas" (South African) player.

Purbrook's Leading Southern, Hampshire and Combination League Averages, 2000-2009

2000   1st XI 5th in Southern Premier League Division 3

			Inns	N.O	Runs	H.S	Average
Batting	11th	**Piet Botha (SA)**	12	1	435	125	39.55
	17th	**Graham McCoy**	13	0	427	64	32.85

Also Billy Hunter: 323 runs, ave 29.37 came 24th

			Overs	Maid	Runs	Wicks	Average
Bowling	2nd	**Mark Stanley**	98	18	344	26	13.23
	7th	**Robbie Charles**	68	8	251	16	15.69
	17th	**Graham McCoy**	127	29	394	22	17.91

Also Steve Brewer: 18 wickets, ave 18.28 came 22nd

2nd XI 16th in Hampshire League County Division 3

Batting		No qualifiers					
Bowling	12th	**Mike Burrows**	116	16	338	21	16.09
	20th	**Phil Andrews**	115	19	409	22	18.59

3rd XI 1st in Hampshire Combination East Division

Batting	Pos'n	**Dave Pugsley**	7	3	194	65	48.50
info not available		**Duncan Garland**	13	6	313	55*	44.70
		Pete de Cambra	7	4	124	45*	41.30
Bowling		**Chris Berry**	55	8	155	20	7.75
		Brian Robbins	74	8	215	25	8.60
		Andy Cragg	135	29	301	27	11.15
		Dave Pugsley	126	40	298	26	11.50

2001   1st XI 5th in Southern Premier League Division 3

Batting	18th	**Jimmy Repsold (SA)**	12	2	371	85*	37.10
Bowling	1st	**Mark Stanley**	112	28	283	25	11.32
	16th	**Graham McCoy**	125	28	419	22	19.05

2nd XI 14th in Hampshire League County Division 3

Batting	5th	**Trevor Pay**	11	2	480	90	53.33
Bowling	14th	**Mike Burrows**	131	21	416	24	17.33

3rd XI 14th in Hampshire League East Division 3

Batting	13th	Pete Martin	10	4	204	55*	34
	20th	Chris Berry	10	3	204	53*	29.14
Bowling	19th	Chris Berry	87	8	381	22	17.32

2002   1st XI 1st in Southern Electric Premier Division 3

Batting	2nd	Will Prozesky (SA)	16	2	988	153*	70.57
		Also **Billy Hunter**: 482 runs, ave 32.13 came 28th					
Bowling	3rd	Will Prozesky (SA)	59	10	234	17	13.76
	11th	Mark Stanley	122	20	485	30	16.17
		Also **Graham McCoy**: 23 wickets, ave 20.91 came 28th					

2nd XI 12th in Hampshire League County Division 3

Batting	12th	Andy Holder	14	1	471	102*	36.23
Bowling		No qualifiers					

3rd XI 5th in Hampshire League East Division 3

Batting		No qualifiers					
Bowling	12th	Dave Pugsley	124	12	442	33	13.39

2003   1st XI 10th (last) in Southern Elec Premier Division 2

Batting	17th	Will Prozesky (SA)	13	0	410	78	31.54
Bowling	5th	Billy Hunter	54	5	261	15	17.40
	6th	Will Prozesky (SA)	112	17	442	25	17.68

2nd XI 15th in Hampshire League County Division 3

Batting	4th	Graham McCoy	14	3	473	68*	43
	5th	Andy Holder	13	2	471	89	42.82
Bowling	14th	Mike Burrows	122	28	399	24	16.63

3rd XI 12th in Hampshire League South East Division 2

Batting	11th	Chris Berry	9	4	193	47	38.60
Bowling		No qualifiers					

2004   1st XI 11th in Southern Electric Premier Division 3

Batting	4th	Will Prozesky	6	1	342	214*	68.40
Bowling	1st	Will Prozesky	29	4	103	13	7.92
	19th	Fuf Engelbrecht (SA)	122	24	455	26	17.50

2nd XI 6th in Hampshire League County Division 4

Batting	3rd	Steve Stone (Aus)	12	0	593	176	49.42
	19th	Andy Holder	12	1	390	81	35.45
Bowling	9th	Mike Burrows	122	13	468	32	14.63
	10th	Graham McCoy	122	24	319	21	15.19

3rd XI 15th in Hampshire League South East Division 2

Batting		No qualifiers					
Bowling	19th	Dave Pugsley	118	15	395	21	18.81

2005   1st XI 1st in Southern Electric Premier Division 3

Batting	1st	Will Prozesky	10	2	961	223	120.12
	12th	Herman Wessels (SA)	14	1	539	80*	41.46
Bowling	4th	Ian Limb	108	16	392	29	13.52

2nd XI 6th in Hampshire League County Division 4

Batting	11th	Andy Holder	13	1	558	132*	46.50
Bowling	2nd	Mike Burrows	107	16	334	29	11.52
	4th	Graham McCoy	128	37	258	19	13.58

3rd XI 12th in Hants League Regional Div 2 South East

Batting	20th	Robbie Charles	9	1	217	57	27.13
Bowling		No qualifiers					

4th XI 8th in Hants League Regional Div 4 South East

Batting & Bowling	No qualifiers	

2006   1st XI 7th in Southern Electric Premier Division 2

Batting	9th	Will Prozesky	14	1	554	100	42.62
Bowling	13th	Will Prozesky	95	13	410	21	19.52

2nd XI 1st in Hampshire League County Division 4

Batting	5th	Andy Holder	11	0	612	116	55.64
	6th	Graham McCoy	12	3	492	83*	54.67
Bowling	3rd	Gordy Charles	108	30	375	25	15
	7th	Steve Matthews	68	3	301	16	18.81

3rd XI 13th in Hants League Regional Div 2 South East

Batting & Bowling   No qualifiers

4th XI 11th in Hants League Regional Div 4 South East

Batting	15th	Joe Slade	Limited info		263	21.92
Bowling	7th	B Hayward	96	13	331	21	15.76

2007   1st XI 7th in Southern Electric Premier Division 2

Batting	15th	Ernest Kemm (SA)	7	0	238	77	34
Bowling	3rd	Billy Hunter	83	17	322	25	12.88
	8th	Steve Mitchell	99	18	378	25	15.12
	15th	Steve Matthews	70	6	255	14	18.21

2nd XI 3rd in Hampshire League County Division 3

Batting	1st	Heini Klaasen	7	3	340	100	85
Bowling	2nd	Graham McCoy	107	17	347	29	11.97

3rd XI 15th in Hants League Regional Div 2 South East

Batting	3rd	Duncan Garland	10	2	369	89*	46.13
Bowling		No qualifiers					

4th XI 12th in Hants League Regional Div 4 South East

Batting & Bowling   No qualifiers

2008   1st XI 10th (last) in Southern Electric Premier Division 2

Batting		No qualifiers
Bowling		Sam Pearce took 17 wickets, ave 20.59 and came 22nd

2nd XI 15th in Hampshire League County Division 2

Batting	10th	Andy Holder	13	4	338	111	37.56
	19th	Chris Berry	11	5	162	41*	27
Bowling	13th	Graham McCoy	122	28	359	23	15.61

3rd XI 13th in Hants League Regional Div 2 South East

Batting & Bowling   No qualifiers

4th XI 17th in Hants League Regional Div 4 South East

Batting & Bowling No qualifiers

2009

1st XI 18th in Southern Electric Premier Division 3

Batting	17th	**Sean Figgins**	16	1	468	106	31.20

Jamie Mitchell scored 368 runs, ave 24.53 and came 27th

Bowling **Steve Mitchell** took 21 wickets, ave 21.81 and came 26th

2nd XI 13th in Hampshire League County Division 2

Batting	5th	**Andy Holder**	15	3	786	139	65.50
Bowling		No qualifiers					

3rd XI 12th in Hants League Regional Div 2 South East

Batting	12th	**Paul Hawkins**	14	2	437	85	36.42
Bowling	14th	**Chris Harrison**	99	29	376	26	14.46

4th XI 2nd in Hants League Regional Div 4 South East

Batting	5th	**Baiju Kurian**	12	2	504	184	50.40
	n/a	**Roni Thankachan**	8	2	275	55	45.83
	19th	**Calvin Charlton**	9	2	157	27*	22.40
Bowling	7th	**Ben Henderson**	81	12	299	21	14.24
	8th	**Sharin Jose**	70	13	200	14	14.29
	18th	**Kyle Ellis**	104	14	444	25	17.76
	19th	**Roni Thankachan**	63	3	341	19	17.95

Key: (SA) means registered "Overseas" South African player.

Purbrook Chairmen and Saturday League Captains, 1991-2010

Year	Chairman	Captains
1991	**Ken Johnson**	1st XI Jon Floyd 2nd XI Brian Robbins 3rd XI Brian Andrews
1992	**Ken Johnson**	1sts Jon Floyd 2nds Bob Smith 3rds Brian Andrews
1993	**Ken Johnson**	1sts Graham McCoy 2nds Bob Smith 3rds Andy Shewring
1994	**Ken Johnson**	1sts Graham McCoy 2nds Mark Howe 3rds Dave Martin
1995	**Brian Robbins**	1sts Greg Carson 2nds Paul McLaughlin 3rds Dave Martin
1996	**Doug Doe**	1sts Andy Holder 2nds Paul McLaughlin 3rds Dave Martin
1997	**Doug Doe**	1sts Graham McCoy 2nds Alan Mengham 3rds Dave Davies
1998	**Pete de Cambra**	1sts Graham McCoy 2nds Mike Burrows 3rds Dave Davies
1999	**Pete de Cambra**	1sts Graham McCoy 2nds Dave Martin 3rds Duncan Garland
2000	**Andy Cragg**	1sts Graham McCoy 2nds Dave Martin 3rds Dave Pugsley
2001	**Andy Cragg**	1sts Graham McCoy 2nds Roger Clarke 3rds Dave Pugsley

2002	**Andy Cragg**	1sts Alan Mengham
		2nds Roger Clarke
		3rds Dave Martin

2003	**Andy Cragg**	1sts Alan Mengham
		2nds Andy Holder
		3rds Chris Berry
		4ths Roy Marsh

2004	**Andy Cragg**	1sts Billy Hunter
		2nds Andy Holder
		3rds Chris Berry
		4ths Roy Marsh

2005	**Dave Martin**	1sts Billy Hunter
		2nds Mike Burrows
		3rds Dave Pugsley
		4ths Roy Marsh

2006	**Dave Martin**	1sts Will Prozesky
		2nds Dave Cleeve
		3rds Ian Colban
		4ths Roy Marsh

2007	**Mark Hamson**	1sts Alan Mengham
		2nds Andy Holder
		3rds Chris Tebb
		4ths Roy Marsh

2008	**Mark Hamson**	1sts Alan Mengham
		2nds Andy Holder
		3rds Carl Marsh
		4ths Roy Marsh

2009	**Mark Hamson**	1sts Alan Mengham
		2nds Andy Holder
		3rds Paul Hawkins
		4ths Roy Marsh

2010	**Mark Hamson**	1sts Steve Mitchell
		2nds Andy Holder
		3rds Paul Hawkins
		4ths Roy Marsh

Long service: Throughout the 20 years covering 1991-2010, Brian Woolley has served as Purbrook's Honorary Secretary (continuous from 1975), and Carol Cooper has served as Scorer for Purbrook's Saturday 2nd XI.

The following people have been Vice-Presidents throughout the 20 years:
Harry Bates, Greg Carson, Andy Cragg, Delphine Sparshatt.

(excludes Appendices and Photographs)